around quitting time

Work and Middle-Class

Fantasy in American Fiction

ROBERT SEGUIN

Duke University Press

Durham and London

2001

© 2001 Duke University Press
All rights reserved
Printed in the United States of
America on acid-free paper ∞
Designed by Amy Ruth Buchanan
Typeset in Minion by Keystone
Typesetting, Inc.
Library of Congress Cataloging-
in-Publication Data appear on
the last printed page of this book.

For my family, and for Liz

contents

acknowledgments

For their critical acumen, wise advice, and steadfast faith in this project, I would like to thank Fredric Jameson, Jan Radway, Tom Ferraro, Susan Willis, and Ken Surin. Phil Wegner, Susan Hegeman, and John Evelev—chefs extraordinaire—provided food for both body and mind, sustaining me still. The protean gang at 819 Clarendon Street offered almost a home away from home, as well as the space for reading groups galore. Thanks to Richard Dienst for facilitating material support. Harris Breslow was always ready to listen, and Evan Watkins came through in the clutch.

Liz Blasco was around to share—in this, and much else besides.

one   *Class, Middle Class,*

and the Modalities of Labor

> There is no permanent class of hired
>
> laborers among us. . . . If any should
>
> continue through life in the condition of
>
> the hired laborer, it is not the fault of the
>
> system, but because of either a dependent
>
> nature which prefers it, or improvidence,
>
> folly, or singular misfortune.
>
> —Abraham Lincoln

"Is there 'class' in America?" asks Thomas Geoghegan in his alternately wry and despairing memoir of being a labor lawyer in Chicago during the Reagan years. "To me, it's such a stupid question, a *hopeless* question. Unfortunately, I'm obsessed with it."[1] Geoghegan describes an unremittingly hostile environment both for workers and for his own efforts to represent them: capital was in flight, the steelworkers' and the air traffic controllers' unions had been crippled or smashed outright, and the egregious Taft-Hartley Act, a Cold War monstrosity that had lain dormant during the "labor peace" of the preceding two decades, was discovering whole new domains of application. Efforts to generate working-class cohesion were rendered virtually impossible, most often because they were simply illegal. Geoghegan nonetheless finds himself at once moved and puzzled by the sudden, fragile, yet vital forms of solidarity he sporadically encounters among the groups of workers he represents, forms which often evaporate as quickly as they had arisen, vanishing, he imagines, into a kind of suburban black hole: "If I go to the Hancock, up to the 95th floor, I can look west over the city and see street-lights, in straight lines, blasting out into the suburbs, out to where the rank and file live. . . . Looking out from up here, I think maybe [history] *is* over. Looking at the lines, perfectly straight, I think of all the people out there watching TV."[2] His lofty vantage point also figuratively encodes his own consciously acknowledged position of relative affluence and self-professed yuppie tastes, marking him in a certain sense as "outside" the very mystery of class he claims enthralls him.

Geoghegan's evocation of the long lines of streetlights heading out into the Chicago suburbs ineluctably recalls Dreiser's remarkable description early in *Sister Carrie* of the lines of streetlamps swaying in the wind, surrounded only by empty prairie. At this earlier moment, neither television nor even the suburb itself had yet arrived. Both scenes participate, however (by way, as we shall see, of a certain updating or refunctioning of an older pastoral dis-course), in a similar production of what I call an essentially middle-class space. In this space—which is ideological, but also material, physical—class itself and the exigencies and investments attendant upon it are, I argue, at once produced but then occluded and rearticulated, to the point where the term "middle class" itself in effect becomes synonymous with "classlessness," an ideologico-practical inhabitance of the world wherein class has been putatively superseded, or at least temporarily suspended. This is a condition or feeling tone of daily life—whose latest systemic mutation would appear to be the sheer voluntarism of the field of "class as lifestyle," suggestively ana-lyzed by Evan Watkins—that can afford people whose own economic status is tenuous at best, who have been used and abused by capital in a host of different ways, the opportunity to consider themselves middle class (and, from the opposite direction, so can wealthy stockbrokers).[3] "Middle class" is then my partial, necessary but not sufficient, answer to the conundrum of class in America—where is it? why is it stubborn and fleeting at the same time?—that Geoghegan invokes.

This is, in one sense, a very familiar territory. The United States has, since the time of the Puritans, been variously conceived of as a providentially blessed nation that has escaped the burdens of history and social division, whose citizens enjoy a birthright of Lockean liberalism and, as implied above by Lincoln, readily achievable upward mobility. This is a set of discourses generally gathered under the rubric of "exceptionalism," great swaths of which continue to litter bookshelves and the brains of media pundits across the country. Exceptionalist discourse has, as Eli Zaretsky argues, "functioned throughout the nation's history to deny and absorb class conflict,"[4] and it constitutes an integral part of that ideological cluster recently addressed by Benjamin DeMott as the "American myth of classlessness," in his symptomatically titled book *The Imperial Middle*. Other ingredients of the myth include notions of limitless personal freedom, an indomitable self which is at once fluid enough to assume a wide range of roles, and the centrality of individual action and the fulfillment of desire.[5] Some of this is quite pertinent in the narrative analyses that follow, for it turns out that many of the novelistic moments we will engage involve precisely the severe problematization of the self and of desire. That is, at the same time that these novels articulate some of the dynamics involved in the elaboration of what Loren Baritz terms the "subjective middle class," they work in different ways toward a (frequently fitful and uncertain) critique of this state.[6]

In general, however, discussions of the forms of exceptionalism tend to be hampered by remaining at the level of ideas and ideologies, where the hegemonic power of the middle class and the commensurate weakness of working-class institutions and ideologies are explained in terms of Locke's greatness or the persistence of conservative strains of Christianity. Political (and religious) ideas and ideologies tend to be rooted in, and take as their presuppositions, the lofty and mystified realm of what Marx described as "political community," wherein man exists as "an imaginary member of an imaginary sovereignty . . . infused with an unreal universality." My sense is, rather, that American novelists and their narratives have inhabited and drawn their vitality from the more profane sphere that Marx counterposes to political community, the sphere of crude economic competition and viscous daily life, namely that of civil society, in which man "acts simply as a private individual, treats other men as means, degrades himself to the role of a mere means, and becomes the plaything of alien powers."[7] What therefore in part distinguishes my approach here is my effort to elaborate some of the material underpinnings subtending and informing what might be called the "semantic complex" of the middle class, the combined histories of narrative and socioeconomic change that converge in its emergence. I explore the middle class not so much as thing or idea, but more as a social-semantic structure capable of a range of investments, and supporting a range of practices and beliefs. The familiar and unassuming phrase "middle class" conceals an almost totemic or talismanic power, and beneath it lies a complex, multivalent, and sedimented history, a history to which certain modern American narratives afford us vital access. In addition, by framing the matter in strong terms, not as some mere weakening of class structure or easing of class tensions but as the felt elimination of these—a freedom from class altogether—I can attend more readily to the strong utopian investments in the middle-class complex (for a classless society is indeed a utopian wish) as well as to the ideological deformations and political scleroses it encourages.

These formulations perhaps risk overstating my case and my findings, though I sometimes think, in a dialectical spirit, that exaggerations often capture the truth of things more so than patiently delimited and circumscribed claims. Nonetheless, on a more sober note, it ought to be stressed that middle-classlessness, given the pressures and contradictions of the social forms we inhabit, can only ever be a limited and intermittent phenomenon. That is, it can never really wipe clean the slate of social class, as a traditional exceptionalist vision might have it. Thus I have no wish to deny, for example, that America has experienced more violent class struggles through its history than virtually any other industrialized country, generally at the instigation of American capital ("I can hire one half of the working class to kill the other half," financier Jay Gould once tellingly put it). Nor do I contend in any way with Fredric Jameson's remark that "few countries are as saturated with undisguised class content as the United States."[8] My emphasis, rather, is that, particularly during the last few decades, very little of this history and these conditions have been translated into public discourse or political common sense (and in that sense the narrative I offer here might best be understood in genealogical fashion, that is, as the uneven emergence of something that has only become "full blown" in the contemporary period).[9] Even if it is the case, as a recent antiexceptionalist study argues, that American workers do often perceive genuine class distinctions in society (as opposed, say, to mobile status differentiations), it remains evident that such perceptions seldom lead to a heightened grasp of structural inequality, or of social injustice or contradiction.[10] Middle-classlessness, along with a host of other forces and possibilities, cuts across the domain of social conflict, disrupting the pedagogical potential of differential class perception. It subsists,

finally, on the very boundary between reason and emotion, between knowledge and affect, providing perhaps an unstable sense more than a clear
certainty of the diminution of class tension—hence my frequent turn in the
pages ahead to a language of affect and desire.

．．．

I pick up the story, then, not with Geoghegan on the 95th floor of the
Hancock (though doubtless with some of the same obsession), but precisely
at that earlier moment, with Dreiser and a rapidly developing Chicago: not,
in other words, when history has seemingly ended, but rather, following on
the great Pullman strike of 1894 and concurrent with the growth of the
Populist and Socialist parties, at a time when it was still very much in the
process of being made. And so the figure of Carrie, leaving her small midwestern city, comes to Chicago to look for a job. As it turns out, Carrie
arrives in the city just at the time of day when everyone else is getting off
work, heading home to dinner and evening amusements (the "enchanted
metropolitan twilight," as F. Scott Fitzgerald, a later and not unrelated con-
noisseur of such times, will call it).[11] This is, as we shall see more fully,
a magical time for Dreiser, full of hope and possibility, and is the occasion
for some of his most intense displays of sentimental yearning. What I take
to be Dreiser's point of departure here becomes our own as well, for it
furnishes us with the first central contention of this study, namely that the
middle-class space that Dreiser explores (allowing us to construct a kind of
Weberian "ideal type" of middle-classlessness in the process)[12] is crucially
organized around the matter of work, or, more precisely, around an imagined zone of interface between working and not working. This space appears, in somewhat differing forms and with altered dynamics, in each of the
novels under scrutiny here, allowing us to test this initial hypothesis in
diverse ways.

By 1900, when *Sister Carrie* first appeared, the American working class
had been thoroughly proletarianized, that is, brought into a regime of wage
labor ("formally" subsumed, in Marx's terminology), which had not been
the case in the earlier decades of the nineteenth century. During the first half
of the century, the spheres of handicraft and agricultural production remained largely in the hands of artisans and small proprietors who owned
their own means of production, and who were for decades the principal

social stratum to which the dominant strains of exceptionalist pastoralism were functionally tied (an ideology that celebrated a kind of individual economic self-sufficiency and a freedom from burdensome work and the exigencies of the bourgeois market). As the century wore on, and large-scale capitalist industry spread, this stratum was relentlessly restructured by the imposition of wage work, effectively eradicating that supposedly naturally harmonious "middling" pattern of social organization, lacking extremes of wealth and poverty, so admired by the likes of Franklin and Jefferson. The "permanent class of hired laborers" invoked disbelievingly by Lincoln had at length come into being, and people now by and large worked for others rather than for themselves, or collectively—the fundamental power dynamic of capitalist society. This historical trajectory thus marks the story of middle-classlessness as essentially a twentieth-century one, as the production of a national imaginary that is no longer simply a kind of plebeian ideology, like labor republicanism (with its own "anticlass" rhetoric of white male unity), now expanded beyond its original context, nor, from the other side, simply the expression of a restricted bourgeois weltanschauung. It is, rather, rooted in material forms of daily life and (sometimes fitfully) practiced by disparate segments of the population.

Such an imposition of an exploitive regime of labor might well be taken as a possible definition of capitalism itself.[13] More precisely, I tend to grasp this peculiar mode of production as something like a giant mechanism for the *capturing of time* via the necessity of wage work (a certain amount of time being just about the only thing we are vouchsafed upon entering this earthly realm). In a now classic study, E. P. Thompson showed how from its earliest days capital has been engaged in the ceaseless restructuring, regimentation, and compression of time, involving a steady increase in the time spent working for an increasing proportion of the population: a striking contrast from the medieval and even early modern periods, when in some parts of Europe feast days and holidays of various sorts made up almost half the yearly calendar.[14] When Marx elaborated his fundamental theoretical categories, seeking to explain the nature of the economic process of capitalism, he too focused centrally on time, specifically the notion of labor time itself, as reflected most crucially in the category of surplus labor. Capital, considered in its purely economic aspect, from the perspective of its "concept" alone, posits the lived time of humans as labor time as such:

the working day contains the full 24 hours, with the deduction of the few hours rest without which labour-power is absolutely incapable of renewing its services. Hence it is self-evident that the worker is nothing other than labour-power for the duration of his whole life, and that therefore all his disposable time is by nature and by right labour-time, to be devoted to the self-valorization of capital.[15]

This is, of course, invoked at a fairly high level of abstraction, and the actual history of struggles over the working day has been complex and varied, with labor resistance in the industrialized core (together with support from some enlightened political and professional groupings) eventually succeeding in reducing average work time from more than eighty hours per week to about forty. But the long-term impetus of capital remains directed toward a longer working day, and recently economist Juliet Schor has drawn attention to the steady increase in working hours and decrease in free time for most Americans over the last fifteen years, as the (always imperfect) postwar social compact between workers and industry becomes increasingly unraveled.[16]

If, as numerous ideologists of exceptionalism (seconded by Marx himself) have maintained, the United States has indeed experienced a starker, unalloyed development of capitalism than elsewhere in the world, then it might be imagined that more intense and substantial practico-ideological means would be devised in order to defuse, neutralize, or otherwise counter the very imposition of work which this development represents. That such a countering would also draw into its zone of effectivity the question of class follows from this, since the imposition of work through the process of production is one of the principal determinants of the class structure itself. This structure can indeed be modeled in its most essential form (useful only as a spare point of departure) as, in the words of the union organizer in filmmaker John Sayles's classic *Matewan*, a matter of "those who work and those who don't," of those who produce surplus value and those who live off it.[17] Imagining a way out of this situation and into a zone of "not working" turns out to be an intensely fraught and complicated affair, owing mainly to the sharp ambivalence of the terms at issue. That is, work is a realm of freedom and of necessity all at once. Under capitalism it is principally exploitive and alienated; however, it is also the central mediation that grounds social organization and through which this last might be changed. Leisure, meanwhile—the principal valorized form of nonwork—posits itself as the simple renunciation or negation of work, thus forfeiting any larger political potentiality and relegating itself to the domain of the private. As Andre Gorz sums it up,

> In our present social environment, only work—however unsatisfactory it may otherwise be—gives men and women the opportunity for collective action, communication, and exchange. The sphere of non-work is a place of solitude and isolation, of enforced idleness for all those who live in the outskirts and suburbs of the major cities.[18]

These two realms, then, are separated by a kind of sociospatial decree, but linked by tantalizing underground energies.

The aesthetic is another sphere of nonwork; unlike leisure, however, its concept retains a vital and tense link with labor, in that it too is frequently modeled as a purposeful interchange between matter and form, nature and culture (even if, as in Kant, no specific goal or end is assumed). Its class codings are also evident, since at one level the aesthetic stands as the specifically bourgeois translation of older aristocratic ideals of noninstrumental or disinterested activity. In any event, whatever unalienated labor would be like has often been imagined in terms of whatever it is that artists do, a notion closely associated, for example, with Schiller, but given precise expression for our purposes by Georges Sorel: "L'Art est une anticipation du travail tel qu'il doit être pratiqué dans un régime de très haute production."[19] The emphases here on art, on practice or use, and on the labor and production process will all resonate with the texts we examine. So too will the more period-oriented notion of modernism, which itself will prove to be a crucial mediatory concept for us (despite, or perhaps because of, its peculiarities in the U.S. context).

Hence, what these narratives attempt involves something rather more complicated than, for example, deploying the images and promises of leisure, let alone of unemployment, for both of these are in their different ways simply flip sides or products of the wage system itself. Rather, a complex circulation and communication amongst these various spheres and modalities must be set in place, otherwise we are faced with a "middle-class complex" too simple or one-dimensional for the multivalent operations required of it. The textual moments and patterns that concern us here thus point precisely toward a shifting and variable state *between* working and not working, en-twining both these states, which suggests in turn a transformed work and a transformed leisure as well. I believe the political unconscious of these texts is materialist and utopian, and in the middle-class imaginary, as in the socialist imaginary (between which I am assuming a kind of ionic or os-motic exchange of energies), what is desired is ultimately the liberation from (alienated) labor as such, in ways that we perhaps cannot at this moment of what Marx called our prehistory fully apprehend or foresee. Not desired here is any kind of utopia of work, wherein happy workers sing as they hammer nails and load crates, as this appears in other, generally more old-fashioned versions of socialism and in some visions of the Protestant work ethic. Once again, it will be through the reconquest of human time that such a liberation from labor must occur.

The invocation of leisure in this context no doubt suggests another per-spective on the general historical terrain this study occupies, one having to do with consumerism and the tendential absorption of a more or less inde-pendent working class into the folds of an ineluctable consumer society, one henceforth grasped as the culmination and central informing instance of what the middle class in America is all about. After all, who intervenes between the moment Carrie boards the train and the time she steps off "around quitting time" but Drouet himself, the traveling salesman and spokesman for the emerging world of mass consumption? The problem of consumerism is indeed important in the chapters to follow, though in a sense I want to circumvent direct consideration of it, or to come at it in a roundabout way. In keeping with the intended focus on the enabling mate-rial and historical conditions of middle-classlessness, my concern is with processes which themselves paved the way for the growth of consumer so-ciety, such as Taylorism, increasing state intervention in culture and econ-omy, and Cold War political repression—in general, processes that in the long run have undermined possibilities for working-class solidarity and collective organization. The writers I consider are all concerned in one way or another with new developments in mass culture and the commodity form, either in broad terms (as spectacle, say) or in terms of their impact on the place of the writer in society. Indeed, this fact provides the most immedi-ate thematic and historical rationale for this particular grouping of texts.

The story I attempt to tell might well be characterized in part as belonging to the Marxian genre of narratives of commodification, but one that employs an alternate conceptual and terminological ensemble—the dialectic of class and middle-classlessness—in order to highlight hitherto underappreciated aspects of this process. My other concern in downplaying the vocabulary of consumerism is with avoiding the temptation to consider consumption in isolation from labor and production, which tends to grant to it an autonomous power and self-sufficient existence, and thinking instead about the kinds of constitutive and evolving interrelationships obtaining amongst the "communicating vessels" of production, exchange, and consumption.[20]

Another principal theme arising in this book is technology, which also emerges from the focus on work and work's deployment in the production process. It is as a moment of production wherein technological developments typically first appear and derive their initial rationale. Nor is this simply a matter of bigger and faster machines of various kinds. Capital has tended to employ technology as a direct intervention into the labor process, such that it might be restructured on terms more favorable to itself: either by reducing the need for workers or, probably more crucially, by reshaping the jobs themselves such that they require less skill to execute. This latter process is generally what is intended by the name Taylorism, something that far outstrips the ultimately fairly limited (and not terribly successful) efforts of F. W. Taylor himself to have industries impose regimes of "scientific management." As David Montgomery observes, only after Taylor's abstract schemata found material embodiment in the physical applications themselves (a development to which Taylor himself contributed little) could Taylorism as such come fully into being.[21]

This, in any event, is the stage or modality of technology with which we engage when we turn to *Sister Carrie*, although even here, by way of what are effectively figurative analogues of Taylorism (rocking chairs, popular magazines—instantiations of that new mobility or flow that Taylorism conceptually encoded), we begin to consider the interface between technology and "cultural form" that Raymond Williams stressed in his seminal analysis of television.[22] In the chapters on Nathanael West and John Barth the interface between technology and cultural production, in the forms of film and television, is interrogated. This boundary line is traversed and complicated by the fact that the cultural forms in question here are those that inhabit what must still be referred to as the culture industry, in which the aesthetic dimension (particularly at the time when West and Barth were writing) is almost wholly subordinate to the profit motive, and the time of leisure during which its products are consumed is more and more structured as an extension of the workday itself. That is, "not working" in this domain continues to be inhabited and informed by the exigencies of labor.

Despite my effort to sustain a focus upon some of the practical and material elements making up the domain of middle-classlessness, the accompanying ideological expressions of these elements do not thereby vanish from sight. Indeed, the reverse but parallel bodies of discourse indicated by the designations "pastoral" and "frontier" remain key reference points throughout. Although the period covered here is from 1900 to 1955—after the frontier technically has "closed" and long after the agrarian world to which the earlier pastoral visions corresponded has disappeared—it is evident, as historians like Richard Slotkin and Michael Rogin have argued, that these ideological patterns have persisted, by way of strategic updatings and fresh figural embodiments, down through the twentieth century. Both ideological traditions participate in the dynamic of class effacement we are analyzing here; however, they operate on the opposite fundamental principle (hence "reverse but parallel"). With frontier mythology, it is precisely movement and dynamism that are emphasized, a continual movement forward that keeps one ahead of the pressures of society, ahead of the inextricable webs of economic dependency and inhabiting an "empty" space suitable for peremptory and often violent acts of self-creation (which inevitably set loose a free-market logic in their wake, which must be evaded yet again). Pastoralism, meanwhile, seeks a retreat from the market (as we indicated earlier) through a strategic inertia, through a small-scale, self-maintaining, homeostatic production system. Putting things like this perhaps affords us one clue about the power of the televisual system, which we encounter in the final chapter on Barth's *Floating Opera*: when channel surfing meets the couch potato, when imagined mobility fuses with stasis, we have an unexpected synthesis of frontier and pastoral, and a cultural form of unusual seductiveness. Versions of this synthesis are, however, discovered throughout the novels at hand—in the form of Carrie's rocker and her department store meanderings, the movies and the crowd scenes in West—which provide us with a crucial Ariadne's thread to help us navigate the narrative complexities ahead.

• • •

A few words should perhaps be said at this juncture concerning some of my own investments in a project such as this and some of the larger political and philosophical assumptions guiding it. First, the reader will by now have guessed that the analytic category of class and the model of the social allied with it, as delineated in the Marxist tradition, are here being accepted fairly straightforwardly. Indeed, Marx's proposal of the struggle between capital and wage labor as a kind of "foundational" contradiction and inner motor for this mode of production (but historically foundational, as a construction in time—one which might eventually be replaced by a different fundamental pattern of organization) still seems more explanatorily powerful and politically consequent than anything bourgeois social science and political philosophy have come up with. Although we are today more fully aware of the many nuances we should attend to when employing this approach—the multiple and contradictory class strata, the many ruses of hegemony—I nonetheless believe that the basic model should be retained.

As far as the supposed untenability of the model's bipolar, "two class" aspect is concerned, I tend to think that worries over it arise from a kind of implicit sociological reduction, of the sort Marx himself (if not some of his followers) usually avoids, wherein class is imagined in terms of preset empirical groups. I would suggest that it is probably more satisfactory to conceive the matter in terms of class processes. While on one hand there may not be two neatly defined classes in any obvious sense, on the other hand there really are only two class processes at work in the capitalist mode of production, known in the tradition as proletarianization and embourgeoisement: imagine these as two great forces, like riptides or gravity wells, pulling (most) people toward the pole of wage work and the production of surplus value, others toward the pole of the appropriation of surplus value, with a corresponding variable proximity with respect to the ownership and control of the apparatuses of production, distribution, and exchange. Imagine, too, individuals and groups either fighting against or colluding with these forces, with widely varying degrees of success—a drama played out across the full spectrum of the highly differentiated contemporary (national and international) division of labor—and one has, I think, a crisp thumbnail sketch of a structure that, while the "product" of human responses to two fundamental forces, can nonetheless display any number of varied and complex locations. All such locations are inherently unstable, and can become subject to the torsional effect of this force field. Indeed, with the recent downsizing of middle management, the increasing technological displacement of engineers and architects, and the sessionalization/detenuring of university departments, positions and locations once regarded as concrete evidence of Marx's errors are today under an intense pressure of proletarianization (which is not the same as saying that these positions will become the social *equivalents* of janitor or autoworker).

Such an overall intellectual orientation faces peculiar pressures these days within the academy (though doubtless this has always been the case to a certain extent). Within the traditions of American culture studies, the place of Marxism has been equivocal at best: when not denounced outright, it has just as frequently been strategically displaced by a left/progressive optic, descending from the cultural criticism of Van Wyck Brooks, Lewis Mumford, and later Popular Front figures. This has tended to operate, as Michael Denning has argued in a well-known essay, as itself a kind of "substitute Marxism" that, while distancing itself from Marxism, nonetheless tries at the same time to make up for the lack of an established Marxist tradition in this country.[23] Meanwhile, the contemporary exploration of the textual and historical imbrications of race/class/gender (a "holy trinity" to its detractors), despite its productive and pathbreaking achievements, has in fact tended to downplay the salience of class. Aside from the difficulties facing Marxism more generally these days, this has to do with the inclination of class to play out rather differently, both conceptually and practically, than discourses organized around race, gender, or ethnicity.

Some might thus be tempted to see a certain incompatibility among these terms, and seek for one or the other a definitive analytic superiority. That way madness lies, however; better, therefore, to become more attuned to the subtle resonances among these key concepts, something we are more fortunately positioned these days to do. Michel Foucault once urged us to contest the subject positions into which we are typically interpellated, to refuse the identities with which we find ourselves burdened. I have often thought that these reflections of Foucault, his own ambivalence about Marxism notwithstanding, represented him at his most Marxist, in that any renovated idea of socialist politics ought likewise to seek a dissolution (or at least a radical rearticulation) of the very concept of identity (and its twin corollary, difference)—political desiderata that align this conception of socialism with broad currents in contemporary theory. It is evident that the hermeneutics of identity are in our society organized to a great degree around work and the division of labor: "what do you do?" is a question never far from our lips, the answer to which (salesman, say, or teacher) then furnishes us with a set of socially fabricated knowledge grids about a person's education, familial background, tastes, gender makeup, and so forth—grids which are frequently not inaccurate, because different forms of work are in fact strong indices of the forms of sociocultural space one inhabits, and really do carry powerful charges of social meaning, which work to fix people in place like insects on a board.[24] The roots of this, I think, lie in the social effects of the specifically capitalist division of labor, in contrast to what Marx called a "natural" or precapitalist division of labor. In earlier societies, tasks were typically sorted out according to identity criteria of gender and age. What one worked at did not particularly reflect on one's identity, since this social identity preceded one's labor. At a later period of historical development, for example under feudalism, some occupational categories began to acquire social content: everyone knew that millers or coopers, for instance, all behaved in certain ways. The capitalist division of labor now generalizes this process across the space of the social, owing to its constitutive, semiautonomous economic moment: purchasers of labor power seek initially a certain ratio of force to skill for a defined task, as opposed to a certain kind of person, even if certain ideologies of race or gender subsequently overcode this process. What this entails, I suspect, is not a further disarticulation between labor and identity but a sharp intensification of the linkage, as a new hermeneutic drive that seeks to read people through the work they do is precipitated. To paraphrase Wittgenstein, to imagine a form of work is henceforth to imagine a form of life.[25] Hence Marx's great passage in *The German Ideology*:

> For as soon as the distribution of labour comes into being, each man has a particular, exclusive sphere of activity, which is forced upon him and from which he cannot escape. He is a hunter, a fisherman, a shepherd, or a critical critic, and must remain so if he does not want to lose his

means of livelihood; while in communist society, where nobody has one exclusive sphere of activity, but each can become accomplished in any branch he wishes, society regulates the general production and thus makes it possible for me to do one thing today and another tomorrow, to hunt in the morning, fish in the afternoon, rear cattle in the evening, criticise after dinner, just as I have a mind, without ever becoming hunter, fisherman, shepherd, or critic.[26]

My sense is that people, whatever their metaphorical proclivities in general, tend these days to approach a passage like this with a resolute literal minded-ness ("but I don't like fishing"), thereby judging it to be rather simplistic. But it is essentially figural in intent, and its radical thrust comes through if we grasp that it specifically targets, besides the division of labor, identity as such: the anticipation, then, of a kind of supreme anonymity, such as one might find—but only fitfully, fleetingly—in our great urban centers.[27] As we shall see later on, consumerism targets identity as well, though in a rather different fashion.

What we might thus perceive as a certain "desire called nonidentity" has clear resonances with other currents in critical thought, most notably queer theory, with its stress on the performative dimensions of gender identity and on the transformative potential of queer counterpublics for refiguring the (hetero)normative frames of bourgeois intimacy and erotic expression. Lee Edelman, in a remarkable recent essay, is even more intransigent in his attack on identity, arguing that any politics depends on a projected futurity rooted in the heteronormative image of the child, and thus questions the very notion of a "queer politics."[28] Edelman counterposes to this what he properly calls the impossible project of the queer, which is to represent or embody the radical irony of the signifier, to become in effect that de Manian aporia or Derridean trace that disables all narratives and disrupts all politics. Indeed, says Edelman, the queer finally figures forth the death drive itself. While I sense here the privileging of a purely intellectualist vision, this in no way detracts from the essay's intense and productive investment in what I am calling nonidentity. Such antireification models of gender and sexuality might be taken as possible (and necessary) cultural analogues to the kinds of new human sociality sought by Marxism through the abolition of private property and the democratization of the labor process.

Meanwhile, Etienne Balibar has in his recent reflections on class as a category proposed a kind of dereified notion of class, shorn of positive "identarian" content. He advises that we stop thinking of class as a particular group invested with a mythic unity and a unique destiny: the proletarian, and invariably masculine, Subject of History. Instead, he foregrounds the shape-shifting manifestations of class struggle—the complex power games and resistances occasioned by the appropriation and apportionment of surplus value—as an irreducible logic that cuts across and disrupts all social and political forms and practices. It is an inescapable and determinate "other" of social action and group identity, a sinuous and mobile terrain on which we move and struggle with our desires.[29] Indeed, the very conceptuality of class, as Peter Hitchcock has noted, is structured by a profound paradox of (un)representability, in that class, as suggested above, does not as a term attempt to name or indicate substances so much as serve as a mediational or translational conduit between economic structure and demographic data on one hand and human and social content on the other. "Marxist critique depends," Hitchcock observes, "on 'grasping' the visible of the invisible— that the illusion of classlessness is a reality of the concept of class, something *both* historically determined and intrinsic to its ambivalent formulation."[30] The manifestations of class, both historically and discursively, thus follow a logic of effacement and return, a properly "spectral" pattern (to invoke Derrida's figure) which, it sometimes seems, American national ideology has exploited more rigorously than any other. All such (queer, Marxian) disruptive logics, finally, imply paradoxical things for the very category of identity: given the fundamentally contradictory nature of the social formation we inhabit, it emerges as something of a permanent crisis term, despised and desired—like so much else—all at once. Imposed upon us, via the multiple modalities of interpellation, in ways not of our own fashioning, still it provides something like shelter in a storm, the appearance of stability in the face of the dislocations and negativities of social logic.

I am not sure, in the end, if what follows really conforms to what Balibar has in mind, although it was certainly motivated by a felt need for new ways of registering the significations of social class, of broadening the semantic field of the concept, in a situation where such methods seemed singularly lacking. Irony of ironies, then, that more often than not in these pages I catch class at the moment of its disappearance, in the process of being volatilized and sublimated into something else entirely, something else that desperately seeks both to preserve and to eradicate the concept altogether. Does this mean that I too have fallen prey to the ineluctable "genius of American pluralism," that contradiction-free domain of interest-group compromise, as Cold War liberal exceptionalists like Louis Hartz and Seymour Lipset might have predicted I would? I prefer to think that, in tracing the complicated circuits of work, leisure, and technology in these novels, I have demonstrated not the weakness but precisely the strength of social class in the "American scene," the unrelenting pressure it exerts on the American cultural imagination. That it is also fictively managed and wondrously neutralized in ever more inventive ways merely attests to this power, and to a political unconscious of class that maintains an intense and insistent relationship with the manifest levels of the texts.

two

The Burden of Toil:

Sister Carrie *as Urban Pastoral*

The wage-earners, the toilers of old,

notably in other climes, were known by the

wealth of their songs; and has it, on these

lines, been given to the American people

to be known by the number of their

"candies"?

—Henry James, *The American Scene*

When Carrie Meeber pulls into Chicago aboard the afternoon train from Columbia City, what sort of a world is she entering? The distance she travels (the kind of journey that had become a stock image in the popular literature of the late nineteenth century) brings her to the brink of, and sometimes across, a series of thresholds, and exacerbates what might be called the qualities of liminality associated with such thresholds. The ineluctable passage from childhood to adulthood, for example, is achieved in the first paragraph: "A gush of tears at her mother's farewell kiss, a touch in her throat when the cars clacked by the flour mill where her father worked by the day, a pathetic sigh as the familiar green environs of the village passed in review, and the threads which bound her so lightly to girlhood and home were irretrievably broken."[1] This achievement is evidently something less than a milestone, our first indication that the sites and contexts of family and childhood are, in this novel, going to be singularly unimportant. It serves only to bring Carrie to the liminal state of temptation, her moral betterment now threatened by the lure of the "cosmopolitan standard of virtue" endemic to the new urban world she is entering.

Other thresholds are present. In a famous passage, Dreiser captures the rapidly developing and, as it were, speculative nature of 1880s Chicago:

> Streetcar lines had been extended far out into the open country in anticipation of rapid growth. The city had laid miles and miles of streets and sewers, through regions where, perhaps, one solitary house stood out alone—a pioneer of the populous ways to be. There were regions open to the sweeping winds and rain, which were yet lighted throughout the night with long, blinking lines of gaslamps, fluttering in the wind. Narrow boardwalks extended out, passing here a house, and there a store, at far intervals, eventually ending on the open prairie. (20)

At least two liminal states are evoked here. One is temporal, and concerns a present condition being eroded from within by an impending future, a present compelled, as Philip Fisher notes, "to live in the near-empty outline of what will someday be real."[2] This is a present, then, that is being flung headlong into the future, bringing to mind the sense of mobility, and of the concomitant insufficiency of the here and now, that finds such intense and diverse figuration throughout the novel. What will meanwhile "fill in" this nearly empty present, at least in this passage, is concentrated human labor itself—labor that, although itself remaining invisible within this image, is busy hammering and sawing just beyond its frame. The quiet inactivity of the scene portends immense energy and bustle.

Here, at the edge of the prairie, we stand at that interface between the metropolis and the wilderness, so prominent in American ideology, designated by the complementary (if reversed) notions of the pastoral and the frontier. The former term connotes the quiet retreat from bourgeois economy, a stillness in the face of the pressures and disruptions of the market; the latter stands as a kind of free-market analogue to this, where a continual flight forward keeps one a step ahead of those same disturbances. Situated as we are so close to Chicago, to burgeoning urban density, the invocation of a notion such as the frontier might seem somewhat out of place. However, as both Mike Davis and Richard Slotkin have argued, not only was the growth of frontier ideologies of social mobility stimulated by the advance of the urban/industrial frontier as much as by the advance of the rural/agrarian one, but frontier mythology enjoyed its greatest period of expansion after the close of the Old West, in an increasingly urban and industrializing era.[3] This last fact is but one indication of the kind of materio-ideological crisis precipitated by the closing of the frontier in the late nineteenth century, when the United States was forced to turn from internal imperialism to a more external variety. Slotkin indeed situates frontier ideology as a version of imperialist thinking, wherein imperialism is posited as an antidote to class antagonism, an interpretation offered originally (if less critically) by Frederick Jackson Turner himself, in his famous paper on the frontier delivered, of course, at the Chicago World's Fair of 1893, a fair attended by Dreiser in the capacity of reporter for the St. Louis *Republic* (the implications of which are taken up below).

For the moment, the passage above evinces a quieter aspect, more pastoral in its inflections. The other liminal state evoked in it is more elusive, but plays perhaps as crucial a role in the novel. To begin, I would ask the reader to reverse directions in the mind's eye, to go back into town, from the open prairie toward the urban center. This provides, I hope, a sense of the city as somehow growing up out of the soil, and points ultimately to some peculiar interminglings of nature and culture, in what seems at first glance to be a resolutely metropolitan narrative. In this regard, Dreiser has, albeit in a very general way, unique raw material to draw on, as William Cronon's recent history of the city suggests. It is the virtue of Chicago itself, Cronon argues, among all the great urban centers of the United States, to have enjoyed a profound and unequaled relationship with its surrounding hinterland, both economically and socially.[4] While Chicago economically dominated a vast territory to the west and south of it, popular images of the city, particularly during its phase of spectacular growth following the Great Fire of 1871, tended to depict in natural terms (volcanic, oceanic) the city's unleashing of productive energy, as well as the overwhelming powers of attraction the growing metropolis displayed. Hamlin Garland, like Dreiser with Carrie, put his character Rose Dutcher on board a train bound for the big city: "It was this wonderful thing again, a fresh, young and powerful soul rushing to a great city, a shining atom of steel obeying a magnet, a clear rivulet from the hills hurrying to the sea. On every train at that same hour, from every direction, others, like her, were entering on the same search to the same end."⁵ Like a great natural process, the popular culture of the day envisioned Chicago as a space where the distinctions between a "machine in the garden" and a more modern "garden in the machine" were beginning to become blurred.⁶

The "hour" Garland invokes in his description of Rose's train ride remains uncertain. Dreiser, in contrast, specifies precisely when Carrie arrives in town, in a crucial passage I want to juxtapose with the earlier vision of empty boardwalks and swaying gaslamps, one that deepens our sense of the type of world Carrie enters. Carrie approaches the city in evening twilight, a time of some significance, it being

> that mystic period between the glare and gloom of the world when life is changing from one sphere or condition to another. Ah, the promise of the night. What does it not hold for the weary! What old illusion of hope is not here forever repeated! Says the soul of the toiler to itself, "I shall soon be free. I shall be in the way and the hosts of the merry. The streets, the lamps, the lighted chamber set for dining are for me. The theater, the halls, the parties, the ways of rest and the paths of song—these are mine in the night." Though all humanity be still enclosed in the shops, the thrill runs abroad. It is in the air. The dullest feel something which they might not always express or describe. It is the lifting of the burden of toil. (13–14)

Despite the characteristic Dreiserian sentimentality present here, I suggest that the utopian impulses at work in such language not be passed over or simply dismissed as insipid. I wish instead to take them seriously, as my sense is that what we might well call a middle-class imaginary takes them seriously as well, indeed treats them in an almost literal sort of way, tying its intended states of fantasy precisely to the affective dynamics of such everyday yearning and anticipation. The transition from work to leisure is here figured in the liminal time of twilight, a time, Dreiser notes with care, during which work is tapering off, perhaps has just ceased, and the approach of leisure becomes palpably anticipated: a fleeting period when labor and leisure effectively interpenetrate one another, the physical memory of work having not yet faded from the anticipation of rest—the burden of toil not lifted, but in the process of being lifted (and in that sense unidirectional—few experience such liminal anticipation on the drive to work in the morning). Dreiser's attempt to give figuration to this phenomenon results in a certain utopian breathlessness, and a striking eruption of desire.

Dreiser is powerfully drawn to the kind of transition evoked here:[7] it appears again, in somewhat more measured terms, two chapters later, as Carrie leaves the factory at which she has just applied for work.

> She walked out into the busy street and discovered a new atmosphere.... She noticed that men and women were smiling. Scraps of conversation and notes of laughter floated to her. The air was light. People were already pouring out of the buildings, their labor ended for the day. She noticed that they were pleased, and thoughts of her sister's home and the meal that would be awaiting her quickened her steps. (31)

Anyone who has ever been downtown in a large city at about five in the afternoon can attest to the accuracy of Dreiser's description here. As in the above passage, he draws attention to the satisfactions of home and, especially, a good meal, images that recur in other writers not normally thought to be very sentimental: I am thinking of Brecht's image of the peasant's soup and cigar, and of Adorno's assertion of the striking quality, at once forceful and "tender," of the utopian demand that "no one shall go hungry anymore."[8] Although Carrie here partakes of this atmosphere of quitting time, the specific referents of home and food (again, anticipated) will quickly cease to strike her fancy. She will in fact never return to them in any imaginative way, because they represent part of the rhythm of the workday, a sphere from which she will try to escape throughout the novel (though she never quite succeeds), an escape trajectory that will bring very different visions of satisfaction before her. Working/not working, then, in the context of capitalist wage labor is one of the central aspects of the ideological imaginary of which *Sister Carrie* traces the essential lineaments.

In attempting to account for the "sentimental power" of the desire embedded in these passages, and to give a more precise configuration of the utopian impulse contained in them, I am drawn to Peter Bürger's thesis concerning the transaesthetic project of the historical avant-gardes of European modernism, namely the effort to *reaestheticize* everyday life. Assailing an aesthetic realm that had been socially posited as autonomous, Dada and surrealism sought, Bürger contends, a destruction of this realm and a return of its gratifications and utopian contents (in particular its Kantian "purposefulness without a purpose") to the material sphere of everyday work and activity.[9] Dreiser is no Breton, of course, but I want to suggest that this programmatic high modernist moment knows (even if it might try to repress) its popular cultural side as well, the evocation of quitting time being the perfect figure of this. I return to that notion of interpenetration introduced above, in that moment of suspension and transition between work and leisure when the immediate and lingering memory of work commingles with the anticipations of relaxation, when the purposefulness of the wage earner's day and the (at least ideal) purposelessness of the time of leisure have not yet been fully separated, affording the slightest inkling of their combination. Here the utopian ambition of the avant-garde project is given more affective, less programmatic expression.

The initial scene of empty boardwalks and swaying gaslamps, together with the atmosphere of the end of the workday, provides us with the essential frame within which the novel's characters will move and act. The former image of the developing prairie can itself be understood to partake of the "lifting of the burden of toil," at least at a certain remove, provided we recall what it is that the incipient labor at its margins will be working toward, namely the construction of a suburb. The suburb has typically been imagined as the negation of urban industrialization, as a pastoral retreat within the confines of urban economic functionality—a greening of the machine. It is also the most exemplary material and spatial correlative to middle-classlessness. As Cronon notes, Chicago in the 1890s was the most extensively suburbanized metropolitan area in the United States, a result of the city's unparalleled railroad infrastructure coupled with the postfire housing boom.[10] The ethos of these new suburban areas was in many ways at odds with what the pop cultural images of the city tended to depict as the core of its greatness: its productive energy and dynamic growth. The suburbs, by contrast, had to banish from their precincts "the one essential foundation of city and country alike: productive labor"—they had to avoid the aspect of a "working landscape."[11]

Such an impulse had long been at the heart of American pastoral ideology, as Leo Marx's great study exhaustively shows. The pastoral realm rejects growth, productivity, the model of *homo oeconomicus*, a pattern first formally codified and elaborated on in the American context in Jefferson's *Notes on the State of Virginia*. The "noble husbandman," the generic denizen of the pastoral, strives only for minimal economic self-sufficiency, a kind of economic stasis that, Marx notes, depends upon a particular dispensation of land ownership:

> By equating desires with needs, turning his back on industry and trade, the husbandmen would be free of the tyranny of the market. Here the absence of economic complexities makes credible the absence of their usual concomitant, a class structure. Jefferson grounds this happy class-less state in the farmer's actual possession of the land; in such a society all men would adopt an aloof patrician attitude toward acquisitive be-havior.[12]

In such a "happy state" one can see how it might be that the pastoral in-habitant can come to enjoy, as Marx puts it, both the "ease of the rich and the simple honesty of the poor": Marx concurs here with William Empson's lo-cating of the key ideological moment of the pastoral, whose "essential trick" was to "imply a beautiful relation between rich and poor."[13] Through the liminal function of the eloquent (and thus civilized, metropolitan) herds-man, or, in his American incarnation, the noble farmer, the pastoral pro-duces a harmonized admixture of urban and rural (or industrial and agrar-ian) which is at one and the same time a meshing of aristocrat and peasant, or bourgeois and worker (but from the ruling class, hence socially conserva-tive, point of view): it is the exemplary middle space or landscape, where invidious extremes of any kind are wondrously neutralized. In this way, the subject of pastoral ideology can enjoy a kind of vicarious solution to the problem of social hierarchy—can experience, as Empson puts it, "a feeling of solidarity between classes."[14] In this perspective, the ideal trajectory of the pastoral would end in an imaginative space that dispenses with the sense that classes exist at all, which is of course the basic frame of our investigation here.

Marx's above comments on Jefferson make clear the material basis of Jef-ferson's Arcadian musings. They are grounded on the putative self-sufficiency of the independent freeholder, whose reduction of desires to needs is in turn made possible by the natural productivity of the land. He owns his own "means of production," and his labor, regardless of its intensity, is gratifying, experienced as a kind of leisure: in a word, it is unalienated. Here is a bourgeois daydream (one of the cornerstones of republican thought) that goes against the grain of some of the more characteristic features of bourgeois ideology, in particular its "frontier" commitment to economic growth and market dynamism (things that elsewhere in his writings Jefferson is happy to endorse). The plausibility of this vision was at the time secured in part by the great demographic fact of the later colonial period and the first decades of the Republic, namely the existence of a uniquely high percentage of the kinds of people Jefferson had in mind: not only independent landholders, but independent yeomen, artisans, and small enterprisers of all kinds, all owners of their means of production and disdainful of what was then still a minority phenomenon, wage labor. This key segment of society tended to uphold conservative and corporatist values, values largely eradicated by the triumphant free-market ideology of the Jacksonian era.[15]

But we are now with Dreiser at the turn of the twentieth century, and if we are to grasp the central impulse of his narrative practice as the exploration of the structure and possibilities of an urban pastoral, then this last must clearly be seen in terms of a certain refunctioning of older discursive materials. In particular, Marx's description of the "reduction of desires to needs" in the Jeffersonian idyll might give one pause, since the figure of Carrie would seem to be strikingly at odds with this process. This is, however, to ignore the figure of Hurstwood, who, in his later phase, not merely reduces desire to need (as evidenced, for example, in his scrupulous returning of exact change to Carrie after his trips to the grocery, and in his refusals of Carrie's offers of extra spending money), but gradually extinguishes even need itself. I treat, then, the two main characters—following the work of other critics (notably Fisher) who have detailed the insistent parallelism of Carrie and Hurstwood—as essentially a dyadic pairing: the noble farmer here split into complementary parts, in order to better map what is now a more complicated and conflicted social and ideological terrain.

The matter of the desire-need coupling, and of the related issue of the "aloof" regard for acquisitive behavior, returns us to the aforementioned material basis of these, the natural and self-sustaining productive power of the land. In the new urban and industrial conditions, this image of the land no longer obtains. Bracketing its literal level, though, allows us to better perceive its function in the pastoral scene, that is, as an image of material security, of individually owned plenitude, which supports a life of ease and happiness: the kind of function that can henceforth be reassumed by the sphere of consumption, and its "basket of goods," once the actual means of production are in someone else's hands. Surrounding oneself with new and better objects works to keep the specter of class society at bay, as the personal plot of land did in the earlier formulation. To Richard Lehan's puzzled question about whether *Sister Carrie* is more concerned with production or consumption,[16] I would respond that, regarding these matters, its primary concern is with showing production *on the way to* consumption, or, more specifically, the ideological function of an older image of idealized agrarian production being translated into the terms of modern consumer ideology, attempting thus to bypass along the way the realities of industrial capitalist production. These are still quite general coordinates—we have yet to locate in the novel, in any systematic fashion, the full range of pastoral sites and their associated energies.

■ ■ ■

That Dreiser's adaptation of pastoral strategies and impulses to an urban setting takes place in what is also a "middling" setting is evident: "Among the forces which sweep and play throughout the universe, untutored man is but a wisp in the wind. Our civilization is still in a middle stage, scarcely beast, in that it is no longer wholly guided by instinct; scarcely human, in that it is not yet wholly guided by reason" (74). Here is a kind of cosmic frame for the narrative, one which might be recast in terms of the transitional space between civilization ("reason") and the wilderness ("instinct"). Its inhabitants are themselves purposefully described. Carrie, we learn at once, is "a fair example of the middle American class," a statement that must at once be coordinated with our knowledge that her father works in a flour mill: the suggestion is made immediately that the "middle class" has as much to do with sensibility and attitude as it does with the kind of work one does. As for Hurstwood, something of a reverse but parallel image is offered. He is, Dreiser says, "altogether a very acceptable individual of our great American upper class," but we know there is something hollow in this. He is not a true bourgeois, for he lacks "financial control" in the saloon or "resort" where he works, and, to underscore the point, all of Hurstwood's property is put under his wife's name. A kind of curious bourgeois retainer, his entire sense of his social position rests on the flimsiest of material foundations. That is to say, he really is "middle class" in the sense we are trying to develop here.

We enter this great middle state, with Carrie, in August 1889. Four years later, the city of Chicago hosted the World's Columbian Exposition, which still stands as one of the most spectacular expositions ever mounted. Dreiser covered the event for the St. Louis *Republic*, and his reports from the scene conveyed a breathlessness and sense of awe in the face of the exposition's highly self-conscious attempt at magnificence. Although we might suspect here a measure of deliberate participation in this attempt on Dreiser's part (that is, his understanding of the reporter's task to be in part to sell the fair to people in other cities), nearly thirty years later, in his autobiographical *Newspaper Days* (1922), he testified that the fair had achieved "a lightness and an airiness wholly at war with anything that this western world had as yet presented, which caused me to be swept into a dream from which I did not recover for months."[17] These sentiments were induced particularly with respect to the White City, the gleaming neoclassical extravaganza on the Lake Michigan shore that comprised the architectural, if not necessarily the ideological, heart of the fair.[18]

This is not to say that there was no explicit thematic intent lying behind the design of the White City. Daniel Burnham, its architect, and Frederick Law Olmsted, its celebrated landscaper, wanted the bright plaster, wide boulevards, and the many green spaces and reflecting pools of the White City specifically to conjure up a sense of the open prairie. To this pastoral invitation, Dreiser responded positively:

> The White City is grand. It is beautiful by day, with the blue sky above, the changing colors of the waters of Michigan to the east of it and the glorious sunbeams flooding its arches and spires, its pillars and domes, as they stand so distinct and clear, out against the sky. There is not one who does not delight in the coolness of the air, the endless splash of the waters on the sands of the shore. None could fail to appreciate the beauty of the well-kept lawns, so richly green, that are curbed in by winding walks, so graceful in their contour and shaded by beautiful trees and shrubbery. Then it is that one is reminded of what the ancient Athenian capital must have been like. How its temples and public buildings, its statuary and its public ways must have adorned the ancient hills of Helias.[19]

Dreiser then goes on, in *Sister Carrie*, to re-create some of this very same language, as for example in the famous passage where Carrie (characteristically peering through the window of her carriage, through the windows of houses), responds feelingly to the mansions of the new northside suburbs:

> Across the broad lawns, now first freshening into green, she saw lamps faintly glowing upon rich interiors. Now it was but a chair, now a table, now an ornate corner, which met her eye, but it appealed to her as almost nothing else could. Such childish fancies as she had of fairy palaces and kingly quarters now came back. She imagined that across these richly carved entrance ways, where the globed and crystalled lamps shone upon panelled doors set with stained and designed panes of glass, was neither care nor unsatisfied desire. (100–101)

One hesitates to draw a direct line of influence from the former passage to the latter: perhaps Dreiser had always responded to stately buildings and manicured greenery in this fashion (later transferring this response to his characters in a relatively unmediated way, as recent critical work on the ambiguous status of the novel's narrator might suggest).[20] Still, the resemblance is striking, and I find suggestive the manner in which Dreiser later recalls his White City response precisely in relation to a suburban scene, as if he had himself grasped that aspect of the fair that Cronon points to, namely its evocation not so much of the prairie, but of the suburb: "In the fair's electric vehicles and lack of horse manure, its carefully cleaned streets and landscaped grounds, its architectural beauty and leisurely crowds, visitors saw an urban equivalent of the suburban ideal."[21] Like the suburb, the fair depended upon the hiding of "productive labor," although sheer productivity, at least—the tremendous development of Chicago itself—was no doubt alluded to through the exposition's size and baroque excess. It is not clear that such a spectacle could have been successfully mounted at that time in any other city.

Other passages, similar to Carrie's tour of the suburbs, are present in the novel, in which some of the more familiar pastoral motifs are employed. Others are cleverly reimagined: the insistent seasonal changes that Dreiser details—the sunlit parks and chill, blustery avenues—emerge, for example, as expressive rhythms of the city itself. I suggest, however, that Dreiser's real innovation with respect to his adaptation of pastoral impulses to an urban setting lies with his invention of a new scene of pastoral typicality, a new site of ambivalent utopian energy, which is the famous and insistent dyad of window and rocking chair (associated with both Carrie and Hurstwood). At the most basic level, windows are the ambivalent threshold (are they part of the inside of the building or not?, Derrida asks) between the inside and the outside, between the built environment and the natural one, and hence partake in what might be termed a certain phenomenology of the pastoral. Recall Benjamin's invocation of the breath drawn at a windowsill, where the spirit is inscrutably quickened and notes of longing and anticipation are struck, a qualitatively different experience from a breath drawn either wholly in or wholly out of doors. Windows are, of course, a prime site for the production of desire in the novel (Carrie's yearning, her envious peering into others' homes), but also, and this is usually not stressed as frequently, desire's extinction (Hurstwood, too, reads and rocks by the window, not only during his decline but all the while in Chicago as well, the first evidence that his "downfall" is not exactly what it seems).

This ambivalence can be linked to another principal function of windows in the novel, which is their symbolic demarcation of those who work from those who do not. Carrie's first forays into downtown Chicago, inhabiting the new and unfamiliar subject position of "wage seeker," are one instance of this: the great sheets of plate glass lining the outer offices of the factories afford Carrie a view of the workplace while positioning her as one who does not yet have gainful employment. Later, having escaped wage work, Carrie imagines a series of work/window images, with herself on the outside:

> Toil, now that she was free of it, seemed even a more desolate thing than when she was a part of it. She saw it through a mist of fancy—a pale, somber half-light, which was the essence of poetic feeling. Her old father, in his flour-dusted miller's suit, sometimes returned to her in memory, revived by a face in a window. A shoemaker pegging at his last, a blastman seen through a narrow window in some basement where iron was being melted, a benchworker seen high aloft in some window, his coat off, his sleeves rolled up: these took her back in fancy to the details of the mill. (140)

Windows consistently position Carrie as outside work or activity, but also somehow near it, in some unclear relation to it, whether, as here, she is imaginatively looking in upon it, or in her rocker, dreaming but not doing, another space of inactivity.

Philip Fisher, following Sigfried Giedion, has analyzed the increasing popularity of the rocking chair in late nineteenth-century America in terms of the pleasurable routinization of the ever more motion-intensive patterns of labor and technology. He then widens the analysis to "that quintessential American image," the rocking chair on a porch, which

> permits the rocker to be in motion and yet never to leave the same place, to be outside the house and yet still in the domestic space, to participate in street life without leaving family safety. . . . The state is one of striking in-betweenness, as though a way had been found to factor out the pleasures of many conditions and fuse them while discarding all of the inconveniences that generally accompany either motion or rest, domesticity or sociability, family life or citizenship.[22]

This is pertinent, so far as it goes, though it remains insufficiently appreciative of the deeper, or at least more basic, process at work already invoked in relation to windows, which is the porch's mediating function between the natural and built environments. Although one might object that the more crucial mediation here is between domesticity and sociality, I am guided by Michael Rogin's observation that this latter split, and related notions of a public/private separation, have, in American culture, been intensely and ambiguously overcoded by the nature/culture division (ambiguously, because the spatial polarities of where "nature" and "culture" are to be located can change in different circumstances).[23]

This mediating function, and the porch's status as among the most intense of pastoral spaces, can initially be grasped by thinking about the necessary structural details attending any proper porch, without which it will simply not feel right (a list that can probably be generated only after having spent considerable time on porches): it must be covered but not enclosed (the screened porch thus being a fairly lamentable innovation in this regard); it must be elevated a couple of steps or so above street or ground level; it should have a railing, although sometimes well-placed shrubbery can fulfill this role; it cannot be too narrow or too wide; and so forth. In other words, a fairly exacting articulation of the inside into the outside takes place in such spaces: one cannot be either too inside or too outside, a point I stress because the "formal demands" of the porch recall, again in a popular cultural or "vernacular" fashion (in the way Dreiser's depiction of quitting time brought to mind the project of the modernist avant-gardes), another high modernist ambition, namely the architectural effort to imagine a solution to the contradiction between the inside and outside (or, more precisely, between the interior and the facade). For the modernist architects, this particular division was not simply an inert distinction. Rather, it became a focal point of intense creative energy, and was grappled with in concrete and utopian terms, the problem being regarded as an invidious separation, a symptomatic blockage, whose solution—framed typically in terms of the need for the interior to "express" the facade or exterior—would have profound consequences (among them, some new relationship to the nonbuilt), recalling that destruction and rearticulation of the split between the aesthetic and the everyday sought by the avant-gardes.[24]

The porch does not of course solve this conundrum, though I think it addresses a related set of problems, at a level different from that of high modernism. Juxtaposing the porch with the modernist concern allows us at the very least to sharpen Fisher's formulation, and to give a more thorough accounting of the peculiar properties of this interesting space (to account for what we might call its "sentimental power," analogous to our discussion of the end of the workday). Fisher sees the porch as a harmonious blending of domesticity and sociality, which factors out the more annoying aspects of both. This is on the right track, but would benefit from a stronger formulation: the porch is first and foremost a negative space, a negation of both the social and the domestic, public and private (in their status as both material and ideological opposites, a symptom of the reifications of class society),[25] which generates in turn a suggestion of their possible refiguration and recombination at a higher level. The porch attracts initially not because it offers a positive blending of social and domestic elements, but because it is *unlike* either of these. Intertwined with this axis of negation/affirmation is the aforementioned, more purely spatial problematic of inside to outside, with the porch a way of bringing the interior out onto the facade, producing (particularly in the situation of the modernizing America in which Dreiser is writing, a situation to which he is sharply attuned) an independent and overdetermining utopian resonance.

In *Sister Carrie*, Fisher suggests, the window substitutes for the porch. This seems accurate, although again attention should be paid to certain nuances. In particular, we must figure in those typical functions of the window noted above, which so often position Carrie in relation to work as well as in relation to pastoral scenes of consumption: near these things, but not yet partaking of them. It is thus possible to see the window, especially in tandem with the rocker, as a kind of condensation or translation of the liminal space of quitting time invoked earlier—the urban downtown around five in the afternoon, the incipient suburb of the undeveloped prairie— which is the new world in which Carrie arrives. Both have in the novel as their internal mechanism the enticing juxtaposition of wage work and lei-sure, of work on its way to leisure, one not fully faded, the other not fully achieved. Complicating things here is that the (finally unsatisfactory, be-cause "realized") kind of leisure activity that crystallizes in the wake of these pastoral moments is typically centered around shopping and consumption, which, we have argued, is precisely the ideological substitute for the realm of production in the older pastoral. So, right behind consumption is labor yet again, and precisely the whole capitalist labor process at that, wherein the essential structuration of social classes is effected and wherein they receive their political and historical potential.

The liminal spaces we have examined so far gesture, in their utopian moment, to both a transfigured work and a transfigured leisure, while their practical ideological course (which we must analyze further) leads either to consumption, with Carrie, or to death, with Hurstwood. Both of these stand as failed negations of the labor process: Carrie wants out of the factory, whereas Hurstwood seemingly cannot get in. That is to say, the trajectories of Carrie and Hurstwood suggest an effort to realize the transient and unsta-ble utopian impulse of the liminal space through a peremptory, and impos-sible, flight or disconnection (of self, of libido) from labor, the precise opposite of the route envisioned by what I take to be the more authentically revolutionary tradition, which prescribes the path to utopia, by which I mean here a successful socialist society, at some essential level as being ex-actly through labor and the production process and on out the other side.[26] This strikes me as one of the central components of the emergent middle-class (as classless) realm that the novel fitfully articulates. The middle-class "imaginary" attempts in effect to posit the meaninglessness of labor, to shift the sites in which humans work out their relationships to being to other domains entirely, sites where, if their affective power is to be realized, translated or recoded images or impulses of work must reoccur or well-up, as a kind of obligatory return of the repressed.[27]

The specific role of the rocker should be briefly addressed, too: it is not simply the window's twin. We have noted Fisher's linking of the rocker to the routinization of the incessant new rhythms of a dynamic society. This observation can be extended with a recent suggestion of Martha Banta's: "Rocking chairs are an American invention. They symbolize the restlessness of the nation's population, urged to attain something unnamed and unreachable even while at rest. Rocking chairs are in constant motion but go nowhere. We might view a woman seated in such a chair the way we view anyone bound to the routine of factory shop or office."[28] Banta's formulation places the effect of the rocker outside it, in some ideal that lies elsewhere, whereas it is intrinsic to it: it resides in the very fact that it can be a kind of rest that teases at the edge of work, figured in the image of static motion. Banta's more interesting assertion is her linking of this motion to a specifically Taylorized workplace, ruled by the principles of scientific management, the characteristics of which we will explore momentarily.

As must be apparent by now, the lifting of the burden of toil in the novel must be a highly ambiguous affair. Carrie flees the shoe factory, but later, after having made a name for herself in the theater, something of that original situation returns: "She could feel that there was no warm, sympathetic friendship back of the easy merriment with which many approached her. All seemed to be seeking their own amusement, regardless of the possible sad consequences to others" (409). Like the "coarse" and "fresh" workers of the factory, from whom Carrie is repelled, these new acquaintances offer only shallow, self-seeking company. A little later, having become the featured lodger, as it were, at a swank new hotel, a certain lassitude begins to overtake her comfortable situation: "Unconsciously her idle hands were beginning to weary" (423). What had earlier been physical fatigue returns in a more spiritual, but still draining, form. These moments suggest that while she has in some sense escaped her former condition, in another sense she is still back in the sweatshop.[29]

Hurstwood's eccentric class status, meanwhile, undergoes a displacement and literalization that renders him incapable of working at or producing anything at all, an escape from toil whose terminus is death. Hurstwood's role in the streetcar drivers' strike is instructive in this context. His appearance as a scab (among his last desperate attempts to secure employment) takes place precisely amidst the breakdown of the labor process. Indeed, from the point of view of the strikers, the labor of the scab is not legitimate, and the scab himself is the most vivid and despised figure for the exploitation and erasure of authentic labor as such. So even when Hurstwood is working, he is not really working, a condition not unlike his earlier position in the saloon, where his task was to be a coordinating image in the image-world of the club (and he later becomes an image yet again, this time for the crowds of strikers who stare at him from the side of the tracks). Amy Kaplan's keen insight that the strike scene, throughout its entire presentation (and not merely by way of this chapter's lack of a sentimental heading), feels "roped off in a separate sphere" strengthens the sense that the sociological actualities of class, whether bourgeois or working class, are being kept at bay in this novel (something long noted with respect to Carrie, whose fortunes as mistress and actress depend on a certain determinate remove from class). This allows *Sister Carrie* to thereby explore a new, ideological world of middle-classness, to which social class as such stands as a kind of constitutive outside.[30] Carrie and Hurstwood both map this domain, which they remain inside of even during the Bowery scenes of unemployment and starvation. Although "real" enough in one sense, these function within the novel's rough mapping of middle-classlessness to dramatize the dystopian face of the attempt to dream oneself out of capitalist wage labor and production, with its attendant paralysis and extinction of desire.

The two characters' ties to their original situations is one index of a more pervasive sameness that attends their pathways through the novel. As Kaplan notes, "Carrie is constantly on the move up the social scale—from one city, one man, one job to the next—yet she always seems to end up in the same place."[31] Like the rocker, she is always moving but going no place, her protean name changes (Meeber, Madenda, Wheeler, Murdock) and stage acting testifying to a certain multiplication of surface identities that remains in thrall to some deeper, less mutable configuration. Hurstwood, meanwhile, starts out as the manager, then remains the "ex-manager" for the rest of the story, a kind of ghostly afterimage of his former situation, indicating that he has not at all transcended this previous existence. These observations might be juxtaposed against what Fisher takes to be the dominant mode of "self" in the novel, a mutable, theatrical, situation-responsive mode he calls the "self in anticipation."[32] This conception of the self conforms well to Fisher's notion of a "dynamic" society, though it ignores the ways in which, at the level of the self, such dynamism is at one with processes that lock the self into rigid molds, which prevent it from being different than itself. That is, Fisher's presentation of the anticipated self in effect ratifies a certain principle of nonidentity, one which might be understood as a central promise of a consumer society (endlessly to renew the self through consumption), a principle that denies that there might also exist in this society any kind of original structuration of the subject, or some process of identity-imposition (of the sort discussed in the introduction), against which the subject might then resist. Although *Sister Carrie* vividly displays the workings of such a nonidentity principle, I am not convinced that it finally endorses it or, more to the point, shows it to be all that effective.

But how, finally, could all these characters not remain the same throughout? It is hard to imagine more formalistically rendered entities—less characters than nodal points on a grid, or, better, a set of names attached to a series of different *spaces*, spaces that accord with varying socioeconomic levels, the successive inhabitation of which then produces the characteristic up/down social momentum (and plot) of the novel. This formalism is no doubt at the base of the famous passivity and emptiness that mark these characters and seem to have been among Dreiser's principal writerly innovations. The parallelism of these traits in Carrie and Hurstwood has also been noted by Kaplan: "[Carrie] falls into success as passively as Hurstwood falls into stealing the money."[33] Characters such as these are bound up in turn with other patterns in the text (whether as effects or as consequences, it is difficult at the outset to say), patterns whose source or motivation seems more complicated and involved than that naturalistic "determinism" to which they have been so frequently ascribed (that is, the characters are passive because they are at the mercy of blind, impersonal forces). Such a deterministic view was no doubt a part of Dreiser's own intellectual makeup, and it is invoked here and there in the story, but it is inadequate to account fully for all that transpires (that is to say, successful aesthetic production involves processes that properly transcend the particular "belief set" of the artist).

Alan Trachtenberg draws attention to one of these related patterns in terms of what he calls the "relative weakness of plot in *Sister Carrie*," that is, "extended complications through which sentient characters work through their relations to each other and to themselves by means of memory and intelligence, [a weakness which] follows as much from the kind of characters Dreiser chose to depict as from his distrust of the neatly rounded-off endings of popular romances."[34] Daydreaming and distracted characters such as these cannot partake of a "stronger" plot, an index of Dreiser's greater interest in objects, in the environment of *things*, which typically "speak" more eloquently than do the characters. But the peculiar shape and inner momentum of a given narrative are the result of more than a set of "interests," and surely derive at another level from certain authorial competencies—what the writer can do and where he or she learned to do it. I have in mind here Dreiser's two-year tenure as editor of the mass-market magazine *Ev'ry Month*, in 1896–97. This magazine, put out by Dreiser's brother Paul's publishing company, was an imitation of such popular monthlies as *Ladies' Home Journal*, and was part of that new wave of magazines of the late nineteenth and early twentieth centuries whose cultural role, as Christopher Wilson has argued in a well-known essay, was to help create both a new kind of reader and a new kind of consumer (who initially was most likely to be a woman, although this would change with time).[35]

I wish to speculate here about Dreiser's immersion in and absorption of what Margaret Morse has called the "concept" of the magazine, at once its technical structure and its abstract essence, during a period of intense activity.[36] Dreiser was not merely the editor: the magazine's tight budget forced him to have a hand in virtually everything, from writing the stories and selling the ads to production design and pasteup.[37] Wilson notes that the goal of the mass-market magazine during this period was to inculcate new reading habits, to undermine older patterns based on long attention spans, quiet reflectivity, and relatively low "information intake." Some of the strategies relating to this goal included using more stories, shorter in length; better integration of advertising and copy space; focus on personalities and gossip; and expanded use of "helpful hints," factoids, and tidbits of all kinds. The aim was a new reading space, one that promoted a more hurried and selective apprehension of the printed material, with an augmented rhythm or flow to it. Indeed, Morse sees in the turn-of-the-century magazine an important precursor and analogue to the flow or rhythm later achieved, at a greatly intensified level, by television—a technology that helps structure everyday life according to a logic of distraction.

Morse describes distraction in terms of an "attenuated fiction effect," akin to the idea of a "willing suspension of disbelief" while reading a novel or watching a movie, but different in that distraction "involves two or more objects and levels of attention and the copresence of two or more different, even contradictory, metapsychological effects." The familiar "space out" effect of highway driving—operating a vehicle at high speed for an hour or more while thinking or daydreaming about something else entirely—would be an obvious example, illustrating a certain "detached involvement" with the surrounding environment. We might well think of Carrie in this connection, as at once a distracted character and a character conceived of in distraction, that is, as a by-product of that new reading space Dreiser himself was helping to create: wandering along the impressive avenues of Chicago and New York, imbibing the stimuli and "shocks" memorably detailed in Georg Simmel's essay on the metropolis and mental life.[38] For Simmel—for whom the city was in effect a modernist text, whereas Dreiser might again be understood to be reading things through analogous mass cultural frames— the distraction of the metropolitan lifeworld entailed a heightening of the role of the Freudian preconscious, that banal psychological level of daydreaming and idle musing in which decision making, and hence action, are problematized, and in which the public object world is flattened to a realm of things all of potentially equal value and meaning. That is, this object world is posited as a source of stimuli that are valuable as such, and a certain cognitive, discriminatory capacity is temporarily suspended (and thus one can perceive in this context the role distraction, however generated, might play as an essential adjunct of commodification, where the subject is open to the "jesuitical" voice of the commodity partly because it has "suspended disbelief").[39]

Another, possibly more suggestive angle on this matter arises from Morse's specification of distraction in terms of the narratological distinction between discourse and story (or narrative). This concerns the relations between two planes of language, a plane of a subject in a here and now, and the plane of a nonsubject in another place and/or time. As Gerard Genette puts it, glossing Benveniste, "in discourse, someone speaks, and his situation in the very act of speaking is the focus of the most important significations; in narrative ... *no one speaks*, in the sense that at no moment do we ask ourselves *who is speaking, where, when*, and so forth, in order to receive the full signification of the text."[40] In the state of distraction, these two distinct levels of language are in effect expressed simultaneously, or there is at least some equivocal alternation between the levels. Trachtenberg points to a similar phenomenon at work in *Sister Carrie*, and indeed locates it as perhaps Dreiser's most striking prose innovation (responsible as well, one imagines, for that "heterogeneity" of raw material and "versatility" of narrative apparatus that Jameson discerns in Dreiser's realism).[41] Throughout the novel there is a persistent fluctuating of the narrative voice, as the narrator moves from objective reporting to didactic and opinionated metacommentary to, finally and possibly most tellingly, a level parallel with and only fitfully distinguishable from the inner thoughts of the characters—where, as Bell observes, despite the narrator's often "overtly distant" stance from the characters, "he seems to be in some covert way identified with them."[42] The move from "no one speaking" to "someone (but who?) speaking" is frequent and equivocal, evidence of a narrative persona itself conceived in distraction: unsure of his exact spatio-temporal location, oscillating uncertainly between a "here and now" and an "elsewhere"—a narrative presided over by a kind of magazine consciousness. In this admittedly speculative optic, it is Dreiser himself, or at least his novelistic self-consciousness, who proves most susceptible to the innovations in magazine conception and production promoted in this period. Such innovations, finally, might also be understood as advances in scientific management, since a number of prominent editors of the time were also vocal proponents of Taylorist philosophy and characterized their editorial practices in these terms. In any case, this mediation of the "magazine concept" in Dreiser's narrative practice gives us a more concrete source for the puzzling passivity of his characters.

. . .

The characters Dreiser creates naturally have a highly uncertain relation to action, to events, and to the representation of these last. Indeed, the novel might be seen as one long "melodrama of uncertain agency," to use the phrase coined by Mark Seltzer in his study of naturalist fiction.[43] We have already noted the image of ambiguous activity in the rocking chair—window pairing and its centrality to the story, an image echoed during one of the novel's most explicit renderings of the site of consumption. Here Carrie, in her familiar habitat of the department store, surveys the display of goods: "There is nothing in this world more delightful than that middle state in which we mentally balance at times, possessed of the means, lured by desire, and yet deterred by conscience or want of decision. When Carrie began wandering around the store amid the fine displays she was in this mood" (67). Here, in what is perhaps the most vivid depiction of the "self in anticipation," is another and important middle or liminal space, in which the activity of consumption at its most intense is itself imagined as a suspended or uncertain activity. The very language of the scene suggests those earlier liminal spaces, with the self "rocking" to and fro, toward the commodities and back again, in a pleasurable suspension, a movement which symbolically mimics the translated productive energy of the rocker. Here is the subject in a new sort of "bower," amid a new source of material security, rearticulating work done (through the wage) as a leisure activity.[44]

If only such a middle state could last forever. Alas, it is inherently unstable: one must eventually take the plunge and buy something, whence it vanishes and one is left with a commodity that is inevitably something less than one thought it would be (indeed, one knew it would be all along, which is partly why the anticipation of the purchase can be so pleasurable). The cycle must then be started all over again. This is but one instance of a model of self-consuming desire that the novel insistently foregrounds, the unfulfillable nature of which is wonderfully captured in Carrie's well-known definition of money, "something that everybody else has and I must get" (63). Once obtained, it isn't money anymore, so one has to keep getting more of it, which will evaporate in turn. Such a purely formal dynamic of increase, incapable of fulfillment or appeasement, is at the center of Walter Benn Michaels's important reading of the novel, a reading that helps us think more clearly about what exactly we mean by the term "consumption," even if we might dissent finally from Michaels's implied political evaluation of the narrative.[45]

It seems to me that if periodizing concepts such as consumer society are to be historically meaningful, they must refer to mass consumption. A growing majority of the population must be engaged in the restless acquisition of ever cheaper industrially produced goods. For this, not only consumers but also industry itself must undergo a certain reconfiguration, something that only broadly happens during the 1910s and 1920s, when rapid technological change for the first time permits enormously increased industrial output without correspondingly increased capital investment.[46] The problem of production thus having been "solved," at least in the view of many at the time, the problem of disposing of the new surfeit of goods could be more strenuously addressed. The habits of consumption thus inculcated should be principally understood not as the expression of a particular ethos or set of norms, but specifically as practices, which are partly enabled through ideological work but assume a semiautonomous dynamic once "launched," henceforth enabling and becoming entangled with a diverse range of normative supports and fantasy investments. That is to say, I believe that a certain constitutive *formalism* of mass consumption should be stressed here, as a way of underscoring its historical originality: the genius of what is generally known as Fordism thus emerges as the strong, if incomplete, linking or doubling of the formalism of the profit motive (the essentially vacuous or content-free necessity of securing more "pluses" than "minuses" on the ledger at the end of the day, or quarter) with consumption itself (the necessity for ever more goods, based on whatever reason or desire one might think of—or sometimes, as with the "shopaholic," for no apparent purpose at all). Framing the matter in this fashion is meant to counter, or at least problematize, analyses of the type offered by Lori Merish, who, in a recent essay, finds a full-fledged consumerist "ethos" in the small towns of 1820s Illinois, in the form of local clergymen urging the newly minted bourgeois of the region to get themselves decent curtains and silverware (a task that has in any case been assumed since time immemorial by the intelligentsia—in particular the clergy—and associated bearers of culture with respect to the comparatively backward aristocrats, bourgeois, and other prospective leading citizens).[47]

These reflections return us to the question of the status of the desire-consumption nexus in the novel, or what might be considered its political valence, something that, following Michaels, has been a matter for debate in recent criticism. Kaplan plausibly suggests that consumption in *Sister Carrie* stands as a compensation for social powerlessness, although she is not entirely clear about the possible (extratextual) sources for this lack. Neil Harris, for one, has suggested that the growth in interest in the purchasing act stems from a declining ability to manufacture one's own material environment.[48] Although generally true, this observation would hold for any increase in the technical level of society, or increased complexity of the division of labor. That is, it does not take into account the shifts in power dynamics and forms of wage exploitation that would necessarily attend such increases under a capitalist dispensation. Exploring these matters would afford the specification of those processes which, as Jameson has recently noted, in closing off collective political movements and opportunities, pave the way for the emergent passion for commodities, understood, again, as a recent historical creation.[49] In this view, consumerism crucially depends on allied political and economic forces and developments to enable its march toward hegemony, a truth sometimes obscured in analyses that emphasize the commodity as spectacle, possessed of a kind of irresistibly bewitching power.

Kaplan also suggests that consumer desire in the novel expresses a longing for change, in a displaced or redirected sense: impulses for social change are rerouted to a consumer sphere where they dissipate and disperse, co-opted by the consumerist promise of eternal novelty (which battles its own principle of identity, the commodity threatening to devolve into the eternal return of the same). Whereas Kaplan sees the workplace as the story's principal site for the production of such longings, our reading here has privileged in this regard those times and spaces of the ambivalent interface of work and leisure (Dreiser's urban pastoral), where both are suggested but neither predominates. Although utopian energies are produced at these sites, it is difficult to see them specifically as a conscious desire for social change. They are perhaps better designated as *gestures of transfiguration*, which demand a political completion, while not themselves issuing in any particular representable desideratum, nor indeed in any concrete will toward any such political issue: the pleasurable stasis-in-motion depends upon remaining at the threshold. The site of consumption, meanwhile, appears from the present vantage point to be a displacement of these pastoral spaces, or one product of their decay (as in radioactive decay), another being, as we have argued, desire's extinction and incipient death (desire and aphanisis being in effect structural parallels in the novel). That is to say, these latter modes strive to retain the ambivalent, incomplete passage from work to leisure and rest; however, each fails in its own way, that represented by Hurstwood the more disastrously because it finally makes no place whatsoever (even ideologically) for work and production.

It is Hurstwood, of course, who dramatically embodies the path of devolution and aphanisis, and might be expected therefore to entertain an even more problematic relationship to the question of agency. The remarkable scene where the drunken Hurstwood discovers the open safe is paradigmatic in this regard, since it foregrounds not only Hurstwood's hesitation and uncertainty but also Dreiser's:

> "I didn't know Fitzgerald and Moy ever left any money this way," his mind said to itself. "They must have forgotten it."
>
> He looked at the other drawer and paused again.
>
> "Count them," said a voice in his ear.
>
> He put his hand into the first of the boxes and lifted the stack, letting the separate parcels fall. They were bills of fifty and one hundred dollars done in packages of a thousand. He thought he counted ten such.
>
> "Why don't I shut the safe?" his mind said to itself, lingering. "What makes me pause here?"
>
> For an answer there came the strangest words:
>
> "Did you ever have ten thousand dollars in ready money?" (243–44)

The peculiar, both personal and impersonal locution "his mind said to itself" points immediately to Hurstwood's divided consciousness, thus preparing for the tortuous equivocations that follow. What is the basis of this division? Hurstwood has been drinking, so presumably we are to understand that he is not in his "normal" frame of mind, money or no money. Indeed, the suggestion seems to be that any actions taken or not taken during this episode are not to be seen as originating from Hurstwood's own will or "self."

More immediately interesting are these voices. There are a fair number of such cajoling voices in the novel, a good deal of insistent whispering in the ear, from the very opening of the narrative (the first voice in the book is Drouet's speaking into Carrie's ear). From one perspective, these might be associated with the twin voices of conscience and temptation, returning us to the liminal site of temptation encountered on the very first page of the novel. Except, here as elsewhere in the novel, there is very little in the way of the intervention of conscience, or of any structure of "belief" to which any force of conscience might be allied, nor can there be given the essential formalism we have been ascribing to these characters. Hurstwood's considerations in this scene are for the most part strategic; his pacing and fidgeting serve as evidence not of a moral quandary, but of a general strategy of the deferral of the crisis of action itself—that is, on Dreiser's part fully as much as Hurstwood's, as if at some level Dreiser is aware that the characters he has invented cannot act in any meaningful sense, and that therefore steps must be taken to delay or defuse this realization. In this context, even Hurstwood's drunkenness appears as a smokescreen and alibi for this underlying "scandal of agency." In any case, any linkage between actions and some conscious structure of belief or intention has here been systematically severed. What results is the now familiar realm of generalized passivity, surrounded by an atmosphere of permanent temptation. Temptation always wins out in this world, save for the signal exception of the strike scene, where the voice in Hurstwood's ear urging him to join the strikers is not only resisted, it seems almost to inspire fear. But this has nothing to do with anything Hurstwood believes; rather, to the extent that he represents one coordinate on a map of the middle-class imaginary, the prospect of crossing over into the proletarian camp is an even greater threat to his existence than penury and starvation.

A more plausible archetype for these voices would seem to be that "voice of the so-called inanimate" (99) whose jesuitical speech Carrie fancies she hears as she wanders down the aisles of the department store, past shelves of glittering trinkets. It is the voice of the commodity, the way each one has of making an individual claim on the consumer: "I'm for you, and you alone." This is the voice that Hurstwood hears before the safe, at least to the extent that we are still within the horizon of the commodity-money nexus. The very words that manifest themselves to Hurstwood ("Did you ever have ten thousand dollars in ready money?"), despite their strangeness, would in the years ahead become exceedingly familiar, for they are a part of the language of advertising itself, of the promise of freedom in credit cards and lottery tickets. In their suggestion of easy money, they are aimed precisely at the sucker, the dreamer or naïf who is incapable of successfully negotiating the pathways of both the workplace and the marketplace. Hurstwood will eventually fulfill this role all too well. His hesitancy while in the thrall of this language is a figure for the more drastic forms of inactivity that grip him later in the story.

Hurstwood's deferment is not interminable. Characteristically, what precipitates the "decision" is sheerly accidental:

> While the money was in his hand the lock clicked. It had sprung! Did he do it? He grabbed at the knob and pulled vigorously. It had closed. Heavens! he was in for it now, sure enough.
>
> The moment he realized that the safe was locked for a surety, the sweat burst out upon his brow and he trembled violently. He looked about him and decided instantly. There was no delaying now.
>
> "Supposing I do lay it on the top," he said, "and go away, they'll know who took it. I'm the last to close up. Besides, other things will happen." At once he became the man of action. (247)

Given what we know of Hurstwood's career and of his ultimate fate—indeed, of the very structure of the narrative—the epithet "man of action" seems singularly incongruous. What could it possibly mean? Inasmuch as he has given himself (or has been given) over to the promise of a "ready ten thousand dollars," he has assumed the role of one who precisely does not act, or is incapable of doing so.

What is striking here are the text's own equivocations with respect to these matters, as is indicated by the plaintive and unstable question "did he do it?" Who asks this question, and of whom is it asked? It seems doubtful, and not merely because of its grammar, that Hurstwood is asking it of himself. Rather, it is as if Dreiser were asking himself, musing aloud at that very point when the realist novelist encounters a kind of void opening up beneath the act and its representability. Here then is the baffled response of American realism to the types of narrative problems being dealt with at the very same time and in a more modernist fashion by a writer like Conrad (as in *Lord Jim*). Eschewing the Conradian device of multiple points of view, and its vertiginous textual productivity, Dreiser seems to want, at least at this juncture, to retain a more stable notion of character, only to have it disrupted by the sudden intervention of the deus ex machina ("the lock clicked"). From this perspective, the expression "man of action" is less a description of Hurstwood than a kind of self-conscious and rationalizing bluster on Dreiser's part, clumsily positing here something Nietzsche decried as typical of the sickliness of modernity, namely a subject of action, capable of serving discursively as both the originator and teleological rationale of events, a reification imposed upon the flux of action. Dreiser, the actual crisis of the decision and the act now passed, can try to cover his tracks by resuming what he hopes to be his surefooted narrative realism; however, the effect turns out to be virtually parodic. Hurstwood formulates an escape plan, tricks and abducts Carrie, and heads off for the train station all in the span of less than two pages, as if Dreiser wants to put this momentary loss of control over the narrative behind him as quickly as possible.

This is not the first time in the story that Hurstwood has assumed the mantle of the man of action. His attraction to Carrie and his decision to win her away from Drouet ("By the Lord, he would have that lovely girl if it took his all. He would act at once" [181]) amount to an earlier rallying to action, one, as Donald Pizer notes, equally fatal to Hurstwood's social position as his flight with the money.[50] As a "man of surfaces," in Ellen Moers's acute phrase, dependent on his social and business milieu's perception of him, Hurstwood fails to recognize the doom inscribed in this initial eruption of desire, another vivid illustration of how in the novel desire is constructed as undecidably productive-destructive, or present-absent.[51] At both moments, then, with Carrie and before the safe, Hurstwood becomes the man of action in terms that signify his eventual torpor and suicide. Indeed, becoming a man of action in this story seems just about the surest route to destruction (hence, at one level, the apparent success of Carrie's playacting in the theater).

Dreiser's writerly uncertainties with Hurstwood arise again later, in connection with that other evacuated category, belief. What occasions the doubts in this context is Hurstwood's own relationship to the strikers, one that, as noted earlier, already positions him as a kind of nonentity, something he admits ("I'm not anything") to the clerk charged with hiring the scabs. Dreiser wonders what Hurstwood himself might "think" about all this, in a kind of puzzled manner reminiscent of the safe scene: "Hurstwood at first sympathized with the demands of these men [the strikers]—indeed, it is a question whether he did not always sympathize with them to the end, belie him as his actions might" (375). Again, for whom is this "question"? Since we as readers are in no position to answer it, and since it grants to Hurstwood a kind of independent psychic existence Dreiser dispenses with elsewhere, it seems once more to be a kind of visible uncertainty on Dreiser's part, wondering aloud about the strangeness of this no-longer traditional character, and still fitfully wanting him to possess that inner life expunged by the narrative apparatus. The settled belief Dreiser finally decides to ascribe to him unsurprisingly turns out to be an utterly divided one, a division that is not attended by any sense of conflict however:

> In his heart of hearts, [Hurstwood] sympathized with the strikers and hated this scab. In his heart of hearts, also, he felt the dignity and use of the police force, which commanded order. . . . The two feelings blended in him—neutralized one another and him. He would have fought for this man as determinedly as for himself, and yet only so far as commanded. Strip him of his uniform, and he would have soon picked his side. (379)

In this remarkable passage, Dreiser imagines most concretely the peculiar mind-set his innovative characters might possess. In essence, we are presented with what amounts to the state of belief commensurate with that pastoral, middle-classless state we described earlier: what might have been a source of tension or instability is instead quietly neutralized, the potentially contradictory poles seemingly shunted to different levels of awareness, a fitting mechanism for an ideological strategy that seeks to dissipate and manage any emergent sense of opposition and structural social conflict. Perhaps, like an infernal machine, such a character will always be able to sympathize with yet act against particular groups or individuals.

So Hurstwood, unperturbed, joins the scabs and plays his small part in the trolley strike, an event whose semantic richness and resonance in the novel we should pause to appreciate. The strike possesses a profound dual valence with respect to the middle-class world of the rest of the story. On one hand, as an image of workers not working, it rearticulates the figure of a lifting of the burden of toil whose inner logic we analyzed in terms of the ambivalent interpenetration of work and rest, of the passage from activity into inactivity. To the extent that we focus on the suspended activity of the strikers as such, it also recalls the moment when the lock of the safe clicks shut, condemning Hurstwood to his downward fate (and indeed, perhaps through some unconscious or subterranean textual current the "locking out" of the safe scene punningly meets the "locking out" of the strike).[52] On the other hand, as an instance of rebellious working-class subjectivity and class struggle it embodies those realities of class that middle-classlessness works to suppress. Here is, for its time, one possible image of the concrete path to utopia, which threatens to unmask the competing ideological pathway. Hurstwood's role in the strike, as we have already noted, is ambiguous, in that the labor of the scab is from a certain perspective not legitimate: while it might be tempting to think that he has again become the man of action in driving the trolley, he has managed to take the one job whose activity is once again, at a certain level of abstraction, not activity at all (in that sense, the work of the scab is—to invoke a Hegelian idiom—the "truth" of middle-classlessness).

．．．

What we have been examining in terms of the evacuation of the categories of belief and agency, and Dreiser's own flustered attempts variously to negotiate and revive them, can be understood as one novelistic figuration of a larger pattern of separation and disjunction that Lukács codified as reification, a concept that includes the idea of a generalized process of social rationalization, a relentless atomization into smaller units in the name of efficiency and control.[53] The separation and cancellation of belief and agency, embodied so strikingly by Hurstwood, also offers a fortuitous analogy to what was among the most important forces of reification during this period, the spread of various Taylorist processes. The central aim of Taylorism was precisely the commandeering—through the time/motion analysis and quantification of discrete job processes—of craft and artisanal knowledge from skilled and semiskilled workers on the shop floor and the reinscription of such knowledges, in a streamlined and putatively more efficient form, in the domain of management. In other words, the link between workers' knowledge and their work—literally, between brain and hand—was to be broken, so that they might become deskilled automatons in the grip of management control.[54] Stanley Aronowitz has pointedly described the consequences of this in terms of the "destruction of worker selfhood" and, ultimately, the "tendency to abolish the subject as an historical actor."[55] By "subject," Aronowitz does not mean the autonomous liberal self but rather the realm of the subjective understood as greater than simply a "moment" in the self-reproduction of capital, and hence as at least a potential basis for an organized self-activity which grapples with the contradictions of class society.

At issue here is the passage from what Marx called the "formal subsumption" of labor by capital, which denoted the introduction of wage labor as such, to labor's "real subsumption," which indicates the active intervention of capital in the labor process. Driven by a rationalizing logic, this intervention "is a means to remove the boundaries, set historically by working-class self-organization, culture, and skill traditions, upon the capacity of capital to become the tendency toward production for its own sake—that is, production as an end in itself . . . becomes a compulsion."[56] The sheer formalism of the capitalist economy, its infernal logic—something of whose cultural ramifications Dreiser has captured in *Sister Carrie*—is fully unleashed. Another aspect of this formalism might be represented by Taylorism's facilitation of the production of abstract labor, that is, the reduction of heterogeneous social labor to quantitatively commensurable units, a process Marx locates at the center of the value form under capitalism. All in all, as Etienne Balibar summarizes this process, real subsumption "goes a long way beyond the integration of the workers into the world of the contract, of money incomes, of law and official politics [that is, the results of formal subsumption]: it implies a transformation of human individuality, which extends from the education of the labour force to the constitution of a 'dominant ideology' capable of being adopted by the dominated themselves."[57]

Despite the tempting analogy between Carrie, tending her rocking "machine," or Hurstwood—his mind (not to mention Dreiser's!) disconnected from his hand—and the Taylorized worker, *Sister Carrie*'s relationship to these processes, which were under way not only (if perhaps most crucially) in the factory but in many social spheres at this time, is more complex and indirect. The novel is responding to, and beginning to explore, not Taylorism as such, but rather a developing sociocultural habitus that Taylorism was itself helping to create and make available. In this sense, the image of this or that putative "agent" failing in some capacity stands not for the dissolution of some ahistorical concept of agency, but rather as the novelistic index for a modernization and homogenization of disparate work cultures that is affecting the tenor and texture of the social at multiple levels. To put this in a stronger form, I would say that the processes of labor subsumption active during the latter decades of the nineteenth century pose the very problem of agency as such, in all its configurations, for the first time in American culture (on the order of the Marxian precept that humankind only poses for itself those problems it is capable of solving).

One possible mediation with regard to *Sister Carrie* would again be Dreiser's tenure at *Ev'ry Month*. As we indicated, in a certain sense the goal of a magazine such as this can be understood to have been to produce a scientifically managed or "Taylorized" reader, passive and lacking older readerly skills, a goal Dreiser himself pursued so vigorously that in the process (and regardless of any wider cultural success of these editorial strategies) he might well have rendered himself something of a Taylorized *writer*: that is to say, minimally at least, a writer whose novelistic techniques, learned (through material practice) under peculiar conditions, fortuitously open out onto similar conditions active in a separate sphere. In this context, the notion of distraction (and its concomitant, daydreaming) might again be useful, if we recall Gramsci's speculation that Taylorism, and its embodiment in assembly-line and related flow technologies, could itself promote distraction in the worker, a worker now absorbed into an external rhythm and whose mind is now free to shift into other registers. Gramsci considered the possibility that this development might in fact help foster revolutionary consciousness, since the worker in effect had more time to think.[58]

In *Bodies and Machines*, Mark Seltzer ties the various "panics of agency" he isolates in realist and naturalist writing in part to what he posits as the uncertain blending of person and machine at work in Taylorism (in this case a kind of technology of writing embodied in the scientific manager's graphs and flowcharts), a reading that is not fully persuasive because it finally misses what is most important about Taylorism. The root issue here, as hinted above, is not a crisis in some abstract conception of individual agency, which is how Seltzer tends to frame the matter, but rather an ineluctable dismantling of any notion of collective agency.[59] What is assumed in Aronowitz's comments above is that the skills and knowledges being undone in Taylorism, and the particular cultures of work and patterns of daily life in which they were embedded, depended on essentially collective modes of social organization and interaction. Atomize and disperse these modes, subject them to "real subsumption," and both the subjective, at the level of the individual, and the domain of collectivity suffer together. When realist narrative begins to map these developments, or the ideological domain opened up by them, it nonetheless does so using those limited and anthropomorphizing units known as "characters," about whom the novelist, like Dreiser, can openly wonder, "what are they really doing? what is going on inside their heads?" It is as if Dreiser, as "author function," if not perhaps as author as such, is responding to the pressure of these social and collective materials upon the narrative apparatus, but, locked into the logic of that apparatus, rearticulates the effects of these materials as a confusion about individual agency (which effectively does not exist in the novel at all).

These uncertainties in part mark the historical limits of *Sister Carrie*'s delineation of an emergent urban and modernized classless imaginary, this last being, in 1900, by no means fully articulated and in place as a component of hegemonic ideology, due to the continued existence of a possible working-class alternative to bourgeois society (this is not to assert that this was likely at this moment, only that working-class existence retained a certain density and recalcitrance that bourgeois ideology could not wholly subsume).[60] Another important and symptomatic indicator of such limits arises in terms of what might be called the "spatial possibilities" of subject positions. I have in mind the pattern of movement instantiated and projected by the Carrie-Hurstwood dyad, which is basically one-way and, as we noted briefly earlier, consistently figured according to the types of space occupied by the characters, and the social milieus associated with these spaces. The process is one of an implacable movement out of one kind of space or milieu and into another, with no possibility, or even desire, of going back: the space of what we might call inhabitance, of where the characters go and with whom they interact, is never really widened, but is systematically recircumscribed with each displacement. It is here, in this context of deterritorialization and simultaneous reterritorialization, to use Deleuze and Guattari's language, that the feminist perspective on Carrie's trajectory must be reckoned.[61] That is, while her escape from the patriarchal family, her personal success, and her discovery of new resources of self-expression in consumerism are all doubtless gains on one level, the novel's tracing of her spatial restriction alludes to the parallel costs of modernization.

So Carrie, having argued with Drouet and unsure of her status with Hurstwood, ponders where to turn for help: "In this situation her thoughts went out to her sister in Van Buren Street, whom she had not seen since the night of her flight, and to her home at Columbia City, which seemed now a part of something that could not be again. She looked for no refuge in that direction" (232). Indeed, she never looks back, nor does she ever want to; Dreiser presents each successive apartment or hotel suite she occupies as a kind of monadic cell that cuts her off from other social spheres. Carrie's indifference to her family thus has nothing to do with any putative self-centeredness on her part, but should be seen more as an effect of structure, as a projection of a certain pattern of spatial description in the novel that effectively eliminates subjective mobility. For his part, Hurstwood must contend with the stigma of criminality, and hence, once in New York, he must avoid "the gay places where he would be apt to meet those who had known him" (284). Such "gay places" had been his principal haunts before, yet his estrangement from them is not necessarily indicative of a constriction of his social world, but rather its reconfiguration. His slide down the social ladder continues apace, until, with another spatial image, Dreiser posits Hurstwood's definitive achievement of a kind of subaltern consciousness: "He began to see as one sees a city with a wall about it. Men were posted at the gates. You could not get in. Those inside did not care to come out to see who you were. They were so merry inside there that all those outside were forgotten, and he was on the outside" (306). This division (which afflicts Carrie in a rather different way) marks the final onset of the extinction of desire that marks Hurstwood, as he becomes ever more at one with the world of flophouses and vagrancy. This division or "outside" is, however, not to be seen as having anything to do with actual working-class existence, as we have been arguing, but is still very much "inside" the middle-class ideological field. This is shown yet again by the kind of spatial separations that obtain during the strike scene, as Hurstwood and the strikers are represented as locked in a specular relationship, Hurstwood aboard the trolley and the strikers lining the edge of the tracks. Gazing at each other with mutual suspicion and incomprehension, the strikers are as walled off from Hurstwood as the strike scene as a whole is from the rest of the novel.

The question of the figuration of mobility is pertinent here because, as Morse argues, mobility is one of the principal constituents of what she calls distraction—it is largely what facilitates the distracted subject's paradoxical engagement with, yet escape from, the here and now. This stems in part from the exploitation of the multiple (and sometimes contradictory) semantic and affective possibilities of mobility itself, which include

> displacement from one location to another, to the freedom of movement which is symbolically equated with social mobility, to the feelings of pleasure in effortless flight which has roots in infancy, to the fundamen-

tal psychic link of motion with causality and subjecthood first described by Aristotle. But mobility also suggests the opposite of subjecthood, the freely displaceable and substitutable part, machine or human, which enables mass production and a consequent standardization brought to the social as well as economic realm.[62]

Like the semiautomated machines that, in Sartre's description, provide the escapist daydreams to the deskilled workers who tend them, the motion that constitutively informs the state of distraction appears, on this reading, to offer a destabilization or bracketing of the here and now that secretly functions to open the subject ever more surely to the exigencies of that here and now. From within its horizons, however, distraction, in terms of its overall solicitation of affect, would indeed seem to project, as its internal ideal, a kind of free-ranging or delocalized subject position, mobile and unfettered, capable of imaginatively neutralizing and evading, while engaging, current circumstances.

Hence the significance of the trajectories of Carrie and Hurstwood evoked above: considered as a kind of spatial allegory, these appear to foreclose on this internal desideratum of distraction (or they at least inscribe its material underside). That is to say, whatever aspects or level of distraction, understood as a constituent of middle-classlessness, that the novel succeeds in capturing and giving figuration to, we do not yet have a unified (however fictively) subject of middle-class ideology. The reverse but parallel up/down momentum of the Carrie-Hurstwood dyad afforded the narrative the opportunity to figure the aporias and inertial dynamics of desire and agency at play in the middle-class ideological field. Yet the same dyadic structure, and the various determinisms and forces of nature it projects as its own manifest level of content (to adopt momentarily a Russian formalist view of the matter), forecloses on the ability to dramatize in terms of sociospatial freedom the contours of a more fully realized "classless" and nominalistic daily life. This might be framed less as historical limit than as outright critique: that is, the novel deconstructs middle-classlessness and shows its aspirations toward a free-ranging or delocalized subjectivity to be illusory. Putting things this way has some force, particularly if we think of the matter more in genealogical terms, in the sense of the novel mapping out initial preconditions and components of this ideological imaginary that are later not overcome so much as recombined and managed in newer, perhaps (but not necessarily) more effective ways. Hence, when we arrive at a more richly elaborated allegorization of a middle-class subject position in West's *The Day of the Locust*, we are offered a kind of "map" of the subjective mobility to which I have been alluding. The attendant constrictions and paralyses are, however, not evaded but refigured and placed as the culmination of the narrative (the novel ends with a violent riot and the protagonist suffers a nervous breakdown).

The limits to the generalizability of *Sister Carrie*'s middle-classlessness might be further specified by briefly considering the popular turn-of-the-century discursive "genre," if that is the right designation, that might be called class tourism. Epitomized by such muckraking, documentary-style texts as Jacob Riis's *How the Other Half Lives* (1890) and Jack London's *People of the Abyss* (1903), the genre—in its putative exposure of working-class existence (which was frequently pictured as more desperate and subproletarian in character) and its exploitation of "seedy" milieus—stands in a privileged relation to realism as one of its essential enabling acts.[63] The genre was essentially the product of a liberal-reformist sensibility and strove to bring working-class life home to diverse strata of the bourgeoisie, but in a predictably ambiguous fashion. From one perspective, the careful framing devices and sturdy moralism of the class touristic text served to keep this lower world at a distance, with a clear cordon sanitaire around it. But the genre did proffer working-class life in the form of a kind of knowledge, and, more importantly, the touristic gaze, with its playing off the boundaries of readable surface versus inner secret and simulation versus authenticity, opens this world up to a range of possible affective investment.[64] Through this genre, the realm of proletarian existence, however sensationalistically or phantasmatically conceived, could exert an unsettling pull on the unwary bourgeois subject.[65] That is, within that sector of bourgeois ideology in this period that handled class demarcation and managed the representation of class structure, powerful and seductive currents of otherness had yet to be neutralized or expunged. This dynamic is vividly captured, for example, in Stephen Crane's Bowery tales of the 1890s, and in one story in particular, "An Experiment in Misery" (1894), the matter is carried to its logical conclusion. Here, a young bohemian (already an incipient class traitor) dresses in rags and spends time among the unemployed, ostensibly to discover their "point of view." By the end of the story, a change has come over the young man, and he is no longer free not to be a tramp: "He confessed himself an outcast, and his eyes from under the lowered rim of his hat began to glance guiltily, wearing the criminal expression that comes with certain convictions."[66]

While in general I would say that such stories (and documentaries) dramatize a certain structural incompleteness or ambivalence characterizing bourgeois ideology at this moment (rather than any literal process of real bourgeois being absorbed by the lower orders), it is nonetheless striking, for our purposes, how something of this afflicted Dreiser himself. Throughout his early journalistic work and first short stories, such as "Nigger Jeff," where a young reporter covers a violent lynch mob, his writing evinces a sharp fear of the prospects of sinking into the undifferentiated and "nameless" crowd, condemned to anonymity and endless toil—in effect, of being proletarianized.[67] Yet we also know that throughout his life Dreiser sympathized with and sometimes worked for left-wing and working-class causes of many kinds. *An Amateur Laborer* interestingly complicates this affective dynamic, as Dreiser seeks out the heteronomy of wage work: imaginarily at first, at a sanitarium where businessmen were infantilized and treated like lackeys by the imperious proprietor, then later at an actual railroad workshop. In the grip of depression and unable to write—indeed, subject to a harrowing inertial torpor—he is drawn to labor (in an "amateur" capacity) as a kind of shock therapy, an immersion in a "destructive element" whose form stands in many ways as the negation of his own self-conception, that is, a professional writer of "genius." Yet the work cure largely succeeds (his depression wanes and creativity returns), thus fortifying our sense of the paradoxically intimate yet also polarized relations among labor, rest or inactivity, and the aesthetic in Dreiser's writerly metabolism.

Hence, finally (to put Dreiser in the place of Hurstwood aboard the trolley for a moment), we hear the radical ambivalence of the voice of the striker in Hurstwood's ear, entreating him to join the cause of the workers, a voice that also inescapably recalls the jesuitical voice of the commodity so prevalent elsewhere in the novel, both laden with the promise of leaving behind that class-bound world forever. Hence, we understand, too, the novel's astonishing evocation of middle-classlessness as such, with its various reroutings and domestications of radical impulses, surely one imaginative solution to the dilemma Dreiser himself acutely experienced.

three

Willa Cather and the Ambivalence of Hierarchy

When Nancy came back after so many
years, though the outward scene was little
changed, she came back to a different
world. . . . The war had done away with
many of the old distinctions.

—Willa Cather, *Sapphira and the Slave Girl*

Tom Outland, the naively charming and doomed young drifter/cowboy/ physicist/archaeologist of *The Professor's House* (1925), had, Cather tells us, an odd way with some people. "He idealized the people he loved and paid his devoir to the ideal rather than to the individual, so that his behaviour was sometimes a little too exalted for the circumstances."[1] Lillian St. Peter, with a characteristic hint of snobbishness, attributes this to a vulgarized "chivalry of the cinema." Godfrey St. Peter, the eponymous professor, finds on the contrary something else at work here, namely lingering habits learned through what he imagines as working-class solidarity, habits now out of place in the narrow, petit bourgeois milieu of the college town of Hamilton: "There is, he knew, this dream of self-sacrificing friendship and disinterested love down among the day labourers, the men who run the railroad trains and boats and reapers and thrashers and mine-drills of the world." Hence, where Lillian sees a certain lack of "class," her husband sees rather too much of it.

Cather's invocation of the cinema in this context resonates interestingly with the St. Peters' interpretive ambivalence with respect to Tom, since it is apparent that the early silent cinema was the locus of intense and contradictory class and cultural investments. Although elements of a corporate-dominated mass culture driven by the ideology of entertainment—notably the studio and star systems—emerged during this period, historians are beginning to analyze the extent to which the early screen was also a remarkable forum for the depiction of all sides of the capital-labor struggle.[2] Prior to the dominance of Hollywood, hundreds, perhaps thousands, of films produced by corporate and government agencies as well as by unions and independent activist filmmakers were disseminated alongside the more familiar comedies and melodramas, to still predominantly working-class audiences. Company and state authorities (including local censorship boards) and working-class groups fought continually over access to production and distribution through to the late 1920s, by which time the forces of "bourgeois hegemony" had emerged in a much stronger position. The working-class habits of Tom that the professor perceives might, in this context, have *also* been due to the "chivalry of the cinema."

Either way, Cather would probably not have approved. She mostly tended to disparage the spread of a "cinema public" (she forbade the filming of her works), which she took to be absorbing those "fine readers" whom she dreamed of cultivating as her intended audience.[3] What Cather meant by the ideal of the fine reader is precarious indeed, something that leads out into the peculiar nature of her novelistic project, as well as the associated problems of the subsequent reception of her work. In essence, she imagined the fine reader to be someone who was at once ordinary but cultivated, possessed of a "richness" of mentality, a "fineness" of spirituality, but not necessarily a traditional high cultural educational background, the aesthetic disposition somehow preexisting any familial or academic inculcation (Cather was notorious for her efforts to keep her texts off high school and college syllabi, fearing that exposure in such an institutional setting would lead students to hate her books). In this sense, her ideal reader bears a certain resemblance to Tom Outland himself, the orphaned "tramp boy" (121) who roams the Southwest and falls in with some priests who clean him up and teach him some Latin (*The Professor's House*, of all Cather's novels, lends itself most readily to allegorization in terms of her own writerly situation, not least because its main character is himself someone whose principal occupation is writing).

Tom, then, stands as some idealized fusion of high and low, a modern-day cultured shepherd of the pastoral tradition, a situation overcoded by a certain ambiguity with respect to class consciousness (perhaps it is intensified, perhaps not). The example of Tom serves as an initial indication of a complex set of positions with respect to matters of class and hierarchy at work in Cather's texts. These positions disrupt in unexpected ways the traditional criticism (true enough at a certain level) of Cather as an irremediable conservative, a term (particularly in its somewhat insipid American usage) that does not do adequate justice to the intense and conflicted patterns of yearning and resentment the texts exhibit. Hence a judgment such as that of Deborah Carlin's, directed at Cather's last two novels but more generally applicable to her work, that they "believe adamantly in hierarchy," is, from our present perspective, not so much wrong as insufficiently elaborated.[4] For Cather, some hierarchies are better than others, and maybe, just maybe, none at all would be best. This vision of classlessness in some ways departs instructively from the general coordinates of our larger analytic frame, a divergent episode in the overall narrative, though as we shall see, the central matter of labor and nonlabor is never far from Cather's mind.

■ ■ ■

Cather's most open, and openly troubled, "endorsement" of hierarchy is probably to be found in the novel she published prior to *The Professor's House*, *A Lost Lady* (1923). With this novel, we can grasp more clearly one of the things that attracted Cather so frequently to frontier settings, namely the stark class structures which tended to predominate in the little prairie railway towns in the last decades of the nineteenth century. In a sense, Cather deploys the frontier as the unspoken antipode of Turner's notion of the frontier as the safety valve that would kick in whenever society "gave signs of breaking into classes."[5] Turner envisioned the incipient eruption of classes as a curse visited principally upon the eastern and midwestern United States; Cather completes the spatial trajectory by imagining the western frontier, as it relieves the pressure of social crisis, as a fictive terrain upon which classes can then "break out" with suddenness and clarity. On the opening page of *A Lost Lady* she writes that, during the 1880s at least, there were "two distinct social strata in the prairie States; the homesteaders and hand-workers who were there to make a living, and the bankers and gentleman ranchers who came from the Atlantic seaboard to invest money and to 'develop our great West,' as they used to tell us."[6] Such a simplified class structure is a function of the frontier itself, as an arena of rapid capital accumulation, and at a point in its development when it has yet to generate, to any substantial degree, those numerous middle and white-collar strata then beginning swiftly to appear in the industrializing eastern and midwestern states.

Accompanying this structural lucidity is a searing, class-driven ressentiment on the part of many of the novel's characters, all directed, in one form or another, toward the leading family of the town of Sweet Water, the Forresters. The townspeople, for instance, particularly some of the wives of those very "homesteaders and handworkers," who elsewhere in the Cather imaginary might well merit considerable sympathy, are here portrayed as sheer vermin whose sole purpose is to invade and bring down the Forresters' once elegant hilltop home, which they have the chance of accomplishing when Marian Forrester falls ill:

> The Mrs. Beasleys and Molly Tuckers had their chance at last. They went in and out of Mrs. Forrester's kitchen as familiarly as they did out of one another's. They rummaged through the linen closet to find more sheets, pried about in the attic and cellar. They went over the house like ants, the house where they had never before got past the parlour; and they found they had been fooled all these years. There was nothing remarkable about the place at all! The kitchen was inconvenient, the sink smelly. The carpets were worn, the curtains faded, the clumsy, old-fashioned furniture they wouldn't have had for a gift, and the upstairs bedrooms were full of dust and cobwebs. (138)

Here is reactionary rhetoric of a classic sort, the justified dislike of one's "betters" refashioned as an evil malignancy. Characteristically, the house is in decline (Daniel Forrester, the incorruptible railroad magnate known mainly as the Captain, has by this time suffered business failures and a stroke), and *A Lost Lady* is indeed a "tragedy" of fading class distinction, the class structure of Sweet Water not so much disappearing as becoming permeable.

Niel Herbert, meanwhile, the young man who at first idealizes Marian Forrester, only to become disillusioned with her once the household begins to decline, is himself marked as déclassé, which at length occasions his own bout of ressentiment. Niel's father has lost his property, and, Niel tells us, "there was an air of failure and defeat about his family" (30). Niel's déclassé status clearly informs his basic perspective: he can libidinally invest in the Forresters as representatives of a realm of wealth and beauty perhaps once but now no longer available to him, only to turn on Marian (after the Captain's death) once the same fate befalls her, as the grip of economic necessity begins to tighten, and grasping arrivistes like the hated Ivy Peters slowly come to prominence. Hence, when we get to the narrator's striking statement that "what Niel most held against Mrs. Forrester [was] that she was not willing to immolate herself, like the widow of all these great men [that is, the bourgeois pioneers], and die with the pioneer period to which she belonged" (169), we can understand this partly as less an exaggerated expression of pain at the passing of obsolete ideals than as an externalization and transference of Niel's own self-hatred, the self-hatred of the déclassé whose imaginary escape from failure has been definitively blocked.

Patterns not dissimilar to these had been seen earlier in Cather's fiction, particularly in her classic *My Ántonia* (1918). Jim Burden, the young male narrator who himself ambivalently idolizes the female figure of Ántonia Shimerda, is a structural counterpart of Niel, though with the polarities reversed: he is younger than Ántonia (though only by a few years), and he is of a higher class than the working-class Shimerdas. One of the dark under-currents of this often bucolically toned novel is precisely the ironic class fate of these immigrant Bohemians, who leave behind the Old World for a life of grim toil on the Nebraska plain. Mr. Shimerda had "made good wages" back in Europe, and "his family were respected there."[7] He is a thoughtful, medi-tative man and an accomplished fiddler, but he finds that such a cultured disposition has no place in his new situation in America, and hence while he has strictly speaking moved out of the working class in acquiring his farm-land, Cather nonetheless imagines him to have suffered a kind of cultural declassing. This is ultimately more serious than his economic status and occasions his eventual suicide, leaving the family in the hands of the grasping and resentful mother. Meanwhile, the daughters of the various immigrant families in time find work in the local town of Black Hawk, imagined, much like Sweet Water, as a place of Victorian repression and ressentiment, though again the overall tone here is rather more reflective and affectionate than in *A Lost Lady*.

In *My Ántonia*, the lost historical moment being mourned is that of Old Bohemia. In *A Lost Lady*, Cather jettisons most of these ethnic/European materials (with one important exception, as we shall see below) and places the golden age in the immediate frontier past, a putatively heroic age on which the novel reflects at some length. Nina Schwartz, in her excellent analysis of the novel, argues that the energy of the text has in this domain a strong demystifying component: that Marian's personification of these ideals, and Niel's and others' investment in that personification, is revealed to rest not upon the innate power of female sexuality as some have maintained,[8] but rather on bourgeois property and its fetishization. Once the Captain's property loses value, any grace, charm, or other powers of attraction commanded by Marian—which are extensively detailed in the novel— also vanish.[9] This argument seems basically right, although it slights somewhat the effort the narrative makes to fashion the Forresters as more than bourgeois but precisely as aristocratic. This is meant here literally (not merely in the sense of donning aristocratic trappings, which is what is usually meant)—that is, as being members of a feudal mode of production.

Virtually every description of Marian in the first half of the novel, not only those that can be ascribed to the perspective of this or that character, works to locate Marian's qualities as natural and effortless emanations of her inner self, as inborn powers of both grace and command that cannot be ignored even by those who would claim to see through them: Ivy Peters (another ressentiment-governed character, crude and ambitious, who is confident that he will one day supplant the Forresters as leading citizen), on gaining entrance to the Forresters', had "intended to sit down in the biggest leather chair and cross his legs and make himself at home; but he found himself on the front porch, put out by that delicately modulated voice as effectually as if he had been kicked out by the brawniest tough in town" (87). Ivy will eventually find his way into Marian Forrester's bed, the contrast with this scene providing us with some measure of the extent of her downfall.

Captain Forrester's infirmity functions here as well. We never actually see the young, energetic bourgeois: within the frame of the story, the Captain has long since suffered the accident that forces his early retirement from the railroad company. On one level, this is yet another symbolic marker of the closing of the frontier itself, and the waning of the age of the Captain and his ilk. It also reinforces the sense of how Cather uses the space of the frontier, deploying it as a realm of rigid class structure; the Ivy Peters who come after the Captain harbor a set of "mass" tastes and opinions which threatens to blur that clarity. On another level, the Captain's slowness, solemnity, and commanding presence work to remove him from the stream of time, from the hurly-burly of bourgeois historical existence, and place him in a naturalized realm, rooted, like one of the great cottonwoods on his estate. At one point, moreover, the Captain's voice is characterized as containing a "lonely, defiant note that is so often heard in the voices of old Indians" (55). Indians are, for Cather (as we will see more clearly in *The Professor's House*), embodiments of a kind of authentic cultural nobility, an aristocracy of the soul, at least, who once had, we discover, an encampment on the very hill where the Forresters' home now sits. But they have been wiped out, suggesting that this business of being an aristocrat is fleeting and precarious.

All of this might escape the average reader, who might complacently perceive here just another pair of leisured bourgeois. This explains why Cather needs literal incarnations of the other pole of feudal society, not merely to complete the circuit, but to recognize the truth of the Forresters *for us*. The Blum boys are sons of poor German immigrants and clearly marked as peasants. Refreshingly undemocratic, and free of the ressentiment that drives their more modernized fellow townsfolk, the Blums realize, as the other residents do not, "that such a fortunate and privileged class [as the Forresters belonged to] was an axiomatic fact in the social order" (20). Later, things are made even more explicit, when, after Adolph Blum happens upon a romantic liaison between Marian and the dashing Frank Ellinger, a bond of conspiratorial sympathy is posited between the upper and lower orders: "But with Adolph Blum her secrets were safe. His mind was feudal; the rich and fortunate were also the privileged. . . . Mrs. Forrester had never been too haughty to smile at him when he came to the back door with his fish. She never haggled about the price. She treated him like a human being" (68). It takes one to know one: although worlds apart in one sense, the two nonetheless inhabit the same class imaginary in the novel.

A Lost Lady is typically taken as one of the pinnacles of Cather's nostalgia, but on this reading it emerges as an oddly distinct form. It harkens back not merely to a golden age of pioneer ideals that may or may not have existed, but to a class structure that certainly never did in this country. This suggests that there is something more underlying this, some more vital (if masked) charge of desire at work—certainly it is not that weak, old-womanish sentimentalism that the leftist critics of the 1930s charged Cather with. They were responding hostilely to her declared lack of interest in realism and social issues, but their confused and regressive gender politics (detailed nicely by Sharon O'Brien) blinded them to what strikes one now as a marked *lack* of sentiment in her fiction, a lucid and even harsh conception of character and social structure.[10] The full ramifications of this can best be grasped in *The Professor's House.*

. . .

This rapid overview of the main lines of *A Lost Lady* allows us to see that its central structures and preoccupations are revisited in *The Professor's House,* but in heightened and intensified form.[11] The Marian-Blum dyad is here represented in the pairing of the professor with the earnest German seamstress Augusta. Augusta is characterized as someone with if not a feudal, then at least a "medieval," frame of mind, in her devout Catholicism and her strict sense of a "great chain" of social and natural being, with herself firmly ensconced a good way down the chain. Indeed, the emphasis on her gravity and rootedness ("seasoned and sound and on the solid earth she surely was" [281]) lends her a touch (despite her foreignness) of the peasant autochthon. St. Peter, meanwhile, with his jet-black hair, dark complexion, and "close-trimmed Van Dyke beard," is "said to look like a Spaniard" (12–13). His students even think he looks like Mephistopheles, a figure whose frequent narrative role—to draw disaffected intellectuals into the realm of aristocratic whimsy and profligacy (as in Marlowe, for example)—further underscores what I take to be the essentially noble accents we are to read here.

What unites the two—aside from the natural bond of sympathy Cather imagines between these disparate social levels—is their sharing, over a period of many years, of the same work space. In this cramped, third-floor room (where they both hover above the rest of the family, toward whom the professor has grown increasingly indifferent) St. Peter has written his magnum opus, the eight-volume *Spanish Adventurers in North America,* while Augusta has sewn skirts and dresses for Lillian and the two daughters. Despite the manifest differences in their work, their labors seem to partake of a similar quality or structure, characterized by the elaboration of a preexisting pattern. Augusta's dress forms (torsolike shapes) stand in the corner of the room, and her dress patterns are mingled with the professor's manuscripts in the space beneath the window seat. The plan for the professor's project, meanwhile, is described as coming upon him all of a piece—a kind of visitation, almost—the subsequent execution of the work amounting to the fleshing out of this originary moment, which adds nothing essentially new. St. Peter here recalls an episode from his days as a graduate student, aboard a boat cruising the Mediterranean:

> One day stood out above the others. All day long they were skirting the south coast of Spain; from the rose of dawn to the gold of sunset the ranges of the Sierra Nevadas towered on their right, snow peak after snow peak, high beyond the flight of fancy, gleaming like crystal and topaz. St. Peter lay looking up at them from a little boat riding low in the purple water, and the design of his book unfolded in the air above him, just as definitely as the mountain ranges themselves. And the design was sound. He had accepted it as inevitable, had never meddled with it, and it had seen him through. (106)

As Marilyn Chandler has persuasively concluded, "The two activities that take place in this room are not conflicting but complementary. . . . Augusta's sewing, with its forms and patterns and routines, is an exact counterpart to the professor's writing."[12]

What is produced in this workroom is of a slightly ambiguous character. The emphasis on forms and on designs written in the air (to which the professor in effect rises as if lifted above the world, as one critic has observed)[13] suggests a certain immateriality at the root of these labors, as if the making of an actual, tangible *thing* were to be regarded with some suspicion. This sense of the immaterial persists in relation to Tom Outland, whose scientific achievement is the discovery of a new type of "vacuum," which, by the time of his death, has been incorporated into a "design" for a new kind of aircraft engine (thus leaving behind solid ground yet again). Such a suggestion of insubstantiality should, however, be balanced against the description of the workroom itself, whose exaggerated peculiarities have often been noted:

> The furnace heat did not reach the third floor. There was no way to warm the sewing-room, except by a rusty, round gas stove with no flue—a stove which consumed gas imperfectly and contaminated the air. To remedy this, the window must be left open—otherwise, with the ceiling so low, the air would speedily become unfit to breathe. If the stove were turned down, and the window left open a little way, a sudden gust of wind would blow the wretched thing out altogether, and a deeply absorbed man might be asphyxiated before he knew it. The Professor had found that the best method, in winter, was to turn the gas on full and keep the window wide on the hook, even if he had to put on a leather jacket over his working-coat. (26)

This scene is typically read as exemplifying St. Peter's essential asceticism, a reading that seems insufficient, even if we grant this latter trait (and the attention paid, elsewhere in the novel, to his well-developed culinary tastes renders the charge of asceticism rather dubious). The hyperbole of this passage concerns the working conditions under which the two labor, conditions that are uncomfortable at best and often dangerous: more than anything else, they connote the *factory*, and proletarian working conditions. Against the suggestion of immateriality, then, arises the space factory production, where the things produced are very material and tangible indeed. Moreover, these things are commodities, fashioned by wage labor and intended for sale, something else with which Cather is not exactly comfortable. Here then is another suggestion of the ambivalent class energy at work in the novel, as a certain fantasy of premodern hierarchical relations calls up its modernized negation from within itself.

In general, at the manifest level Cather would seem to be pushing the description of St. Peter's and Augusta's labor toward a certain ideal of handicraft, an ideal figured in the stress on pregiven forms and emblematized in economic terms in the professor's valorization of "purely cultural studies" over and against the "new commercialism" in education, which is designed only to "show results" (140). The handicraft or artisanal ideal is here embattled through its involvement in what might be termed a crisis of pastoral withdrawal from the market. The terms of the pastoral are familiar from our analysis of Dreiser—we have already noted Cather's imaginative reconciliation of the upper and lower classes (here figured in a specifically feudal sense). Whereas Dreiser, in *Sister Carrie*, elaborated the novel's engagement with the pastoral along a work/leisure axis, the governing axis in *The Professor's House* might be more adequately described in terms of circulation/stasis (although a certain pattern of movement/stillness was also implicated in *Sister Carrie*). The image of handicraft labor itself stands as a kind of fusion of high and low, of complexity and simplicity: while possibly artful, handicraft work remains, in the terms established in the novel, the elaboration of a set pattern, rather than that expression of the new as advocated by the aesthetic ideology of modernism.[14] Hence handicraft is effectively allied in the novel with the pastoral impulse of classless harmony. Cather, unlike Dreiser, tries to imagine a kind of production whose products would not circulate on the market (or only with great difficulty), or things that are not exactly thinglike, because only this kind of production can forestall entry into the realm of circulation, a realm whose social consequences are disastrous and wholly decipherable in terms of that very "modernized" class passion of ressentiment. The social and political faculties of the text in effect grasp the capitalist marketplace as the fruit of an underlying process, namely the stamping of social production as uniformly commodified. The resultant imaginative effort to conjure a different process is unsurprisingly fraught with peril, as the shadow cast by the factory upon the professor's workroom may already have hinted.

Indeed, the novel is obsessed at every turn with the prospects of circulation in general, and the dire effects it everywhere generates. The dresses Augusta makes do not circulate; they remain within the confines of the nuclear family, which is here a kind of paradigm of an arena of noncirculation. St. Peter's books, meanwhile, after many years finally circulate sufficiently to garner him some attention and win him a cash prize, a prize subsequently translated into a new house that he refuses to move into, jealously defending his traditional work space (and thus furnishing the immediate pretext for the narrative). Kathleen and Rosamond, the two daughters, circulate all too successfully outside the family. Rosamond marries Louie Marsellus, a successful Jewish engineer/entrepreneur whose "only Semitic feature," we are told, is a nose that rivals that of *The Great Gatsby*'s Meyer Wolfsheim ("it grew out of his face with masterful strength . . . like a vigorous oak tree growing out of a hillside" [43]). Kathleen, meanwhile, is married to Scott McGregor, a bitter, underemployed writer of newspaper filler who, like his wife, resents Marsellus's exploitation of Tom's legacy. These attachments cause no end of strife and recrimination.[15] Professor Crane, meanwhile, who acted as mentor to Tom in the laboratory, and his wife, feeling that they should receive a share of the riches the posthumous development of Tom's inventions is generating, venture forth from their sheltered lives toward the sphere of circulation, only to have their worst (bitter, grasping) selves exposed (an "adventurer" and a mere "salesman," Mrs. Crane calls Louie). And Tom, finally, desires that the Indian artifacts he and Roddy Blake have discovered on the Blue Mesa remain within the non-circulating realm of the museum, a desire thwarted when Roddy sells them to a German collector, ending their friendship.

The general pattern of these crises of circulation suggests the paradox that, although the true value of something resists circulation, it is nonethe-less the sphere of circulation which affords the apprehension of this true value in the first place. It is not merely Tom's discoveries, of course, that subsequently find material embodiment and success on the capitalist mar-ketplace: Tom himself undergoes a kind of resurrection in the form of "Outland," the lakeside estate Louie and Rosamond build with the profits reaped from the marketing of Tom's work, an estate essentially dedicated, as is underscored repeatedly in the novel, to displaying the Marselluses's new wealth. This situation prompts a lament from Kathleen, who imagines a "true" Tom drawn back within the noncirculating realm of the family: " 'Yes, ' " she says to her father, " 'and now [Tom's] all turned out chemicals and dollars and cents, hasn't he? But not for you and me! Our Tom is much nicer than theirs' " (132). Meanwhile, Tom arrives at what he believes to be a genuine grasp or perception of the mesa only after Roddy has transformed the artifacts into commodities and then departed: "I remember these things, because, in a sense, that was the first night I was ever really on the mesa at all—the first night that all of me was there. This was the first time I ever really saw it as a whole. It all came together in my understanding, as a series of experiments do when you begin to see where they are leading. . . . It was possession" (251). So, only after Roddy has indulged in a bit of "new com-mercialism" can Tom go on to indulge in some "purely cultural studies" for the remainder of his stay on the mesa (he says that this period "was the first time I'd ever studied methodically, or intelligently").[16] These studies afford him a certain communion with the vanished natives themselves, who, in the "patience" and "deliberation" (craft virtues, again) with which they fashioned their attractive dwellings and implements (they had a "feeling for design" [203], Tom notes), represent another combination of the cultured and the primitive, much as Tom himself does. In both these examples, then, the positing and perception of genuine value does not arise despite a debased realm of circulation but precisely because of it, thus paralleling in this movement that shadowing of the professor's workroom by the factory we noted earlier, and calling attention to a split within the ideological imaginary of the novel whereby what is disavowed at one level is posited as necessary at another.

Another crucial result of circulation, and one which will allow us to begin to specify more concretely some of the historical content of the narrative, is the eruption of hierarchy out of what had hitherto been a plane of equivalence, something that follows from Cather's apperception of the workings of the market. In these instances, of course, hierarchy does not signify the valorized and naturalized feudal dichotomy typified by St. Peter and Augusta, which encodes a certain motion toward self-transcendence through harmony, but rather what the text posits as an invidious hierarchical dynamic whose center of gravity pulls in the direction of antagonism. This process has two distinct domains of enactment. The first of these arises in the wake of the decay of the family, as we started to see above, as the prominence of the Marselluses and their ostentatious display of wealth breed jealousy on the part of Kathleen and hasten the steady drifting apart of the professor and Lillian. This domain is corrupted by ressentiment, and represents the space of an emergent, and still sociologically contentious and vexing, professional/managerial class stratum. The growth of the professional/managerial class during the first decades of this century represented a major development in the complexity of the class structure of American society, greatly expanding the political and cultural centrality of what Erik Olin Wright, in a major Marxian effort to unlock the structural puzzle of the middle classes, has termed "contradictory class locations," wherein people occupy ambiguous social positions that are at once exploitative and exploited.[17]

The informing presence of this newly central class formation in Cather is consistent with her own evident antiprofessionalism. In *A Lost Lady*, the supreme embodiment of ressentiment was Ivy Peters, a lawyer, whose crime lay in his belief that he himself might someday occupy the same leading political and social position as the Forresters. Other characters in the novel were also lawyers or judges, but they all perceived their social standing to be essentially adjunct to that held by the Forresters. Ivy does not at all respect the traditional divisions. In *The Professor's House*, meanwhile, Louie is at once engineer and businessman, combining in himself both the professional and managerial roles. He becomes increasingly central to the social life of Hamilton, and foreign academics begin dropping by Outland for lunch, as if his estate and not the university were the prime site of academic life. St. Peter, of course, resists, defending an older or "preprofessional" conception of the noninstrumentality of work practices against the "new commercialism" taking hold at his school, this last—with its business of "showing results" to the state legislatures—being a part of the first great wave of professionalization in higher education occurring in the 1910s and 1920s. Teachers in higher education sought to demonstrate the social utility of their labors, and hence claim a share of social spending in exchange for some semblance of the continued autonomous organization of work practices.[18] Of course, for the liberal arts such a demonstration has always been especially problematic; these disciplines as often as not resort to an anticommercial rhetoric that has little by little become a part of the professional ethos of the humanities. Thus the professor's anticommercial stance, like so much else in the novel, itself pulls in two conflicting directions.

The other domain of sudden hierarchization, which stands in a certain opposition to the first, can be observed in the crystalline air of the Blue Mesa, in one of the novel's more striking moments. This occurs after Tom has explained to Roddy (who imagined that he had done well to earn a tidy sum from the sale of the artifacts) that he intended to garner no profit through their recovery: "I supposed," Roddy says, that "I had some share in the relics we dug up—you always spoke of it that way. But I see now I was working for you like a hired man, and while you were away I sold your property" (245). Tom in effect betrays that dream of solidarity the professor had earlier imputed to the day laborers of the world like Roddy Blake. Unlike the bickering of the familial realm and of Hamilton in general, there is here the suggestion of some more fundamental split, a purer break (Roddy disappears over the edge of the cliff and is never heard from again), against which the ressentiment occasioned by the professional/managerial formation emerges as so much inauthentic white noise, a pattern of complaint and frustrated desire or intention with no particular issue. That is to say, this moment on the mesa appears as something of a demystification of the other realm, whose full implications we must try to grasp.

Roddy's statement is peculiar, in the sense that it positions Tom (who insists he wants no profit) precisely in the role of capitalist entrepreneur. Tom contends that he had never regarded the relics as his property—something Roddy assumes. However, in claiming the artifacts as his "inheritance" (243) he nonetheless implicitly arrogates to himself a certain right as to their ultimate dispensation. This turn of events, which relocates putative equals as a worker and a capitalist (that is, a nonworker), had in a way been foreseen by Roddy himself, a premonition rooted in his perception of the piecemeal liberal arts education that Tom has managed to pick up: "[Roddy] said if I once knew Latin, I wouldn't have to work with my back all my life like a burro. He had great respect for education, but he believed it was some kind of hocus-pocus that enabled a man to live without work" (188). This implies that the "respect" Roddy possesses is less for the content of education than for the cultural capital it grants, and for the social mobility—a rise from the working class into the "work free" realm of the middle class—this cultural capital was said to make available, at least according to the ideologies of education and its social role that were becoming predominant during this period.[19] Roddy thus regards education as one possible escape from the burden of toil; however, he places himself firmly outside its purview.

At the conclusion of this southwestern adventure, then, a situation not unlike the one that befell the original native cliff dwellers themselves arises. Cather does not posit a homogeneous native civilization extending across the continent, a fantasy of bucolic primitiveness, but rather a situation in which primary and invidious hierarchizations have already taken place. The people of the Blue Mesa, according to Father Duchene, an archaeologically savvy local priest, were "too far advanced for their time and environment," and were "probably wiped out, utterly exterminated, by some roving Indian tribe without culture or domestic virtues, some horde that fell upon them in their summer camp and destroyed them for their hides and clothing and weapons, or from mere love of slaughter" (221). The savages, lacking in "culture and domestic virtues," also presumably lack access to craft skills, as defined earlier, with their unstable and implied relation to a kind of "non-productivity," to a kind of work that results in "immaterial" products and fitfully suggests an aestheticized transcendence of itself. More sharply still, these hyperprimitives can be seen as lacking "education," in Roddy's sense, which is to say that, within the ideological imaginary of the narrative, they are *workers* (and as plain dwellers, only too obviously positioned as "low" with respect to the "high born" cliff dwellers).[20] Like the "cinema public" invoked by Lillian St. Peter (but in reference to Tom), they have no use for purely cultural studies, and they certainly (much like the townspeople with respect to the Forresters in *A Lost Lady*) do not recognize quality when they see it. So Roddy, finally, by dispersing (as commodities) the relics and hence making disappear a portion of whatever existence the cliff dwellers still clung to, in effect repeats the earlier eruption of primal class violence, his status as worker vividly reconfirmed in the process.

We are now in a position to begin to specify more precisely some of the characteristic patterns and sets of distinctions *The Professor's House* insistently mobilizes, patterns and distinctions whose ambivalent logic tends to produce what would initially seem to be the unintended opposites or contraries of the initial terms. People and objects marked for withholding from circulation and commodification—St. Peter's books, his daughters, Tom's inventions, the native artifacts—nonetheless tumble into this latter sphere, with unhappy consequences. At the same time (and as a partial consequence), groups that had initially been construed along a certain plane of equivalence—the family, Tom and Roddy—and that had enjoyed a harmonious existence, undergo a kind of internal distantiation and subsequent "violent hierarchization" and move toward more antagonistic relations.[21] Whereas this hierarchization in the domain of the family and Hamilton more generally is governed by ressentiment and its attendant interminable ill will, the example of Tom and Roddy (overcoded as it is by the violent native "primal scene" of the destruction of the cliff dwellers), together with the harmony of the professor-Augusta dyad, figure forth as a kind of alternative pathway. What I am suggesting is that the antimodernism of the imagined feudal harmony of St. Peter and Augusta (like that of Marian and the Blum boys earlier) stands opposed to the "bad modernity" of the professional/ managerial formation, with its instrumental reason and essentially false dynamism: its (comparatively) wealth-besotted production of unhappily permeable class fractions (the kind of permeability already apparent in *A Lost Lady*) spins acrimonious dramas of social rise and fall, of chasing after new status opportunities, but the basic script remains forever the same. The deeper political energies of the text then produce, on the far side of such bad modernity, the radical modernity of the labor-capital contradiction, whose secret link to the feudal moment lies in the promise of transcendence encoded in each: feudal relations point "beyond class" because of the bonds of natural sympathy they foster, whereas class under capitalism, despite the manifest antagonism, represents a universalizing political dynamic that promises the eventual end of all hierarchical social relations.

These patterns or movements of the text—the insistence with which valorized sites are disrupted by contradictory pressures—testify in part to the very intensity and generative power of Cather's class investments. While seeking out and vigorously attempting to imagine moments of harmony and of pastoral retreat and sanctuary, the implacability of the social and ideological vision at work goes on to produce not merely the "negations" of these initial spaces but their effective conditions of realization, in the sense that commodification and class antagonism must be faced squarely and gone through in order to reach that realm of social peace and aestheticized labor (in whatever forms this might be realized) which was initially valorized. Cather herself in effect "misrecognizes" this process of undoing, marking its moments in the darkly ironic terms of modern "corruption" (the novel thus remaining at least manifestly "conservative"), and fails to grasp that they are at one with the text's strongest utopian energies. To put it another way, Roddy's angry confrontation with Tom and disappearance over the cliff is from this perspective the happiest moment in the novel.

The relationship between St. Peter and Augusta seems to remain relatively free of the kinds of disruptions and reversals just described; from the opening pages until the end, it appears as a site of relative stability. It is menaced, of course: the workroom that makes the relationship possible in the first place is in the professor's old house, in which he no longer lives. Still, a note of continuance is struck at the end, as St. Peter reflects on his diminishing ties with and obligations toward his family. "There was still Augusta, however; a world full of Augustas, with whom one was outward bound" (281). This thought occurs only after the unreliable old gas stove in the workroom has blown out and the professor has been overcome by the fumes (Augusta pulls him to safety). That is, only after what we earlier termed the "shadow of the factory" has been cast once again can this thought take shape. In this sense, the professor's near-fatal accident appears as only the most distant or mediated echo of that primal scene of class violence encountered, and repeated, on the Blue Mesa, a primal scene that inscribes a note of melancholic uncertainty upon these words. The phrase "outward bound" indeed suggests a steady fade-out, an image of riding off into the sunset, perhaps, only to disappear on the sinking horizon. The professor survives, but he and the Augustas of the world—and the peculiar and always already obsolete feudal space Cather tries to place them in—nonetheless seem doomed, as in *A Lost Lady*, to a certain extinction, erased by inexorable and competing modernities.

Another aspect of the "noncontinuability" of this dyad and the ideals it represents, emphasized throughout the narrative, has been its essential sexlessness, which underscores the difficulties it faces with respect to its further propagation through time. Augusta herself, her general stolidity aside, is metaphorically allied with those aforementioned dress forms, naked female torsos that are distinctly, albeit surprisingly, unpleasant to the touch:

> Though this figure looked so ample and billowy (as if you might lay your head upon its deep-breathing softness and rest safe forever), if you touched it you suffered a severe shock, no matter how many times you had touched it before. It presented the most unsympathetic surface imaginable. Its hardness was not that of wood, which responds to concussion with living vibration and is stimulating to the hand, nor that of felt, which drinks something from the fingers. It was a dead, opaque, lumpy solidity, like chunks of putty, or tightly packed sawdust— very disappointing to the tactile sense, yet somehow always fooling you again. (18)

This pretty much drives out any libidinal associations one might see in Augusta. St. Peter, meanwhile, has throughout the story been characterized in terms of increasing fatigue and diminishing masculine vigor, a pattern capped by Lillian's pointed comments: "Two years ago you were an impetuous young man. Now you save yourself in everything" (162). The nonreproductive quality of this pairing is echoed in Tom's narrative by what Eve Sedgwick has aptly called the "gorgeous homosocial romance" between Tom and Roddy, facilitated, for a time, by Henry, their amiable cook and housekeeper: "Life was a holiday for Blake and me after we got old Henry . . . the three of us made a happy family" (197–98).[22] These examples of nonreproductive relationships need to be juxtaposed with the Marselluses, who sail off to Europe and engage, as Benn Michaels tellingly phrases it, in the "production of a young Marsellus,"[23] which strikes a note of terror in the professor and which, given the consistent role assigned both to Louie and Rosamond and to production itself throughout the novel, cannot be wholly counted a good thing.

Subtending all this, finally, would seem to be a valorization of non-reproductive sexuality, something consistent with the ambivalence displayed toward production as such, and something that might plausibly be taken as an informing instance in the novel of Cather's own lesbianism (the very existence of which remains open to some speculation). The debate over the relation between Cather's sexuality and her writing continues strongly to-day.[24] Although I have no definitive solution to offer on this problem, I would in the present context merely observe that we can discern here a certain homology between a nonreproductive realm of sexuality and human intercourse in general, and a realm of imagined work practices in which production, or the product, is deferred and implicitly dematerialized. Sexuality perhaps offered an enabling "lens" to Cather through which she could then imagine this sort of work, a vision that could then intersect in compli-cated ways with her (related but discrete) imagination of class. In any case, what is enabling to the narrative is in the end not controlling, since things do eventually get produced and the nonreproductive relationships shatter and fade away, and hence we are left, at this juncture, suspended uncertainly between the various options and outcomes.[25]

• • •

We introduced Tom at the beginning of the chapter in the context of a certain ambivalence as to the "charge of class" he carries: that is, whether he represents an imagined dynamic of homogenizing mass culture (as typified, perhaps, by Scott McGregor and his newspaper jingles) or, on the contrary, a path of deocculation and heightened class consciousness, as manifested in lingering working-class habits. The affair with Roddy on the Blue Mesa, meanwhile, strongly classed him by momentarily placing him in the position of the capitalist exploiter, yet, on the other hand, his scholarly bent and rough-hewn ways mark him as a kind of ideal synthesis of the professor-Augusta dyad, both suggesting a potential resolution to hierarchical conflict rather different from the one that might be imagined issuing from the putative entropy of mass culture. In still another register, his inventions mark the place of the emergence of the novum, an appearance whose dialectical ambivalence is sharp indeed: on one hand, it is allied with aesthetic modernism and its general hostility to the capitalist marketplace; on the other, it is evident that the necessary systemic expansion of capitalism relies in good measure on the innovations of science and technology, for new products and new production techniques alike. Although Tom himself dies before his discoveries become commodified—luckily enough, for he is thus able to retain and occupy a certain space of purity with respect to the circulation process—the intervention of Louie Marsellus, acting in effect as Tom's surrogate in this regard, nonetheless retroactively "classes" the deceased Outland via the generation of new riches.

All of this indicates that at a certain level Tom is less a character than a shifting narrative crisis point, a signifier that differentially inhabits all of the text's multivalent possibilities of hierarchical production and class distinction. In relation to our earlier invocation of the professional/managerial class, Tom emerges as a kind of literal embodiment of the notion of the "contradictory class location." Although Louie Marsellus might be the resident "professional/manager" of the story, it is through the figure of Tom Outland that the text attempts to articulate a more concrete sense of the contradictoriness of this position, indeed to the point of its outright impossibility, at least in the unconscious judgment of this narrative. That is, the unstable and ambiguous class valence of Tom can be read as a way of at once imagining and refusing this particular class complication, his insistent absent presence in the novel—dead before it opens, yet still lingering in everyone's thoughts— thus signaling both an acknowledgment of, and a retreat from, his inescapable modernity or contemporaneity, a quality partly disguised by his knack for Latin and his embrace of dead Indians.[26] These things render him at once the figure of greatest hope and greatest anxiety, at one with the novel's most powerful utopian and ideological energies, and all told it is little wonder that he motivates what is frequently taken as Cather's most substantial departure from more familiar narrative practices, that is, the insertion of Tom's first-person account between the opening and closing sections of the novel. Like the monstrous vermin which precipitates dramatically in the first sentence of Kafka's *Metamorphosis*, Cather's aesthetic imaginary calls up this charged narrative marker from a site of intense productivity and incipient rupture, then proceeds with the dual effort to give it meaningful figuration yet contain its explosive implications.

We noted at the outset as well a certain congruence between Tom and what Cather imagined to be her ideal reader, that person of fine imagination who acquired his or her sensibility honestly, not in school but through the ordinary travails of daily life. But just as Tom is dead before the novel even begins, in practice Cather's ideal reader has tended to bifurcate (in yet another eruption of hierarchy) into two separate audiences. These have been acutely characterized by Christopher Benfey, invoking the analogous situation of Robert Frost, as "a popular readership that would take nostalgic themes at face value," specifically in the earlier novels of struggling and noble prairie pioneers, and "a more sophisticated and skeptical circle of readers who could be counted on to find the hidden pitfalls and ironies."[27] One audience who paid the bills, then, and another, much smaller, who would recognize the true worth of her work: perhaps an ungenerous way to put it, but certainly some such tension was inherent in the very project Cather self-consciously set herself, which was, on one hand, to reach a wide popular readership (and her novels were in fact consistent best-sellers, and continue to sell well today) and, on the other hand, to be considered an uncompromising literary artist of the first rank. This latter ambition has been more equivocally realized. Although highly regarded during the 1910s and 1920s, her reputation suffered somewhat in the decades following, and her status has only begun to recover during the last twenty years or so, in the wake of the canon debate and the revalorization of diverse modes of writing. Still, ambiguities and uncertainties surrounding her place in American fiction persist, the discussion of which has become something of a staple of recent Cather criticism.

The analogy with Frost might in this context be pursued a bit further. Frank Lentricchia has recently invoked the phrase "low modernism" to characterize the peculiar status and achievement of Frost's poetry.[28] Low modernism amounts essentially to a modernist and high culturalist disposition that, in order to make writing a viable way to earn a living (a way of "buttering the parsnips," in Frost's typically homely terms), has effected a strategic rapprochement with the literary marketplace, of the sort consistently shunned by the various high modernisms, which could then proceed to elaborate their formal innovations at a constitutive semiautonomous remove from the commodity form. While wanting to reach a wide public (and, at a certain level, to be wealthy and famous), Cather also extensively praised and sought to emulate various modernist and protomodernist writers (Flaubert, James, and Proust are among those she mentions most frequently). Such a dual ambition led, for both authors, to a strategy of "hiding" the more subtle verbal and narrative ramifications beneath an apparently straightforward surface. The question that continues to nag at the edges of Cather criticism is whether in the end she was so artful at concealing complexity that the very measure of her novelistic accomplishments is put in doubt.

The writerly situation in which Cather was enmeshed doubtless placed peculiar pressures on her narrative practice, and it is tempting to read *The Professor's House*, among all her works, as the most elaborate allegorization of this situation. This line of interpretation, while seductive in terms of the clarity of the allegory (indeed, almost *too* clear), should nonetheless be grasped as but a discrete moment in the overall interpretive economy we are proposing for the narrative, an economy overdetermined fully as much by the particular range of class investments we have mapped thus far. In any case, the parallels might by now be evident: the convergence between Tom and the ideal reader has already been noted, yet what is also apparent is the whole matter of circulation—the products that only slowly and with some resistance find their way into the marketplace (they seek a certain "delay of convertability," as Bourdieu might put it). But it is not, as we have seen, their true value that finally circulates, as this last is imaginatively withheld from the circulatory fray for more discerning tastes to appreciate, a pattern that perfectly describes the contradictory task set before the low modernist artifact. Even the manner in which Cather often described her approach to writing—as the subtle ringing of changes on a delimited and unvarying set of narrative and stylistic devices adopted early in her career—bears a strong resemblance to what in the novel we described in terms of the ideal of handicraft, a quasi-aesthetic practice whose full opening onto the realm of art (understood, again, in explicitly modernist terms as the achievement of the new) is interrupted by a disciplined adherence to an inherited pattern or form.

Like the reluctant commodities of *The Professor's House*, Cather's books must circulate, but not too well; indeed, her aesthetic project extends into an attempt to control the dissemination of her work, and hence to a certain extent to establish the conditions for its reception. We noted at the outset Cather's efforts to keep her novels off school curricula,[29] and the ban on movie versions (although she did eventually permit *A Lost Lady* to be filmed). Meanwhile, Dorothy Canfield Fisher, one of the principals at the Book-of-the-Month Club and a good friend of Cather's, labored long and hard trying to convince Cather to allow the club to feature her work, something she finally relented to beginning with *Shadows on the Rock* in 1931. Cather regarded the club, despite its assurances of offering only "quality literature," as yet another species of the "new commercialism" she tirelessly derided, and she wished to maintain her distance from it. The Book-of-the-Month Club, however, was not mere garden-variety commercialism, as recent work by Joan Shelley Rubin and Janice Radway has demonstrated. Rather, it was at the cutting edge of that new middle-class cultural formation, the middlebrow.[30] The promoters of middlebrow culture generally attempted to combine a commitment to high culture with a desire—often based on laudably democratic impulses—to make art and literature available to a wider audience. This is somewhat at odds with the logic of Cather's project, since, at the end of the day, what she fantasizes as the "aesthetic" or the true value of the work is precisely what is not widely circulatable.

Cather's project and that of the Book-of-the-Month Club, however much they subsequently diverge, would seem to derive some inspiration from Van Wyck Brooks's famous call for the elaboration of a cultural "middle plane between vaporous idealism and self-interested practicality," in his 1915 essay " 'Highbrow' and 'Lowbrow.' "[31] Highbrow, for Brooks, designates the realm of academics and other guardians of official culture, whereas lowbrow refers essentially to homely business pragmatism (the theologian Jonathan Edwards and Benjamin Franklin are his representative embodiments of the two spheres). Thus what must be observed at once about the distinction Brooks elaborates is that, from a sociological perspective, both poles lie within a broad middle-class domain, the terms being more descriptive finally of class fractions than of classes as such (one is surprised, then, to discover Brooks arguing finally that the middle plane he seeks implies the achievement of socialism, since the whole question of working-class politics and culture is wholly absent from his essay). In this context, the efforts of the "makers of the middlebrow" might be read in terms of the creation of a compromise formation with respect to Brooks's ideal—that is, quality culture that sells—whereas Cather seems to imagine, in *The Professor's House*, a certain radicalization of Brooks's terms. In the harmony between the professor and Augusta, in the impossible and unstable figure of Tom Outland, the novel furnishes more concretely dualistic class content to the Brooksean distinction and imagines a more thoroughgoing articulation of the contradictions at issue. In Tom, indeed, we see nothing less than a striking fantasy of the recombination of intellectual and manual labor, a healing of the fundamental division that since the advent of priestly castes and the state has informed all class and caste hierarchies through history.[32]

This "strong utopian" interpretation of this facet of Cather's novel acknowledges the distinctive modernist energy or dynamic articulated in her writing. This energy is in turn deflected by the very contradictions that generated it into allegorical images and patterns, away from formal experimentation, and into a zone where it is open to a certain recuperation by the middlebrow. I have in mind here not only the Book-of-the-Month Club, but also more recent developments like the Willa Cather Pioneer Memorial Society and Education Foundation, which promotes Cather's life and works, sponsors tours of the Red Cloud, Nebraska, area (site of much of the fiction), and operates a little museum complete with wax-figure dioramas of scenes from the novels.[33] I also have in mind that prominent strain of Cather criticism which at least implicitly allies itself with this version of Cather's life and work, critics like Merrill Skaggs and Susan Rosowski, whose work strives to construct a kind of cordon sanitaire around the narratives, positioning them as serene, jewel-like masterpieces shorn of tension and contradiction.[34] A virtual *reductio* of this strategy is offered by David Stineback, who argues that the emotional subtlety of Cather's fiction is so great that it is bound to "frustrate" the rationalism of academic scholarship and "resist" any "abstract intellectual restatement." He proposes instead that the medium of popular book reviewing has been and should continue to be the most fruitful domain of correct interpretation.[35] On this view, and indeed as Cather herself might have imagined it, her work finally has no proper place within the academy.

The title of Stineback's essay invokes the problem of "professional evaluation," which is instructive because the question of professionalism is, finally, a kind of subtext underpinning these issues. The conservative mode of criticism we have just invoked seems marked above all by a deliberate and studious avoidance of anything resembling contemporary theory, something no doubt necessary to preserve what is seen as the calm unity and exquisitely balanced symbolism of Cather's fiction. The advent of theory, meanwhile, has recently been analyzed by John Guillory in terms of the attempted reprofessionalization of the literary academy, one response to the progressive marginalization and perceived irrelevance of the humanities over the last twenty years or so.[36] It is all the more striking, then, that the object of these critics is a writer like Cather, whose own antiprofessionalism was evident, perhaps nowhere more so than in *The Professor's House*. In the 1980s, official Cather studies produce a Cather about whom it is extremely difficult to be "theoretical," that is to say, professional. The final irony attending all of this has once more to do with Cather's uneasy relation to the middlebrow and professionalism. Janice Radway's research on the middlebrow attempts to show that the middlebrow might in the end be thought of as the cultural formation functionally suited to precisely that emergent and vexing class fraction, the professional/managerial class.[37] This last, of course, was already present in *The Professor's House*, where it became the object of fairly intense narrative figuration and ideological disapprobation. The novel instead sought out starker feudal and capitalist class patterns, moments of purity to be counterposed against the newer class fractions (represented by the Marselluses, and imaginatively refused in Tom Outland). These fractions, products of corporate organization and the expanded production of wealth, remain mired in the frenetic dance of status and in a sour ressentiment without issue. They thus mitigate against both nostalgia and revolution alike, the two opposing paths that, as we have seen, lead in their different ways through antagonism to harmony. The way this is enacted in this novel, and in others by Cather, nonetheless grants them an unwanted place (but never wholly unwanted) in the cultural self-reproduction of the professional/managerial class.

four

New Frontiers in Hollywood: Mobility and Desire in The Day of the Locust

> From the form of a city, the style of its
> architecture, and the economic functions
> and social groupings it shelters and
> encourages, one can derive most of the
> essential elements of a civilization.
> —Lewis Mumford[1]

Nathanael West begins his 1939 novel *The Day of the Locust* this way: "Around quitting time, Tod Hackett heard a great din on the road outside his office."[2] The unassuming phrase "around quitting time" seems in the context of the novel as a whole to be a peculiarly resonant and symptomatic one. What exists around quitting time, particularly for an office worker such as Tod, is a brief space of transition, in the first instance between a time of work and a time of leisure, between something structured and rule-bound and something at least putatively unstructured and open. For a novel which will proceed to offer a punishing meditation on the nature of a culture industry whose products increasingly occupy the time of that leisure, this is fitting indeed. Tod, of course, is himself a worker in that culture industry, which at once diminishes our sense of the magnitude or genuineness of the transition in question. Meanwhile, the very raw materials of leisure time—a costumed cinematic army, on their way to the film set—are tramping by on the road right outside his window; their work, in this context, itself occupies a peculiar zone of interface between labor and its cessation.

All of this recalls, of course, our analysis of *Sister Carrie*, the burden of which was, in part, to show how Dreiser's project in that novel was deeply informed by the dynamics of quitting time. This is at least less visibly so in *The Day of the Locust*: after this initial invocation, this image and its associated impulses sink from view, slipping beneath the surface of the text, where they begin to interact with other currents and hence work themselves out in ways rather different from *Sister Carrie*. This process of working out, however, retains a certain linkage to, and involvement with, what might be called the essential problematic of the earlier novel.

What can at this juncture be observed about West's opening scene concerns its "middling" setting, in the sense that we are now in an office, removed from the rigors of the assembly line and its Taylorist discipline. The setting connotes a certain relaxation of work rhythms, an absence of punch clocks, with perhaps small groups gathering around water coolers and chatting as the end of the day approaches. This is not, however, to suggest that factory-like conditions were unknown to white-collar work sites. Indeed, insurance and accounting firms had pioneered the kind of "assembly-line office" grimly parodied in King Vidor's 1928 film *The Crowd*, where, in a cavernous, hangarlike office, row upon row of desk-bound, number-crunching clerks hunch silently under the stern eye of their "foreman." We might keep in mind here as well the sorts of stories recounted in Otto Friedrich's anecdotal feast *City of Nets*. Here, screenwriters and other "creative" Hollywood studio workers of the 1930s and 1940s tell of the thoroughly proletarianized and often quite harsh conditions under which they labored (though at least some of this might be the sour grapes of those whose identifications with "aesthetic" production would perhaps have made them chafe under routine studio discipline).[3]

Tod's rising from his desk and wandering over to the window to observe the "troops" for a few moments would seem to demand a less regimented context, and hence evokes a place somewhat higher in the division of labor: the realm of bureaucratic officials, of technocratic experts and their minions, a realm of greater creative expression and control (and perhaps West, working as a screenwriter himself, is here briefly projecting a less demanding office from within his own more hectic context). Such a realm, in the 1930s, more precisely embodied the dream of middle-classlessness than sheer white collardom as such, since its inhabitants seemed to many to occupy a unique new position within the social system as a whole. Entering the decade, these "technical" strata were still largely a novelty, and the crisis of the Depression touched off an enormous flurry of speculation about them, from every imaginable political viewpoint. The very fate of the nation—whether it would survive the economic catastrophe, whether it would follow the path of revolution or reaction—seemed to hinge on the choices ultimately made by what was understood at the time as a radically ambivalent political and economic formation. The positions adopted in this debate could generally be sorted out according to their initial methodological choice, that is, whether the problem of the middle classes was one of structure or ideology, of objective situation or subjective belief. This basic divergence led in turn to differing assessments of the essential stake the middle classes held in either the maintenance or alteration of the socioeconomic system.

The "objective" position corresponds of course to the Marxian one, such as that typically offered in a text like *The Crisis of the Middle Class* (1935) by Lewis Corey. Corey lays out a broad but careful history of the middle class, from its older incarnation as a class of small enterprisers, owners of their own means of production (flourishing in this country in the 1820s and 1830s), through to its newer dispensation under monopoly capitalism, where such small enterprisers have been largely eradicated and only a disparate range of salaried, propertyless employees remains. Corey's principal thesis is thus straightforward: because they are propertyless, and are too heterogeneous to possess a definable set of class interests, the new middle classes have no real stake in the system, and thus it remains for them either to join the workers in the struggle for socialism, or to retreat toward fascism, which would benefit only what few small enterprisers remain as well as the upper ranks of the salariat. The other strata would be destroyed. Corey implores the new middle class to opt for the former path.[4]

The problem of ideology receives little attention in Corey's hands, an oversight avoided in *Common Sense* editor Alfred Bingham's remarkable *Insurgent America: Revolt of the Middle Classes* (also 1935), a classic embodiment of what Alan Lawson has identified as the "independent liberal" strain active in American political thinking at the time. Lawson sees such independent liberalism as a sequel to the Progressivism of the 1890–1917 period, and concerned with forging non-Marxist alternatives to capitalism (he includes Stuart Chase and Lewis Mumford under the rubric as well).[5] This is also consistent with Paul Buhle's discussion of attempts to imagine an "unembarrassed radical middle class" in the 1930s, wherein viable left strategy was redefined as the demand for a fair share in the national abundance (that is, middle-class comforts for everyone, leaving aside any talk of "liberation"), a strategy that was, by the latter half of the decade, being proffered in the name of Marxism as much as the various liberalisms.[6] For his part, Corey inveighed against such "revisionism" throughout the decade, accurately forecasting that, with any economic upturn, such leftism would implode into consumerism.

I call Bingham's book remarkable because it is an early and exceptionally clear statement of certain problems that are still very much with us. To begin with, it is among the first articulations of what we would today call new class theory. In the very first chapter, Bingham (who does style himself a radical) bids farewell to the working class, which "can no longer lead and dominate a social transformation," that is, it has been permanently supplanted as the prime mover of radical politics. Yet, if "the original Marxist concept of a class rising from functional supremacy to political supremacy be followed, it leads today to the conclusion that *the technical and managerial middle classes are slated to be the next in the sequence of ruling classes*."[7] Bingham speaks here as an advocate of Technocracy, a curious movement that had substantial but fleeting currency in the early 1930s, where it was imagined that groups of experts, somehow coming to occupy positions of power, could, through technical management and planning, abolish "the price system" and reinstate "production for use" (these terms derive from Veblen, who was a chief inspiration of the movement, in particular from his 1921 book *The Engineers and the Price System*).[8] Bingham also speaks in the wake of Taylorism, whose very purpose, as we saw in our discussion of Dreiser, was to effect the transfer of skills and expertise from workers to machinery and the technical-bureaucratic strata in the first place. This was undertaken, of course, in order to strengthen capital accumulation and control over the labor process, but the Technocrats evidently envisaged such fruits of Taylorism being turned precisely against capital. In any event, the notion of some professional/managerial class formation being the real holder of power and key to social change has become much more popular since Bingham wrote.[9]

Bingham is also clear that "for purposes of social and political action classes are entirely a matter of psychology" (65). No reckoning of the putatively objective stakes and interests of a class is of any use in regard to this problem—the weight of ideology is paramount. Hence Bingham seeks to produce a thorough delineation of the contours of middle-class consciousness, several aspects of which will prove to be relevant to our reading of West. He stresses the desire for security on the part of the middle class: "It is security—security of income, security for home and family, security for old age, security of position—that the middle class type craves" (73). Subsequent historical investigation has tended to confirm Bingham on this point, even if this work locates the sources of this craving in the effects of the economic crisis rather than the inner genetic code of middle-class ideology. On this reading, the overarching desire for security emerges as a tendentially conservative impulse, wary of anything beyond the here and now, whose widespread appearance during the decade partly belies the progressive or radical cast frequently imputed to this time period.[10] I would stress, however, at least the potential political ambivalence of this impulse, since socialism itself projects as one of its goals a thorough, cradle-to-grave security—the question being, then, what or who is to provide this security.

This drive for security, Bingham thinks, naturally disposes the middle class toward a planned society, over and against the anarchy and destructiveness of capitalism. Such planning can assume different forms, however, a fact that helps anchor yet another facet of the radical political ambivalence of the middle-class ideological formation: on the very same page of the book, Bingham tells us that on one hand, "middle-class America is more ready for socialism than other countries," whereas on the other hand, "the American middle classes are in fact ripe for Fascism" (97). There is a basic confusion here, common enough among left-liberal intellectuals of the period, having to do with seeing socialism and fascism as simply variants of some overarching notion of (technocratic, top-down) "social engineering," corporatist and antidemocratic in the case of fascism, enlightened and egalitarian (but still fundamentally authoritarian) in the case of socialism. This underscores what might be seen as the essential formalism of this kind of thinking, and makes apparent what is lacking from it, namely the entire dimension of "cultural revolution," in the sense of the vast production of new habits and modes of behavior that would be an integral (and doubtless temporally distended) part of any large-scale political movement toward socialism.[11] Such thinking, in any case, leads Bingham to the still scandalous idea that the Nazis, quite against their intentions and wholly by accident, might in fact be the first to achieve a genuinely free and egalitarian society (he thinks the chances of this occurring are slightly better than even).

Beyond the dimension of cultural revolution, we must open a parenthesis here to register the material effects, on the context in which both Bingham and West were writing, of the lack of "actual" revolution, including what might be seen as having in part substituted for this last. I have in mind here Perry Anderson's argument that one of the essential coordinates for the full development of European modernism was the "imaginative proximity of social revolution,"[12] during a period (roughly 1900–1920) when remnants of the ancien régime were being challenged by bourgeois and proletarian forces alike. Together with the tremendous development of new technology during this time, a unique historical conjuncture was produced, characterized by an exhilarating "*openness* of horizon, where the shapes of the future could alternatively assume the shifting forms of either a new type of capitalism or the eruption of socialism."[13] This conjuncture fostered one of modernism's signal ambitions, namely the retotalization of what was perceived as a frag-mented and degraded ("detotalized," in effect) cultural sphere, a utopian remaking of the world, at the level of the aesthetic, analogous to the social restructuring projected by the various political revolutions of the period.[14]

West, of course, did not have this particular historical conjuncture avail-able to him. That the 1930s were a time of tremendous political and cultural ferment is apparent, a ferment that can be traced in some measure to the economic crisis itself. Yet more crucial, for our purposes, might be what historians are coming to understand as the central and deeply ambivalent role, in the historical life of the period, of the New Deal. In its complexity and extent, the New Deal, when grasped in the full variety of its manifesta-tions, can be understood as having projected its own particular political and cultural totalization, not along the axis of class movements and revolution, but along that of the modern state.[15] More must be taken into account here than the novelty of state intervention into the economy (including the Works Progress Administration [WPA]), although this is crucial, since it was precisely the kind of ambivalent deployment of the state apparatus that was both applauded and denounced along all points of the political spectrum (as variously the destroyer of capitalism, its savior, communism, fascism, and so forth).[16] Also at work were the various state-sponsored cultural projects (the writers' project, the theater project, among others) which, in their various ways, touched millions of people during the latter half of the decade. These intersected with the flourishing cultural nationalism of the 1930s, which, sparked by the Depression and given further stimulus by the rise of Fascism, went on to become a prominent part of the public philosophy of the New Deal, and whose irony lay in its journey from reformist and often radical beginnings to a reaffirmation, as Charles Alexander has put it, of "almost everything about America and Americans."[17] Finally, we should note the Roosevelt administration's innovative use of new media technology (as with the famous, and hugely popular, fireside chats), which has been taken as indicative of an incipiently hegemonic state-media coupling emergent at this time.[18]

All of these elements, in sum, represent various potential axes of (re)totalization, which had the effect of at once stimulating yet containing diverse political and cultural currents, generating material and ideological effects of both centralization and dispersion/polarization, and opening up, for a great many people, that kind of undecidable horizon—socialism, or a new capitalism?—invoked above by Anderson for the European context. Yet the dynamics of the American experience had their own specificity. In hindsight we can recognize that the New Deal—however it might have functioned, at this moment in the development of the advanced capitalist state, as a space of mediation between classes and class fractions, and whatever temporary openness it might have displayed toward initiatives from "below"—ultimately represented the initial, constituent template of that integration of the state and big business known as Fordism (and whose cultural implications are examined more closely in the next chapter). Although the 1930s did not fully arrive at this latter social configuration, the openness of horizon invoked here is rather less open than its European counterpart, its bourgeois character somewhat closer to the surface. For our purposes, this implies that the impulse toward modernist retotalization that suggests itself to West (in his own overdetermined situation) and with which his novel grapples is of a different character, one indeed more crisis-ridden (in the sense that this statist totalization cannot in the end really function as a substitute for what Lukács called the "actuality" of political revolution), than that facing the European modernists.

Bingham's own response to the conundrum of a new capitalism versus socialism is finally a very American vision of "classless capitalism," whose theorization in Europe, one imagines, would have been a rather more problematic matter. As a corollary to his insistence on the determinant role of ideology (what he calls "psychology"), Bingham emphasizes that "it is necessarily the nature of the 'middle' classes that they do not recognize classes" (47). If even the most minimal definition of class consciousness must make room for some awareness of class status on the part of the members of that class, then middle-class consciousness must paradoxically constitute itself as an anti–class consciousness, as a release from everything that the existence of classes might imply. This no doubt undergirds Bingham's judgment on the readiness of the American middle classes for socialism, but the limits of this type of premature utopianism (where material constraints are nullified in thought but not in reality) are given in another striking and telling comment. Organized labor, Bingham asserts, returning to the "new class" aspect of his argument, will no doubt play a key role in the eventual abolition of capitalism: "But neither as a class nor as a class movement will labor play the leading role. If it threatens to do so, the great bulk of middle-class conscious people will make Fascism inevitable" (43). Here then is the deciding factor, which will determine which path the middle class will follow, and the moment when all the most grievous contradictions of Bingham's "independent liberalism" are laid bare. This is a disturbing moment, as it points toward the depth of ideological investment in such premature utopianism, and the intensity of the ressentiment it invariably conceals. Middle-classlessness is in Bingham's scheme essentially progressive, even radical—that is, until such time as some radical, class-conscious alternative arises, one giving lie to the promises of such utopian liberalisms by reawakening the painful sense of the sheer burden of class, of necessity and limits, at which point the peaceable middle class will unhesitatingly embrace the most destructive and hateful of ideologies.

All of this, finally, returns us to where we began, around quitting time, an evocation of liminality which is subsequently withdrawn into the interstices of the text. This fleeting moment has been taken as an invitation to speculate on a certain context from which *The Day of the Locust* in part emerges. We must now turn to the precise forms and strategies with which the novel engages this context, and with which it participates in a new dispensation of class and technology.

. . .

Some care should be taken in defining the precise setting of the novel. It is conventionally and superficially characterized as that of Hollywood, its film industry, and the sleaze and degradation associated with the latter, a Hollywood in which resides "whatever is most extravagant, spoiled, and uncontrolled in American life," as Alfred Kazin has put it.[19] This scene (already, by 1939, the stock-in-trade of the Hollywood novel)[20] then serves as the forum for West's (and his critics') frequent moralizing and attitudinizing, pursued typically along the axis of inauthenticity, from the "genuine relics of the old west" at Tuttle's Trading Post, to the imitation dead horse in Claude Estee's pool, to the absurdly eclectic domestic architecture against which "only dynamite would be of any use" (61), through finally to the "natural" environment itself: "It was one of those blue and lavender nights when the luminous color seems to have been blown over the scene with an air brush" (149). Hollywood is by definition the very seat of sham and artifice, a prime source of that "surfeit of shoddy" drowning the country West had satirically detailed in his previous novel, *A Cool Million* (1934). None of this is wrong, necessarily, though it is not evident that such attitudes are any longer of much interest at this late (postmodernized) date. I propose rather to defamiliarize and reassemble such moralizing judgments as so many pretexts or "motivations of the device" which enable the text to fashion a deeper and more consequent meditation on the structure of culture and society in the period.

In addition, we will be able to address certain features of the text that have long exercised critics, particularly certain filmic elements in the narrative, constructions of scene or point of view indebted to the production techniques typical of the Hollywood studio system in which West himself worked as a screenwriter. James Light, in one of the earliest monographs on West, noticed a "roving, panoramic technique" at work in the novel, as the shifting perspectival construction alternately zooms in and out of the events at hand, generating contrasting effects of participation and distance.[21] Thomas Strychacz has recently returned to and extended this line of inquiry, tracing the text's "cinematic modes of narration," which perform a kind of ideological critique, "uncovering the fact of Hollywood representation."[22] Conspicuously intertwined with these discussions is a persistent and often exasperated question about aesthetic value: if the novel is somehow "like" a Hollywood movie, can it still lay claim to the status of art? Is the text cheapened through its contact with mass culture, or is this finally a paradigmatically self-consuming artifact that renders the whole problem undecidable? I shall here attempt to recast these problems as instruments rather than as the results of interpretation, such that they might afford us a more concrete sense of the novel's fraught engagement with the mass cultural realm, and of its historical situation.[23]

Hollywood, meanwhile, is merely one aspect or index of a larger social space, that of southern California itself, with which the novel is concerned. This, too, is largely a symbolic space, a land of sunshine and opportunity, to be sure, but more centrally a space of promise, a vague but compelling promise of some singular fulfillment or realization, at once symbolized and satirized most effectively by the instant religions and miracle diets West shows sprouting there like so many hothouse flowers ("Dr. Know-All Pierce-All," the "Tabernacle of the Third Coming," "Brain Breathing, the Secret of the Aztecs," and so forth). This promise is inevitably and implacably betrayed, of course, something figured most insistently through the image of failed or frustrated desire, of an inability to realize desire in the world (a shattered promise also indicated by West's original title for the book, *The Cheated*). But there is another debilitating gap here as well, one posited by W. H. Auden in his well-known description of what he called "West's disease," namely one existing between what he termed wishes on one hand and desires on the other.[24] Wishing, as I interpret it here, stands thus for a certain blind or inchoate yearning and unfocused anticipation (related to the affective charge of Dreiser's description of quitting time), and is bound up with a properly utopian impulse that, because it cannot be realized here and now, must of necessity be subject to betrayal when it crosses over to desiring and a regime of objects and their partial fulfillments. From this perspective, the space of southern California is not to be indicted on the basis of the cheapness or inauthenticity of its satisfactions, but rather because its purpose is to stress and unduly amplify the faculty of wishing, over and against which any object or commodity would at once appear as the cruelest sham or fraud.

Echoes of the Frankfurt School abound here, and indeed, as Mathew Roberts notes, "it would be difficult to find a work of American fiction more plainly resonant with Adorno's culture industry thesis than *The Day of the Locust*."[25] The invocation of Adorno in recent West criticism has become almost routine, as it should be, though I will try to specify a slightly different connection between the novelist and the dialectician.

Homer Simpson appears to be the most striking victim of West's disease.[26] He does not appear to possess anything that might be called a "desire," at least in any positive sense. Even his attraction to Faye Greener appears unmediated by this category; the speechless awe with which he approaches her seems closer to sheer terror, bound up with a sense of his own imminent destruction ("he somehow knew that his only defense was chastity" [101]), and the abuse she subjects him to functions only to confirm the inadequacy and duplicity of any object in which wishing attempts to realize itself. Consumed utterly by some insensate yearning, he is figured as trapped in a passivity bordering on paralysis. Homer's condition is underscored by his pained, cryptic outburst to Tod toward the end of the novel, after Earle and Miguel have fought and Faye has left: "The words went behind each other instead of after. What he had taken for long strings were really one thick word and not a sentence. In the same way several sentences were simultaneous and not a paragraph" (168). In this description, Homer stretches the bounds of language and the symbolic, groping toward some new structure of expression that might accommodate and body forth the content of his singular psychic torment. Such language-transmuting or form-breaking, as a radical and utopian strategy of escaping the reifications of desire, is a familiar item of modernist practice, which is here assigned to Homer in a kind of secondhand way (we do not actually see what his weird, spatialized language looks like), and hence foregrounded or thematized in a peculiar manner. For his part, Tod is placed in the position of the temporarily frustrated reader of the modernist text, as (to invoke one of Jameson's figures for the modernist artifact) he goes about uncovering for us the "cancelled realist" narrative that exists beneath the obscure linguistic exertions of the text's manifest level, making "the usual kind of sense" out of Homer's speech by refashioning it into a coherent, "realistic" account.[27] This little mise-en-scène gives us our first indication of the novel's remarkable engagement with the problematic of modernism, one whose specificities we will attempt to theorize more completely as we move along.

■ ■ ■

The southern California that West presents no doubt also occupies some privileged place in the ideological elaboration of the American Dream, a magnetic lure to West's stereotypical midwesterners, who "scrape and save" all their lives so that they might reach "the land of sunshine and oranges" (and whom critical discourse invariably characterizes as "hapless"). The promise active here is bound up with one of the primal building blocks of American classlessness, which is the notion of a generalized and available sociospatial mobility (wherein spatial mobility, and indeed individual motion itself, can figure forth fantasies of social mobility). The overdetermination of simple geography is thus crucial: as the terminal point of westward migration in America, as the place where the frontier comes to a halt on the sun-drenched beaches, southern California naturally became amenable to a host of fantasy investments and projections concerning the success or imminent failure of the American Dream.[28] Once there, one either makes it, keeps moving, in some new and often unclear way, in a southern California that must be continually rearticulated as a "space of migrancy," or, as West grimly suggests, one simply dies. It is as if this space solicits some new kind of "frontier principle" of mobility and expansion, the material need for which had been evoked in Gilbert Seldes's chronicle of the first years of the Depression, *The Years of the Locust* (1933), a book known to West and whose title had inspired his own. "The capital fact of American history," Seldes said, reflecting on the ultimate sources of the climate of crisis in the early 1930s, "is that the land rush ended in the 1890s."[29]

Indeed, it is evident that, since the closing of the real frontier in the 1890s (which precipitated a crisis in American ideology), America has continually sought to reconfigure and rearticulate a frontier principle independent of any actual supply of available land. By the 1930s, there was certainly no shortage of substitutes being proffered. There was the New Deal itself, of course, as embodied in Roosevelt's own public rhetoric and codified in brain truster Henry Wallace's *New Frontiers* (1934). Wallace's chief political goal was the "balanced operation of our economic machine," to be attained through the production of new "social machinery," that is, through the manifold expansion of the state apparatus, which, as we have already noted, was one of the hallmarks of the New Deal.[30] The rhetoric of machines here suggests, however, that the New Deal was itself drawing upon the intense social imagination of technology in the period, which fueled cultural production in all domains, including the political. We have already touched on the language of the Technocrat movement, which typically employed images of modern technology together with the latest scientific management techniques, the two combining to produce a "new freedom" (echoing Woodrow Wilson's rhetoric) of limitless expansion and (deliberately unnatural) harmony, thus negotiating again that mutually supportive interface between pastoral peace and frontier dynamism examined earlier.

If the Depression seemed to be placing a material brake on motion and social mobility, the realm of technology—its promises, its possibilities, its sheer material embodiment—offered to the culture of the 1930s fresh possibilities for reimagining these. This might best be registered initially by way of the notion of visual style, as the look of the life world itself underwent striking changes over the course of the decade, changes that held peculiar implications for the field of cultural production. Let the 1934 "Machine Art" exhibit at the Museum of Modern Art stand as a kind of talismanic marker of this process: here, gleaming propellors and curvaceous springs and turbines hung on the walls, evidence of an uneasy relationship between the ambitions of the aesthetic and the realm of daily life and the utilitarian. A certain signification of power and speed was evidently expressed in the style of these various industrial implements, which found increasingly diverse expression throughout the decade.[31] By the mid-1930s, as Dick Hebdige reminds us, Streamform design principles, which had been developed to enhance aerodynamic performance in aircraft, were being applied to automobiles and, with even less engineering rationale, increasingly to sundry gadgets and household appliances of all kinds, connoting and promoting the fashionable ideals of speed and efficiency.[32] The design aesthetic of streamlining, of course, informed the familiar period style of art deco, which Fredric Jameson has reinterpreted in terms of a genuinely global period style, capable of being "generalized across the whole international spectrum of representationality in the 1930s."[33] Art deco strives to transmit the essence of the "visible machine as it radiates speed and energy through [and this last point will prove symptomatic for us] its forms at rest."[34]

These examples serve to underscore the position of technology as a further axis of totalization operative in this period, whose presence is henceforth registered in numerous and disparate macrological and micrological domains. It is an axis that seems, as we have hinted throughout, to maintain a privileged relation with the modern state, the two combining into a kind of mutually overdetermining symbiotic system. And not merely the New Deal (where, aside from Roosevelt on the radio, we should also keep in mind developments like the rural electrification projects and the Tennessee Valley Authority [TVA]). Stalinism and Nazism alike, as Jameson notes, also depend crucially on the modernizing dynamic of technology. As with the state, however, it is an axis whose fundamental ambivalence is evident, both aesthetically (hovering uncertainly between toasters in the kitchen and the Museum of Modern Art), and politically, where it can be read as at once revolutionary and regressive, on one hand reshaping human life in a utopian manner or, on the other, squeezing out the last vestiges of human culture and agency.

What resources do the unlucky denizens of West's fictional realm have at their disposal to recapture, even imaginarily, the energy, the movement, of the frontier? The movies are one. I mean this initially in the simplest sense of all, that is, the medium itself, as a series of still photos which, when run through the projector, produce the illusion of motion. I believe that the novel reflects upon this purely formal, technological fact and attempts to add content to it, content that in turn deepens the meditation on class the book undertakes.

But movies also mean the culture industry, the nature of its products and the system that produces them. While the basic lesson the book has to offer us about the culture industry (on which it focuses directly only at a few key moments) can be summed up in terms of its production of pseudosatisfactions, things are ultimately more complicated than this. The problem of the culture industry is analogous to that of southern California, as something that makes promises that cannot be fulfilled because their only issue is in the structurally incomplete form of desires and their objects. This emerges with Faye Greener and her movie-script ideas, which she describes to Tod and of which she claims to have hundreds. Her stories are all deliberately stock-in-trade affairs, which show a marked indifference to endings or closure. "Well, he marries her, of course, and they're rescued. First they're rescued and then they're married, I mean," she says, as Tod presses her for the conclusion of one particular story, a romantic adventure set at sea. "Maybe he turns out to be a rich boy who is being a sailor just for the adventure of it, or something like that" (106). At one level, this is indicative of the general process of standardization at work in the culture industry, something Horkheimer and Adorno, in the very chapter of their *Dialectic of Enlightenment* where they coined the notion of the culture industry, analyzed in terms of the confusion or blending of wholes and parts, or universals and particulars. What they had in mind is the formulaic grid of set styles by which the culture industry organizes its production. Whereas what they would consider genuine aesthetic objects approach the matter of general style warily, and incorporate it only to contest it (through the logic of the object's specific content), the products of the culture industry conform to the imposed styles to such an extent that henceforth no distinction holds between a style and its particular incarnation. "The reconciliation of the general and particular, of the rule and the specific demands of the subject matter, the achievement of which alone gives essential, meaningful content to style, is futile because there has ceased to be the slightest tension between poles: these concordant extremes are dismally identical; the general can replace the particular, and vice versa."[35] The argument holds fully as much for calculated deviations from the norm as well, and one could imagine one such style being the "weird/innovative" program, whose effects would in the end be essentially as predictable as any other culture-industry product.[36] Horkheimer and Adorno treat these grids or formulas ultimately as the mediation linking culture-industry artifacts and the labor process, in that they reproduce the regimes of Taylorist organization at the level of cultural production.[37] From this vantage, then, the realm of work can be darkly glimpsed just beneath the shimmer of the California sun.

But Faye's script ideas display a somewhat desultory or aleatory approach to narrative closure, at odds with the predictable narrative satisfactions no doubt demanded by any resolutely formulaic production pattern. As if in response to the potential frustration signaled by such abrogations of the narrative covenant, Tod, immediately following the indifferent ending of the sea-rescue tale, has one of his more graphic fantasies about Faye. It initially posits Faye as a kind of living embodiment of culture-industry narratives and desires:

All these little stories, these little daydreams of hers, were what gave such extraordinary color and mystery to her movements. She seemed always to be struggling in their soft grasp as though she were trying to run in a swamp. As he watched her, he felt sure that her lips must taste of blood and salt and that there must be a delicious weakness in her legs. His impulse wasn't to aid her to get free, but to throw her down in the soft, warm mud and to keep her there.

He expressed some of his desire by a grunt. If he only had the courage to throw himself on her. Nothing less violent than rape would do. (107)

West takes pains to embellish Faye with the Freudian trappings of the "phallic mother," a dynamic, autonomizing narcissism that at once excites and frustrates Tod: "It was her completeness, her egglike self-sufficiency, that made him want to crush her." This only underscores the futility, at this level of the text, of reconciling objects and desires in the domain of the culture industry, the unattainability of satisfaction, confirmed finally by Tod's failure to act ("he did nothing and she began to talk again").

On this reading, however, the random conclusion of Faye's story, which in its disruption of the predictability of the formula marks it precisely as not typical of the usual culture-industry narrative, triggers Tod's fantasy, which is really about just such standardized product. This does not, however, exhaust the full meaning of this aleatory dissolution of narrative. One line of inquiry concerns the violence of Tod's fantasy. I would suggest first, however, that this is another condensed or shorthand thematization of modernism, analogous to Homer's cryptic speech noted earlier. That is to say, again, that we are not shown an example of a modernist practice so much as a paraphrased, descriptive invocation of one, a casually ironic gesture toward the modernist ambition to disrupt and shatter narrative.

This thematization in particular allows us better to grasp the specific dynamics of West's writerly situation, read as gesturing toward an avant-gardist ambition. It is the surrealists (whose work West knew and admired) with whom we associate the most thoroughgoing undermining and repudiation of narrative, as members (along with Dadaism and Russian futurism) of a historic avant-garde that attempted, to return to Peter Bürger's compelling and productive thesis, to smash the bourgeois institution of autonomous art and return the aesthetic to daily life.[38] Again, however, West does not share the exact situation of these European avant-gardes, and hence his novel's offhand reference to their practices must be read as symptomatic of a rather different predicament. Most tellingly, Faye Greener, of all the figures in the novel, is the one who most identifies with the culture industry, who lives and breathes its fantasies, and hence her "modernist" parapraxis emerges from its very heart. This provides us with a rather vivid index of the essential instability of the aesthetic situation West inhabits, indicative, perhaps, of a dawning awareness of the degree to which this modernist goal is in fact being realized, not through revolution, but through the development of mass culture itself (and hence with effects rather different than those envisaged by the avant-garde).[39] West is indeed writing in a period during which—consistent with the incipient Fordism invoked above—norms of mass consumption are being strenuously promulgated across the culture, the culture industry itself being one of the principal agents of their dissemination. Such developments can, I believe, be positioned as another axis of totalization operative in this period. West's previous novel, *A Cool Million*—a cruelly funny satire on the burgeoning commodification of U.S. society—makes it clear, however, that this particular totalizing power did not strike him as "ambivalent" in any way, that its wholly capitalist character was clear from the start.

Many others were less sure. Indeed, Gilbert Seldes himself was among the most vociferous of the many social critics in the 1930s who argued that the Depression had its origin in overproduction and thus the only sure way out of it was for the public to buy and keep buying until totalitarianism was averted and everything was back to normal. His 1938 book *Your Money and Your Life: A Manual for the "Middle Classes"* (the quotation marks indicative of the still-incomplete shift from an empirical to an ideological conception of the middle class under consideration here) elaborates nothing less than a whole theory of a newly empowered consumerist middle class that can bring governments and corporations to their knees with the decision not to consume (the mass strike thus mutating seamlessly into the mass boycott), and hence usher in a new age "beyond socialism and capitalism" alike: "Production may be left in the hands of the few, but the use of things has to be distributed more and more to the many. The ultimate economic power shifts into our hands. . . . If we deliberately chose to deny ourselves everything but the actual necessities of life for six months—that is, *if all of us went down to the scale of living of the least favored in our own population, we could wreck the whole economic oligarchy.*"[40] This argument toys with a positively Nietzschean conundrum: the weak who become strong, while secretly remaining weak.[41] In order to guarantee their political hegemony, the new middle classes in the 1930s must effectively internalize the Depression. The crisis of demand that precipitated the economic catastrophe (and that receives an echo in West's midwesterners, who have "scraped and saved" to reach California) must be self-consciously rearticulated as power *not* to buy. Consumers not consuming, then—this might sound merely like an updating of workers not working, but it must be noted that radical working-class action is predicated, at least in part, upon the necessity of fashioning new production relations, and a new culture, out of the ruins of the old. Seldes's theory, by contrast, amounts finally to a purely destructive, Samson-pulling-down-the-temple strategy that only ensures its impotence: the weak, though "strong" now, remain weak. This gives us another perspective on the ineradicable moment of paralysis and failure genetically encoded in middle-class ideology. But perhaps the most immediate and bitter historical irony attending Seldes's theory is that he thinks consumerism will in the long run be the most effective guarantor of an engaged and politicized citizenry, able to grasp the essential connections among the most disparate economic and social phenomena.

Faye's narrative indifference, meanwhile, in its inextricable entangling of a commodified culture with an aesthetic program frankly hostile to this last, tells us still more about the exigencies of the novel's aesthetic moment. It can be taken as an acute moment of narrative self-awareness, as the text foregrounds, in a manner at once literal and oblique, something both constitutive and agonizing for modernist aesthetic production, namely its secret identity with, despite its manifest difference from, the commodity form itself. This proposition is one of the central insights of Adorno's version of the dialectic of the modern, one most germane in the present context. For Adorno, the key dynamic at work in both modernism and the commodity is the process of abstraction, which at the level of the economic involves the commensuration of social labor and the subjection of humans to "alien powers," whereas in art it denotes a new and intense self-consciousness of form and a parallel ideological inflation of the aesthetic itself:

> The residue of abstraction in the concept of the modern is the tribute levied on this last by the commodity itself. If what is consumed in

monopoly capitalism is no longer use value, but exchange value, by the same token the abstractness of the modern work—that irritating indeterminacy about its nature and function—becomes the very index of what it is.[42]

For Adorno, such "awareness" of this subterranean identity between modernism and the commodity ideally is fully sublimated into the very form of the works themselves; for West, this appears not to be a possibility, and the matter, along with other indices of modernism, falls out into the content of the narrative, becoming a matter of thematic self-consciousness, and being backhandedly invoked by this or that character. All of this, finally, takes place in a setting which itself immediately imbricates the mass cultural field.[43] Taken together, these elements again dramatize what is in West an incompletely realized modernist sphere, in which the possibility of revolution and of genuine cultural renewal is absent, yet has been partially displaced onto a new and multivalently totalizing state-technology coupling. In this situation, West's narrative practice at once seeks out and condemns all the various options, insistently thematizing a modernism that is not fully attainable, while at the same time taking as its principal subject, and finally drawing its aesthetic power from (as we shall see more clearly below), a commodified cultural realm it grasps as sham and empty and from which it can only fitfully distance itself. This is a veritable fury of simultaneous affirmation and negation, undermining all potentially stable bases of operation, which perhaps presages not so much postmodernism (with its aesthetic of the anarchic productivity of the signifier), but rather the bleak late modernist landscapes of Beckett and the *nouveau roman*.

Our reading of these issues here should be sharply distinguished from the kind of approach taken by Thomas Strychacz, who in his recent book also spends considerable time pondering the question of West's relation to modernism and mass culture. For Strychacz, the problem of whether West's work "is" more modernist or mass cultural is finally undecidable on its own terms; it ends up *seeming* more modernist only because the academy, and its venal and invidiously canonizing critics, in effect "bestow the aesthetic" upon it. In this view, there never really *was* anything like an "aesthetic sphere" that, in the form of local and inherited artistic problems, might have confronted West, or any other artist at the time, as a material dilemma to be worked through, a proposition testified against by all of the multifarious strainings and searchings of image and form during this period. This line of reasoning leads Strychacz ultimately to suggest that there is no essential difference between *The Waste Land* and a Spielberg adventure movie that quotes liberally from the filmic tradition (any difference arising, again, thanks to the elitism of the academy).[44] This simply ignores the vastly different contexts in which each is produced, the history of film existing as an unproblematic plenitude for Spielberg, to be playfully raided, whereas Eliot's situation with respect to the literary tradition clearly brings to mind something closer to Marx's invocation of the "tradition of all the dead generations," weighing down like a nightmare.

. . .

The other interpretive pathway invoked above in connection with Tod's fantasy had to do with its violence, which we can now use to grasp the significance of Faye's narrative subversion in still another way, and to lead us into another strand of the novel. The fact that virtually every scene in the novel is marked by, and almost every human interaction moves ineluctably toward, a violent or near violent outcome is of course one of its most striking aspects. But it is the violence of automatons, passionless, seeking nothing, with no issue except laughter, as for example when Calvin and Hink try to provoke fellow "cowboy" Earle Shoop:

> It was another joke. Calvin and Hink slapped their thighs and laughed, but Tod could see that they were waiting for something else. Earle, suddenly, without even shifting his weight, shot his foot out and kicked Calvin solidly in the rump. This was the real point of the joke. They were delighted by Earle's fury. Tod also laughed. The way Earle had gone from apathy to action without the usual transition was funny. The seriousness of his violence was even funnier. (111)

Earle's reaction seems basically involuntary, detached from any conscious intention. The phrase "without the usual transition" suggests a machinelike spring into motion, and indeed this metaphoric characterization has been among the more common applied to the various figures in the novel, following the lead of West himself (Harry Greener is likened to a wind-up toy at one point).[45] Although the metaphor of the machine ought probably to be invoked with caution, because of its "colonizing" power (anything can be made to seem machinelike), I want to show that its application is more than gratuitous.[46]

The novel's rendering of violence does not seek to excite or titillate, but rather to evoke a kind of sinking feeling in the gut, as if in response to the utter frailness of the body: "Miguel grabbed Abe by the throat. The dwarf let go his hold and Earle sank to the floor. Lifting the little man free, Miguel shifted his grip to his ankles and dashed him against the wall, like a man killing a rabbit against a tree" (164).[47] In this context, the substance of Tod's imaginings has little to do with sex, and still less with pleasure (even in a negative or sadistic sense), and is much more concerned with the sheer mechanical wrestling and colliding of bodies. I am not suggesting that there is no charge of affect here, but rather that the clipped astringency of the language of the fantasy does try to squeeze out affect. Like Homer's tortured regard for Faye, it would be difficult to say that Tod in this fantasy "desires" Faye in any substantive way, that he invests in her as an object of some positive or negative "fulfillment." What then drives this imagery, and the violence in the novel as a whole?

"In America," West once remarked, characterizing a certain texture of everyday life in this country, "violence is idiomatic."[48] But this statement can be taken in two ways, as a comment on social existence or on the language peculiar to it, a language that itself dwells upon violence as a response to unique social conditions. Here we might return to an earlier episode in which Tod thinks about Faye. He is looking at a photograph of her, in which she is trying to look sultry and "inviting." Typically, however, sexual connotations give way to violent ones:

> Her invitation wasn't to pleasure, but to struggle, hard and sharp, closer to murder than to love. If you threw yourself on her, it would be like throwing yourself from the parapet of a skyscraper. You would do it with a scream. You couldn't expect to rise again. Your teeth would be driven into your skull like nails into a pine board and your back would be broken. You wouldn't even have time to sweat or close your eyes.
>
> He managed to laugh at his language, but it wasn't a real laugh and nothing was destroyed by it. (68)

Tod recognizes the sheerly unmotivated, hyperbolic quality of his language, disconnected as it seems from anything in the photograph itself, lapsing into it "idiomatically," yet he does not thereby "delegitimate" it—there is still something serious at work here. Perhaps then the content of the photograph is not at issue, the key point instead being that it is "a still from a two-reel farce in which she had worked as an extra" (67). From this perspective, Tod's language is a way of animating an immobile image, surrounding it and shaking it, its static nature soliciting an embrace of violent imagery, the specter of immobility producing an imaginary response that manages to "keep things moving." In essence, there is something about the "stillness" of the still to which all this violence represents a kind of response. At this point, however, we must return, by an admittedly circuitous route, to that other, more utopian component of affect in West that Auden called wishing, and confront the nature of the film medium itself.

For these purposes, I focus at some length on the scene in which Tod goes to watch a pornographic film at Mrs. Jennings's high-class brothel. There are some interpretive risks here, because it is really just a brief scene and not a great deal happens; indeed, I think that what is not present is at least as important as what is. Nonetheless, one hint that West intended this as a fairly crucial moment comes when the film projector breaks, and someone in the crowd yells, "Cheat!" This reminds us once more of *The Cheated*, the original title of the book, and establishes the fact that we are at some level not to understand these high-living Hollywood socialites as distinct from the scrambling lumpens who populate the rest of the novel, that some deeper functional identity unites them. This is underscored through the figure of Claude Estee (Tod's link to this milieu) who, much like Harry Greener, is figured as a kind of windup toy, relentlessly exhausting the comic rhetorical possibilities of ideas and images fed to him. Such an osmotic exchange of metaphorical energy between the Hollywood insider and the washed up outsider complicates what West terms the "mock riot" precipitated by the projector's breakdown, that is, the crowd's self-conscious pantomime of a nickelodeon audience, which in this view fails to differentiate them clearly from a regular (lower-class) group of cinema patrons.

The scene is simple. Tod settles down to watch the movie, *Le Predicament de Marie, ou La Bonne Distraite*. The setting of the movie is established, with the sober bourgeois family, all of whom secretly desire the maid, Marie. The movie slips momentarily into a farcical vein, with family members entering Marie's room one after the other, with Marie frantically hiding them away in various locations. Just as the main sexual "number" is about to begin, the projector fouls up. Tod goes outside for a cigarette, then returns to watch the rest of the movie, which the reader is not "shown." The most obvious semantic level of this little parable is one many critics point out: a kind of joke at the (presumably male) reader's expense, receiving a build-up with no payoff. The reader is implicated in the thematic of desire we have been exploring, himself receiving an object lesson in the problematization of desire in the culture industry. Pornography is especially useful in this regard, dramatizing as it does the gap between desire and its potential fulfillment in its very form: rather like propaganda, pornography points toward certain extratextual or extrarepresentational actions needed in order to complete itself and have it serve its purpose. But this gap between desire and action itself begins to suggest larger, social and public, considerations.

Taking this porn movie (or stag film, more correctly) only as some avatar of the culture industry thus proves inadequate. The story of Marie, and its interruption, can be thought of as another of the text's second-level evocations of modernism, in several ways. It represents a sheer breakdown of narrative, to be sure, but this is also a silent film we are watching—in what is evidently a kind of modernist salon as well, something not wholly appreciated by its patrons: "They wanted to talk about certain lively matters of universal interest, but she [Mrs. Jennings, the proprietor] insisted on discussing Gertrude Stein and Juan Gris" (73). It is useful to recall, as Linda Williams does in her remarkable analysis of filmic pornography, that the hard-core stag movie, under the pressure of censorship, did not enter the full-length and full-budget realm of the talkies until the early 1970s.[49] Until that time, it existed as an underground holdover from an earlier era of cultural production, remaining clumsy and makeshift while the rest of the culture industry underwent successive sea changes, a level of primitiveness I suggest symbolically marks it as more modernist as well. I have in mind the notion, associated variously with Benjamin and Andre Bazin, that the greatest achievements in filmic modernism belonged to the silent era, a site of aesthetic possibility that was effectively liquidated by the arrival of sound in the late 1920s (which constituted a revolution in form and not a mere technological addition). I am also thinking, in relation to the comic element of *Marie*, of Jameson's observations on the "preestablished harmony," in the sense of a shared episodizing and autonomizing logic, between modernism and farce (Chaplin being the signal embodiment here).[50] Hence, in the context of Mrs. Jennings's "salon," the stag film emerges as something of a modernistic "protest" against the norms of the classical Hollywood cinema regnant in the 1930s.

This argument can be pursued further, right into the unseen sex scenes. For, as Williams also reminds us, the sexual numbers in stag films were often the moment of greatest narrative disruption. Even though there is of course no essential requirement for narrative continuity in sex scenes, the incoherence could be so pronounced (hitherto unseen actors, sudden scene changes—testament to the precarious production conditions) and distracting that the very ability of the scene to titillate could be undermined. The projector's cutting off Marie's tale is therefore merely an index to the impending dissolution of the story within the frame of the film itself. So we have what is at once the most intense thematization of modernism and (these are still filmed sex scenes, after all) the most telling figure for the commodifying effects of mass culture, in irresolvable oscillation: a kind of primal scene that itself cannot be shown (signaling the "impossibility" both of modernism, and, behind that, of revolution), but whose absent presence informs the rest of the text, and that is itself a thematization of that "irritating indeterminacy" of the modern which, in Adorno's argument, stands as the secret source of its aesthetic achievement.

Finally, I want to make use of Williams's genealogical return to Eadweard Muybridge's stop-action motion studies of the late 1870s and early 1880s, which were inaugurated when Leland Stanford wondered whether during a fast trot all four feet of a horse left the ground for an instant. After determining that they indeed did leave the ground, Muybridge left horses and moved on to the human body and its movements.[51] At this crucial moment in the prehistory of filmic technology, the mystery of motion itself is at issue: the insistent freezing of motion, its analytic decomposition into its basic units, followed by the attempt to turn these moments illusionistically back into motion again. The obsessive subject of the first motion pictures was motion itself, the technological form initially secreting its own content.

But this is also, and equally as importantly, a fetishistic reduction to the body as well, particularly the female body, as Williams argues. Here the link to pornography is made, the latter being understood as but the logical result of the technological incursion (or implantation, in the Foucauldian sense) into the body made by the filmic apparatus. Williams charts a kind of dialectic of progress, whereby what began as purely formal and "scientific" investigations come little by little to acquire various narrative motivations, taking on the trappings of scene and character ("the lovers"). But pornography is not the only manifestation of such a reduction to the body—clearly violent representations can be too, which is what receives emphasis in *The Day of the Locust*, initially as a kind of inversion or erasure of any connotations of "fulfillment" generated by the sexualized body of pornography. Both pornography and representations of violence in any case find their genealogical roots here in a reduction to the *still* body-as-image, no longer, as in this text, the possessor of anything like a "self" or of "personhood," and which must then be reanimated, either in technology (the filmic apparatus) or in language. Once only bodies remain, the novel seems to suggest, the only thing left for them to do is have sex (but that is ruled out here) or smash into each other with increasing ferocity, index of an emphatic separation of bodies that henceforth demand "recombination."

Or they can shake, twirl, and gesticulate in various ways. This is another dimension of the reduction to the body under consideration, with bodies in the text insistently figured as escaping conscious control and subject to erratic motions of all kinds, which, like Galvani's twitching frogs, disguise a fundamental inertness. Homer's quivering hands (on loan from *Winesburg, Ohio*'s Wing Biddlebaum) are only the most famous instance of this phenomenon, which encompasses Faye's elaborate panoply of tics and gestures, Harry's uncontrollable whirling and laughing, and Abe's springlike resilience.

The central point at this juncture of our inquiry is that the violence in *The Day of the Locust* has little to do with some putative lust for violence on the part of the inauthentic masses, although such conservative and moralizing connotations are probably unavoidable. It is first and foremost a matter of language, the "idiomatic" response to and figuration of a particular reduction to the body whose "secret" is the medium of film itself, as if the text were trying to think, in *linguistic* terms, the formal nature of this radically different apparatus, with its frozen images that appear to come to life. Movies, then, do indeed "keep things moving," and represent a new technological "frontier principle" that nonetheless encodes stasis at its very heart (things must first be "made photographic" [131], to use West's image of the reduction of "dreams" and fantasies to their embodiments in cheap Hollywood sets), which representationally solicits the familiar tandem of sex and violence. It reiterates, too, in its own peculiar fashion, that classic American frontier pattern of "regeneration through violence" analyzed by Richard Slotkin.[52] The novel in this sense emerges as the dystopian critique of those utopian energies embodied in the totalizing presence of 1930s technological fantasy, the reification of motion and mobility furnishing another ideological antidote to a depressed and (in ultimate economic and political terms) stasis-ridden American reality.

This is a stronger argument than those formulations about cinema and the novel noted earlier. Rather than a mere transposition of technique, what is being suggested here is that the very shape and movement of the sentences has been informed by the nature of the film medium as such, considered here as a powerfully overcoded site during this period, a site where technology and the culture industry meet in an intense conjoining. The sentences in effect try to probe the dynamics of film, posited as the ultimate or prime "mover," in that it can seemingly make "dead" things come to life. That is, it promises to make things happen; it has unlocked the secret of the temporal category of the event, that eruption ("without the usual transition") into the routinized, homogeneous time of the everyday that the bored denizens of Los Angeles so crave. We can now grasp how the particular relation between Hollywood and southern California noted earlier is essentially the same as the relationship between movies and migrancy, the latter pole in each case representing a stalled motion in need of reactivation. From this molecular or sentence level of the text, dependent on a certain mediation of technology, we can now turn to a larger molar or narrative level, to investigate finally the other forms of social content vehiculated in the novel, and to grasp more concretely the whole issue of state and revolution.

• • •

Let us return for one last look at *Le Predicament de Marie*, if only to take brief notice of its class setting: the "normal" bourgeois household, with Marie, no longer as indentured servant but as wage earner. If, as I argue, *The Day of the Locust* presents a historical complication of the ideologeme of class tourism examined in our chapter on *Sister Carrie*, then "pornography" in this context symbolizes class tourism of an unusually intimate kind, indeed. Such a bourgeois setting also contrasts markedly with the rest of the novel, where any similar representations of class do not obtain at all.

Pursuing this dimension of the argument returns us at once to the problem of motion and mobility, the conundrum of how to go about "continuing a migration"—a migration to which West insistently draws our attention in the story—once it has at least literally ended. If in the previous section we attempted to think about this in terms of "the movies," we now focus on those other entities, mobile by definition (and etymology), called mobs. Gilbert Seldes, writing in *The Years of the Locust*, had himself invoked a "new kind of mob" that had appeared in the 1930s, evidence of an economic but also spiritual drift affecting people. "All over the country," he wrote, "men were so little attached to any place, because their jobs had failed them, their homes been taken away, their families dispersed, that they were prepared to go anywhere."[53] The Depression plays a central role in the destruction of place—as concrete, lived-in, and affect-laden—in favor of space, as abstract, which facilitates and encourages transience. Thus a certain mobility is predicated here, at once reflecting and making available new social conditions and arrangements, which the novel attempts to reflect upon as well.

There was of course also a mob present around quitting time, suggesting, again, a certain link between mobility and the classless dream that quitting time figuratively evokes: "An army of cavalry and foot was passing. It moved like a mob; its lines broken, as though fleeing from some terrible defeat. The dolmans of the Hussars, the heavy shakos of the guards, Hanoverian light horse, with their flat leather caps and flowing red plumes, were all jumbled together in bobbing disorder" (59). Mobs, in the middle-class imaginary, are typically anxiety-laden figures of working-class unruliness, but West's use of the cinematic army suggests a symbolic erasure of the proletariat rather than its militant uprising. This becomes clear during the scene of the filming of the battle of Waterloo. These unionized actors are in fact the only real workers present in the text (apart from Marie), figures for a class whose mutation into a Hollywood army signals both its literal expendability on the battlefield (and in the factory, or in this case on stage, which collapses and injures a number of people), and its ideological erasure via the products of the culture industry. The collapsing stage also, as Strychacz acutely notes, wrecks this Hollywood attempt to narrate a historical event, underscoring the historical amnesia that Hollywood products foster.[54]

The cinematic army, however, is not the most prominent mob in the book. This is doubtless the crowd gathered for the movie premiere before Kahn's Persian Palace Theatre, at the end of the novel. The crowd is composed of those cheated and frustrated souls who so intrigue Tod Hackett, the ones who "have come to California to die." In one sense, the fact that they have come to California in the first place might be their most salient feature. Here we pick up on the thematics of westward migration with which West is playing, and the problem of mobility one faces when one runs out of real estate. The mob in front of the theater does indeed represent some new possibilities of motion. In general, the people are held fast, unable to move themselves but carried along by the crowd as a whole. Out of this, a violent but oddly calm sociability begins to grow:

> Another spasm passed through the mob and he was carried toward the curb. He fought toward a lamp post, but he was swept by before he could grasp it. He saw another man catch the girl with the torn dress. She screamed for help. He tried to get to her, but he was carried in the opposite direction. This rush also ended in a dead spot. Here his neighbours were all shorter than he was. He turned his head upward toward the sky and tried to pull some fresh air into his aching lungs, but it was already heavily tainted with sweat.
>
> In this part of the mob no one was hysterical. In fact, most of the people seemed to be enjoying themselves. Near him was a stout woman with a man pressing hard against her from in front. His chin was on her shoulder, and his arms were around her. She paid no attention to him and went on talking to the woman at her side.
>
> "The first thing I knew," Tod heard her say, "there was a rush and I was in the middle."
>
> "Yeah, somebody hollered, 'Here comes Gary Cooper,' and then wham!"
>
> "That ain't it," said a little man wearing a cloth cap and pullover sweater. "This is a riot you're in." (182)

This banter continues for a bit, with people musing on the potential for fun in ripping up a girl with a pair of scissors, the men all the while casually groping the women. Thus while powerful forces control the movement of the crowd as a whole, implacably directing its ebbs and flows down alleyways

and over parking lots, at a more local level a casually carnivalesque atmosphere reigns, and all sorts of interesting things are possible.[55]

Tod perceives the crowd to be essentially "lower middle class" in composition, a perception complicated a few lines later by the narrator's observations on the daily routines of those in the crowd: "All their lives they had
slaved at some kind of dull, heavy labor, behind desks and counters, in the
fields and at tedious machines of all sorts" (177). This diversifies considerably
our sense of the class composition of the crowd, which is undercut by the
impersonal and homogenizing sense of fun West evokes, and begins to suggest that the novel is trying to imagine some larger mechanism affecting the
experience and representation of class in this period, a mechanism whose
ideological face can be seen in that imaginary neutralization of the class
structure Bingham and Seldes had variously articulated.

As we have noted, what is conspicuous by its absence from the rest of the
novel is any sustained focus on the "middle class" as such, that is, in the
empirical or sociological sense. Much more striking is the virtually exclusive
focus on leisured but impotent elites on one hand—various inexplicably
monied hacks and hangers-on—and what we would today call the underclasses on the other, lumpen or subproletarian groups on the fringes of wage
labor and economic stability. This recalls, in a degraded and latter-day fashion, those "mythic landscapes of tramps and millionaires," mobile and unfettered, and both free, in their distinct ways, from the burden of toil, which
Michael Denning has shown to populate so many of the nineteenth-century
dime novels.[56] West's novel thus displays a certain historical self-reflexiveness
with respect to the progressive institutionalization of the culture industry;
early components of it are here rearticulated in the service of critique. In
terms of the theme of mobility, what is crucial to note about these groups,
and in contrast to their earlier dime-novel avatars, is their essential immobility. Stuck in the rounds of monied decadence and economic degradation,
these are people who are, we might say, going nowhere fast. Circulating and
mediating between these polarized zones is the figure of Tod Hackett (sometimes accompanied by his reverse but parallel alter ego, Homer Simpson), a
kind of surveyor or "mapper" of this static social geography.[57] In his slightly
detached manner, Tod is less a character than a kind of roving receptor site,
instantiating a particular formal pattern of high to low and back again, a
pattern to which content must in turn be added. West's narrator does tell us

that Tod is "really a very complicated young man with a whole set of personalities, one inside the other like a nest of Chinese boxes" (60), and indeed,
some commentators have taken this at face value, neglecting to unpack these
Chinese boxes, at which point we of course realize that they are all empty.

Philip Fisher has argued that the use of a blank or passive character
(Carrie Meeber is one of his main examples) is typical of certain popular
forms in this country, such as historical and sentimental fiction; these figures
aid in the registration of new cultural possibilities and experiences that
Fisher sees as the chief task of such popular forms.[58] This further suggests
that the novel remains indebted to earlier elements of popular culture that it
then rearticulates as critical reflections when this culture becomes industrialized (which the dime novel, invoked above, was almost from the beginning). More precisely, such popular borrowings are used to vehiculate new
historical content that itself questions and implicates mass culture in wider
social processes. Linking such "mass culture rising" (in the sense of becoming self-reflexive) together with the paraphrased and thematized "modernism descending" examined earlier offers another striking allegory of the
cultural moment in which West worked, and marks *The Day of the Locust* as
a pivotal "work of the break." This maps some of the necessary preconditions for what will later emerge as a central component of postmodernism,
where all culture has definitively fallen into the world of commodities (and
begins to occupy the space of the real itself), yet deploys some of the formal
strategies pioneered in modernism (while altering their function and meaning). Such a transition is by no means complete in West, where the "spheres"
of modernism and mass culture, under conditions of an incomplete differ-
entiation, are at once hurtling toward and hurtling away from each other, in
a contradictory and highly charged manner which, although characteristic
of the modernism/mass culture split as such, is in West uniquely visible and
indeed almost palpable in its generation of tension.

The possibilities Tod enacts, which themselves display the patterning of a
high/low split in crisis, have to do with a space of inclusion, which can
seemingly accommodate a range of social forms and experiences. A character like Tod is by no means unique in American literature—an earlier avatar
of him might be seen for example in the figure of Bartley Hubbard in
Howells's *A Modern Instance* (1882), articulating the contradictions of an
earlier moment of historical development. Bartley, a journalist, embodied

those commodifying forces of mass culture that on one hand so threatened the moral and aesthetic seriousness of Howellsian realism, yet on the other hand stood as the very vehicle for creating that "commonplace culture" of class harmony that was its principal political desideratum in the first place. Sensing the tensions, Howells abruptly killed him off (only to resurrect him briefly in *The Rise of Silas Lapham*), foreclosing on any opportunity to explore the implications of such a figure, one that, with respect to the realm of mass culture, remains at the level of symbolization only.

West, unlike Howells, is careful to put his protagonist in a more frankly allegorical class setting. Not only do the high and low strata in the novel seek to evade the scope of empirical class designations and find ironic unification in their subordination to the mocking vicissitudes of desire in the culture industry (they are equally "cheated"), the composition of the rioting mob itself manifests a distinct semantic charge. "They don't know what to do with their time," West observes of the largely retired and semiretired crowd. "They haven't the mental equipment for leisure, the money nor the physical equipment for pleasure. Did they slave so long just to go to an occasional Iowa picnic?" (178). Here the pastoral thematics we have been tracking emerge once again, in a now grimly distorted fashion, as West presses the initial terms of this libidinal formation toward a kind of vanishing point. Thus work, while being performed, takes place solely with a view to its eventual cessation; once it ceases, the fantasized leisure never materializes. Figured here is a liminal suspension that eschews the positive admixture of polarities found in Dreiser, seeking instead, in consonance with the strategies of the novel in general, a kind of representational productivity out of sheer negation. The mob signals a failed (or anti) pastoral, something underscored by West's cruel troping on the foundational pastoral figure, the cosmopolitan rustic: "Every day of their lives they read the newspapers and went to the movies. Both fed them on lynchings, murder, sex crimes, explosions, wrecks, love nests, fires, miracles, revolutions, wars. The daily diet made sophisticates of them. The sun is a joke. Oranges can't titillate their jaded palates" (178). Alas, no eloquent shepherds, these: lacking the right "mental equipment," their sophistication is marked as so much hollow resentment, a resentment whose secret ("they have slaved and saved for nothing") stands revealed as nothing less than alienated labor itself.

There is a structural, fully as much as a "personal," source for these notes of elitist pessimism. Following Jameson's well-known formulation of the self-reflexive or boomerang-like quality of attributions of ressentiment, it appears that the mob's resentment is but a mirrored displacement of the frustrations of West's own peculiarly ambivalent position as a writer and intellectual whose political proclivities were at odds with his aesthetic sensibilities (U.S. artists and writers in the 1930s, much like their counterparts in France during the Dreyfus affair, were socially interpellated precisely as intellectuals). As he told Malcolm Cowley in 1939, he was unable to coordinate these two dimensions of his self:

> What I mean is that out here [in Hollywood] we have a strong progressive movement and I devote a great deal of time to it. Yet . . . I find it impossible to include any of those activities in [my novel]. I made a desperate attempt before giving up. I tried to describe a meeting of the Anti-Nazi league, but it didn't fit and I had to substitute a whorehouse and a dirty film. . . . When not writing a novel—say at a meeting of a committee we have out here to help the migrant worker—I do believe it [left activity and symbolism] and try to act on that belief. But at the typewriter, by myself, I just can't.[59]

Thus West could not take part in the generalized pastoral impulse so evident in the cultural production of the 1930s—the attempt to imagine, if not eloquence (though sometimes this, too), then at least a certain nobility and heroism amongst the "folk" of the nation. Such antipastoralism and its attendant bleakness emerge as a kind of translation or rearticulation of what is finally a felt absence of linkage between the intellectual and the masses, imbued with the dire problematization of both individual and collective agency such a perceived failure of social connection represents (a failure of "contact," to recall the title of the little magazine West coedited with William Carlos Williams in the early part of the decade). West's split sensibility thus issues in a kind of structural ressentiment that becomes a part of his representational metabolism, allegorically limning the incipient failure of 1930s political movements.

This antipastoral impulse resonates throughout the book, implicating much of West's portrait of Hollywood, and leading us to a final axis of totalization at work in the novel. If I have stressed such axes throughout this discussion, it is because, as I hope has become clearer by now, nothing less than the question of the totality, and of a possible representational access to it, is at stake in the allegorical registers of West's fiction. His conflicted aesthetic set finds in the Hollywood setting its most productive object of expression, its cultural and social dimensions affording a conduit to larger issues of the historical trajectory of the period. Of the many features of West's portrait, I want to draw particular attention to West's emphasis on Hollywood as a vast cultural clearinghouse where all imaginable aesthetic and cultural forms coexist and interanimate each other. Music, writing, painting, photography, theater—films by their very nature cannibalize other cultural products, in a sense extracting their aesthetic use value, which the movies then incorporate into their own (ultimately profit-driven) designs. Meanwhile, dead aesthetic labor piles up on back lots:

> He pushed his way through a tangle of briars, old flats and iron junk, skirting the skeleton of a Zeppelin, a bamboo stockade, an adobe fort, the wooden horse of Troy, a flight of baroque palace stairs that started in a bed of weeds and ended against the branches of an oak, part of the Fourteenth Street elevated station, a Dutch windmill, the bones of a dinosaur, the upper half of the Merrimac, a corner of a Mayan temple, until he finally reached the road. (131)

West does not mention here file cabinets, in which dead labor, in the form of never-to-be-filmed scripts, was also amassing, something with which he was all too familiar. In contrast to the realm of culture-industry products themselves, I am stressing here the novel's vision of the industry as a whole, which stands as a figure not merely for industrial capital as such, but also for some great, organized expansion of the entire cultural sphere, which tendentially saturates every crevice of society.

This cluttered, backlot landscape across which Tod wanders is famously described by West as the "dream dump," where the mass of people's wishes lie entombed in "lath and plaster," having been "realized" but also falsified and emptied.[60] Beyond this level, however, we can perceive this as the last moment of modernist thematization in the novel. If Faye's subversion of B-movie stories gestured toward the avant-garde, the dream dump gestures instead toward the other pole of modernism's paradoxical aesthetic engagement, namely the dream of a book of the world, a work so complex and multivalent that it would effectively "contain" all of reality (Joyce and Pound come most readily to mind, though the notion itself is traceable to Mallarmé). This would not, as with the avant-gardes, be initially a strategy directed *against* the autonomy of the aesthetic, but rather a hyperautonomous ambition, which would ultimately annul the aesthetic by enlarging it to the dimensions of the real, a strategy equally as vulnerable to "realization" through commodification as was its opposite number. Indeed, the precise ambivalence of the modernism-commodity nexus pervades the very built environment of Los Angeles itself, as we can now interpret those "Mexican ranch houses, Samoan huts, Mediterranean villas, Egyptian and Japanese temples, Swiss chalets, [and] Tudor cottages" (61), whose tackiness and "monstrousness" the narrator famously condemns, as themselves implicated, within the context of the novel, in a thematization of the book of the world. Hence, finally, we comprehend the deeper narrative motivation of some of these judgments of taste, as "excuses" for elaborating lengthy catalogs of assorted curios, bric-a-brac, architectural styles, and studio lot paraphernalia, which in *A Cool Million* were merely indices of the "surfeit of shoddy," whereas here they are also gestures of drawing the world into the text.

Such an impulse to generate lists implicitly allies West with the great cultural project of the second half of the 1930s, namely that of the documentarists, despite whatever West might have consciously thought of them (many artists in the period regarded the documentarists as essentially middlebrow). Alfred Kazin, in his still vital *On Native Grounds*, strikingly characterized the documentary project as a great "tagging and indexing" of the country, which regarded the country as "one vast national park," replete with endangered species of the sociological or anthropological type who had to be captured with word or image before their disappearance.[61] This project, Kazin observes, could itself sometimes be at odds with the demands of narrative, and often enough remained at the level of the sheer enumeration of objects and people, propelled increasingly by an indiscriminate nationalism: "America was everywhere, in everything; America was people everywhere; people on farms and on relief; people on the road; farmers in town standing before store windows; the girl on the bus who was going from town to town to look for work."[62] This formulation is deceptive, however, and Mike Davis provides the necessary corrective when he argues that what effectively emerged from the 1930s was an ideological space which for the first time was broadly inclusive of large sectors of the white working class, a historic invitation into the charmed circle of middle-classness from which blacks and other minorities were still rigorously excluded.[63]

For Kazin, even those examples of the "literature of social description" that were not photographically illustrated—such as Edmund Wilson's *American Jitters*, James Rorty's *Where Life Is Better*, and Louis Adamic's *My America*— nonetheless partook, in their effort to "catch reality on the run," of the basic essence of the documentary project, which he strikingly characterizes as "the New Deal plus the camera" (bringing to mind another ambivalently pragmatic and utopian intersection of politics and technology, which is Lenin's dictum that communism equaled "the soviets plus electrification"). Given the terms of our argument thus far, the radical aesthetic ambiguity of this conjuncture should be apparent, and indeed its instability could move toward both cliché and easy sentimentality (as in Caldwell and Bourke-White's *You Have Seen Their Faces*) and anxiety-ridden modernism (Agee and Evans's *Let Us Now Praise Famous Men*), an instability that finally doomed its culturally totalizing ambitions. Tod Hackett, as a wanderer among disparate cultural collections, and as a roving gatherer of cultural material for his painting, "The Burning of Los Angeles," thus seems to occupy a similar structural position to, and to be a kind of reflexive parody of, the 1930s documentarist. That the "camera" of this text is of the moving-picture rather than still variety affords a further engagement with the cultural thematics of mobility and migration, which themselves, as we can now demonstrate, resonate with the ultimate political ramifications of the New Deal.

And so at length we return to the crowd in front of Kahn's Persian Palace, in a better position now to understand this scene as West's vision of the collective consequences of Tod's allegorical mapping of a middle-class subject position, with its commensurate neutralizations of class boundaries. I want to suggest that this crowd is, like the cinematic army at the opening with which it is functionally allied, itself "around quitting time," in its pointed figuration of combined activity and immobility, a combination whose inner referent remains the time of transition at the close of the workday. The mob is at once an antiproletariat and an antibourgeoisie, positioned neither in work nor in leisure, instantiating instead a third space that borders on the Imaginary. At a certain level, the novel here rearticulates the peculiar anxieties of an earlier generation of realists in their attempts to imagine the crossing of class boundaries. For writers like Crane, Dreiser, and London, some vision of the immediate and irrevocable absorption into the lower class often attended their attempts to represent such crossings, an absorption that unsurprisingly occasioned both fear and excitement (the generic trappings of class tourism). Venture out among the tramps, and you just might become one. In West, such dangers are rather more mediated; Tod enjoys a mobile subject position at length before finally being swept up in the mass and suffering a nervous breakdown. Class tourism emerges here in a historically more developed form, which must first pass through some larger social apparatus—imaged here as the mob—before its full nature can be grasped, and its threat to the individual subject can be gauged. This amounts in the end to an ideological erasure of class that strips the individual of any dimension of collective action, affording it a new range of subjective possibility while rendering it powerless before the structural exigencies of the social whole.

This effect is produced in part through the novel's intense exploration of mobility as such (in both movies and mobs), to the point where it anticipates in the mob scene the more full-scale reification of motion that Lawrence Grossberg has theorized as one of the central components of contemporary daily life, namely disciplined mobilization, defined as "a situation in which a particular structure of territorialization is established in which every moment of stability is dissolved, leaving only paths of constant mobility."[64] The *locus classicus* here, perhaps unsurprisingly, is Disneyland, with its perpetual flow of customers. Such a notion highlights the utopian principle of dereification at the heart of American ideology (the frontier principle being among the most crucial incarnations of this), a principle that longs to dissolve stasis into flux, and materiality into ideality. It achieves this, however, at the cost of reifying mobility itself, freezing it over into a kind of image of itself and eradicating its deeper roots in the longing for social evolution, producing the sort of stasis-in-motion pattern or figure that we see operative in the mob at the novel's end (and in film, if in a different way).[65]

For the lesson about failed desire *The Day of the Locust* has to offer has less to do, finally, with the disappointments of consumption and mass culture than it does with the failure of the possibility of collective action as such, and the commensurate weakening of the individual. The mob is neither incipiently revolutionary nor inherently fascistic; paradoxically, its violent energies portend a sharp constriction of the political horizon. The stormy cultural and political ambivalence of the decade, so acutely allegorized by West, was real enough, and productive of any number of remarkable cultural achievements, as Michael Denning's recent and vital work of recovery has amply shown.[66] Nonetheless, *The Day of the Locust* prophesies the eventual implosion of this peculiarly unstable situation (a failure even Denning acknowledges), blackly dismissing its radical pretensions and pointing to the advent of a depoliticized complacency. If West seems to anticipate the views of Warren Susman and other more recent historians of the period, who hold that the era of the New Deal and the Popular Front fatally undermined radical politics in this country for a time, fostering an uncritical nationalism allied with consumerism ("America" now effectively equaling the "middle-class consumption basket"), it is not because he believed that the progressive political and cultural imagination of the decade was (as the historians often maintain) inherently compromised or corrupt; rather, it is because the larger structural forces allegorized in his novel, however "undecidable" they might have seemed at the time, were in the end functionally tied to a mutation within the capitalist mode of production itself, something captured by the sensitive recording apparatus of West's conflicted aesthetic. Hence, finally, we have the social side to the pervasive violence of the novel, understood now as a rage at the "missed opportunity" of the decade (the revolution that never came), a failure that is at one with the difficulties and paradoxes of the novel's tortuous engagement with modernism.[67] All in all, it is a complete and agonized allegorical summa of ambivalence and frustrated possibility. It is hardly surprising, then, that it reaches its climax, with the riot and Tod's breakdown, in apocalypse and madness (grim parodies of social or psychic "revolutions"), two outcomes which threaten to eradicate the moment of the event fully as much as they darkly insinuate its coming.

five

Into the 1950s: Fiction in the

Age of Consensus

No man who owns his house and lot can

be a Communist. He has too much to do.

—Levittown developer Bill Levitt, 1948

In the summer of 1950, General Motors (GM) and the United Auto Workers (UAW) signed a five-year wages and benefits agreement that became known as the Treaty of Detroit. The agreement, spearheaded in part by UAW head Walter Reuther (who ten years earlier had been tagged by auto executive George Romney as a "revolutionary" and "the most dangerous man in Detroit"),[1] was widely hailed as a victory for all sides, as it offered labor peace to the corporations and a hitherto unmatched standard of living to the workers. *Fortune* magazine, meanwhile, in attempting to assess the full meaning of the agreement, focused on the following striking details, rich in political and cultural implication: "It is the first major union contract that explicitly accepts objective economic facts—cost of living and productivity—as determining wages, thus throwing over all theories of wages as determined by political power and of profits as 'surplus value.'"[2] These "theories" that

Fortune so optimistically regarded as having been consigned to the ashcan of history are of course those associated with the socialist tradition.

One could scarcely imagine anything more apt than this agreement, a kind of symbolic marker of the onset of high Fordism in the United States and of the "definitive" absorption of the American working class into a hegemonic middle-class ideology; versions would soon be acceded to by millions of workers in a range of key industries. The economic conditions at the time were certainly propitious for prompting these ideological concessions.[3] As Alain Lipietz reminds us, the key economic indicators relating to productivity, consumption, profit rates, and the composition of capital (ratio of machinery and raw materials to labor) were all rising together from the late 1940s until the late 1960s—the Fordist golden age—an unprecedented situation in the history of world capitalism and indeed almost "miraculous."[4] The uniqueness of the postwar American boom—dependent on many factors, including a bombed-out European industrial infrastructure, U.S. political supremacy, and a strong, Cold War–inspired desire for domestic tranquillity—has not, naturally, prevented this period from becoming stereotyped as the "norm" of the U.S. economy, as what it is regularly capable of achieving, later periods of recession and stagnation being henceforth regarded as simply short-term setbacks or detours.[5]

So, surplus value is no longer the source of profits: at a stroke, any hint of even lingering suspicion between capital and labor (let alone any deeper sense of a fundamental antagonism) is erased from the public sphere, and with it any possible grasp of the unique historical vocation of the working class, or, better, the political possibility immanent within the situation of those who produce surplus value. Indeed, by submitting to this discursive rearticulation of the labor-capital relation, the workers in effect forfeited their status as living labor as such, which capital imprisons and exploits, and instead found themselves equated with dead labor, "constant capital," or in effect with machines, which are themselves incapable of creating new value. It might be objected that this is to read too much into this situation, that an artifact like the GM/UAW agreement simply caps a process that had been under way for fifteen years, granting to workers (who never had anything radical about them) a set of demands that placed them squarely within the fold of middle-classlessness. This would be the perspective, common on both the left and the right, that sees the course of the labor movement in

America (save, perhaps, for heroic but comparatively miniscule endeavors like the International Workers of the World) solely as an exercise in "business unionism," which was never really suspicious of capitalism and only wanted to secure its piece of the economic pie (as if this last goal itself lacked any political resonance). Although there is a measure of truth in this position, I think it is important to try to maintain a more dialectically ambivalent perspective. In general, when the capitalist system is challenged locally, it can respond in several ways, usually by fighting back and suppressing the challenge, but sometimes, given special circumstances, it can accede, at least partly, to the demands being made of it. The resultant "give and take" rhythm, characteristic especially of the industrialized First World countries, can appear (given hindsight and the persistence of the system as a whole) generally to benefit the capitalist class, but it should be recognized that, at the time, the various challenges that were mounted created disruptions and instabilities within the system whose outcomes were unpredictable. For example, the great wave of labor activism of the mid-1930s associated with the first years of the Congress of Industrial Organizations (CIO), epitomized most dramatically by the sit-down strikes and factory occupations pioneered by Reuther and the UAW, depended upon radical new organizing strategies, and called upon new human solidarities, in order to achieve its victories and build momentum.

By the 1950s, such activism seemed to have served its purpose and outlived its usefulness (and was in any case becoming more problematic, as the antilabor backlash of the Cold War set in—the effort to "illegalize class solidarity," as James O'Connor has put it).[6] Things could quiet down, and visions of American civilization as calm and contradiction-free could emerge: Louis Hartz on America's ineluctable and elastic liberal essence, Richard Chase on the American novel's negation of politics and society, and Daniel Bell's sweeping and symptomatic portrait of "political exhaustion," *The End of Ideology*. Bell ascribes to the 1950s a "certain slackening" (to borrow a phrase Jean-François Lyotard attributed to postmodernism as such),[7] as the hegemony of liberal capitalism steadily dampens and douses all politically charged discourse, politics in Bell's view destined henceforth never again to be a realm capable of sustaining radical investments (on the left or the right). As with the Treaty of Detroit, a kind of political and discursive "flattening" is at work, implying that there will no longer be any fundamental political divisions between the strata of society, and that a general liberal pragmatism can effectively contain any more local political problem—the very ground of "consensus."

There is a striking (and suggestive, for our purposes) insistence in Bell's text on the need to disarticulate "intellect" and "emotion." For Bell, the need rigorously to divest thought from any emotional resonance or affective charge is quite clear: reason allied with passion essentially means communism. This is not so much argued for as such as it is narratively enunciated, in particular in the chapter of *The End of Ideology* where he discusses the "failure of American socialism."[8] The theoretical deficiencies of their political outlook aside, the deep flaw of those who fought for socialism in this country, as Bell's relentlessly millenarian and hyperbolic rhetoric insinuates, was the fact that they were all demented zealots, well-intentioned lunatics whose supposedly scientific analysis of society was simply a front for an irrational utopianism whose appeal was strictly emotional. The rhetorical overkill in this chapter is as curious as it is grotesque, contrasting as it does with the social-scientific stolidity of the rest of the text. The one analysis that unmistakably implies that reason should not be infected with emotion is the one analysis that itself has strong affective currents flowing through it. From this chapter, the book can then coast onward to the positive serenity (mixed with vague regret) of the brief final chapter, where the end of ideology thesis is formally announced for the first time. It is as if these two moments constitute the essential poles of the book, which, were they subjected to some improbable alchemical process, would combine to produce a curious mood of "unenthusiastic excitement," one we shall discover presently in *The Floating Opera* as well.

But there is more going on in Bell's text than the usual anticommunism (however charged). It has less often been noticed that the real heart of the book, and in its own way an equally strong source for the subsequent conclusions on "political exhaustion," is the long, wide-ranging, and meditative chapter on work. This is essentially an extended reflection on Taylorism, its more sociological component concerning itself with advances in automation and the fetishization of efficiency (along with the crucial insight that, by this time, the unions themselves have largely become part of the "control system of management"), all of which combines to produce a pervasive and increasing loss of job satisfaction (by no means a new topic in the sociological literature).[9] One perhaps anecdotal (but still telling) index of the latter that Bell invokes is the increase in the professed desire of members of the working class to rise out of that station and become business owners (however small), a desire that appears previously to have been characteristic of segments of the petit bourgeoisie but which by the mid-1950s seems to have decisively migrated over to the workers. This wish for what amounts to a measure of economic power and control over one's destiny strikes one as a reflex of the mounting sense of powerlessness and constriction workers were experiencing on the job, a wish, however, no longer directed at expropriating a share of power from the owners of capital but rather at gaining some control over other workers.

Accompanying this sociological level of analysis in Bell's chapter is a more philosophical one, concerned with the place and meaning of work as such, both in American society and within the tradition of Western thought more generally. For Bell it is apparent that the growing "desemanticization" of work or its neutralization as a site of conscious personal fulfillment for the American worker is also partly a cover (or disavowal mechanism) for a strongly negative relation to work, which propels the worker toward the immersion in leisure time pursuits, activities whose value, as a satisfying substitute for work, Bell doubts. Whatever bourgeois paternalism might be detected here, or fear of the weakening of a productive work ethic, Bell is raising a real concern, namely the possibility that this society might be shrinking, rather than expanding, the range of interesting and satisfying activities in which humans can engage. Work thus is here the privileged locus of what Marx described in terms of the full panoply of "sensuous human activity," which is invaded and structured by the particular demands of capital. Toward the end of the chapter, Bell introduces an existential twist to the proceedings when he notes that, since the decline of religion, work has been a way of "confronting the absurdity of existence and the beyond." After recalling Freud's remark that work is the "chief means of binding an individual to reality" (shades of Marlow in *Heart of Darkness*, and his coveted rivets), he then concludes with the plaintive and uneasy question "what will happen, then, when not only the worker but work itself is displaced by the machine?" (262). Bell writes, of course, before the advent of post-Fordism, when some of this becomes clearer: namely that automation has not at all eradicated work. Rather, its spread has been accompanied by vast new realms of unskilled and sometimes only spottily regulated toil. Indeed, recent research has indicated that the majority of the American labor force works longer, harder, and frequently for less real income than it did twenty years ago.[10] But Bell's description of the process whereby people both dislike the conditions under which they work and find their work itself less interesting is doubtless more true today than it was in the late 1950s.

So, a sense of slackening, of weakening, of tensions eased: how is the vocation of narrative production to negotiate this new landscape? The 1950s do tend to stick out as a kind of baleful time for the novel, with something pinched and constricted about the work of this era, positioned unfavorably between the great interwar period on one hand and the exuberant metafictional and multicultural bounty of the postmodern era on the other. But failure and blocked pathways can often be as instructive as success: let us see what can be learned.

. . .

The most symptomatically marked genre of discourse in John Barth's first novel *The Floating Opera* (1956) is, perhaps unsurprisingly, that of history: as with the end of ideology, there is a question here of what can actually happen anymore. The question of historical understanding and representation is extensively fretted over by the narrator, Todd Andrews, as if the possibility of grasping any kind of historical truth has at this moment suddenly undergone a peculiar problematization. For Todd, all of this takes the form of biography and autobiography—the novel itself being cast as an autobiographical moment in a larger biography of his father. Todd is obsessed with what he calls that most "elusive" of all things, "the cause of any human act."[11] What is the nature of that gap between the moments of "before" and "after" that tell us that an "event" has occurred? How is it that anything "happens" in the first place? To this end, Todd is preparing a vast *Inquiry* into the circumstances surrounding his father's suicide (the immediate, if insufficient, occasion of which was the loss of his business in 1930), a project which is itself merely a prelude to the aforementioned and even vaster biography of his father, which is in turn preparation for the enormous and properly interminable *Letter to My Father*, designed to explain Todd fully to his father and to correct what he perceives to have been the persistent "imperfect communication" between the two. These projects, he realizes, must willy-nilly draw into themselves the entire history of the period in question (basically from the end of the Civil War onward), and be, in some measure, a meditation on that history. The irony, too, is readily apparent, in that this ostensible attempt to improve communication will never be read by his father (and indeed, the reader slowly realizes that the novel itself is but a fragment of the *Letter*—an attempt to "explain myself to myself," as Todd puts it—which will never be read by its intended audience, a metafictional conceit that dramatizes the separation between all writers and readers).[12]

In any event, the novel itself focuses on one day in Todd's life—either 21 or 22 June 1937, he cannot remember which, thus opening a characteristic hole in time that installs a note of undecidability at the center of the narrative—a day upon which he experienced a "change of mind," when, after failing to commit suicide, he revises one of the "philosophical" conclusions of his *Inquiry*. These conclusions are fairly sophomoric, and are evidently indebted to a certain existentialist "period rhetoric" Barth imbibed at Johns Hopkins in the early 1950s (they include items such as "nothing has intrinsic value" and "there's no final reason for living"). As such, they have more to do with the distinction Fredric Jameson has made in terms of the ideology of existentialism, with its characteristic evocations of the meaninglessness and absurdity of existence, with whom we associate figures like Camus, and existentialism as a technical analytic, concerned precisely with the problem of time and the interrogation of the act and the event, as in the work of Heidegger and Sartre.[13] These two levels together with that of narrative proper (Todd wishes his story to unpack and explain the "event" of his change of mind) all coexist uneasily in the novel. It is one thing to have a set of propositions about the absurdity of life, but it is quite another to try to write a novel that in some measure "illustrates" or embodies these principles (that is, somehow detaches itself from "meaning," in the language of the story itself), as seems to be Todd's intent. Indeed, the dilemma here recalls that reportedly encountered by Flaubert during the writing of *Bouvard and Pecuchet*: after a while, he no longer knew whether he was writing a book about stupidity or whether he was writing a stupid book.[14]

Todd's ambition involves in part the attempt to structure the narrative around not events but nonevents. The beginnings of this are in the first pages of the text, with Todd's little disquisition on his own name:

> So. Todd Andrews is my name. You can spell it with one or two *d*'s; I get letters addressed either way. I almost warned you against the single-*d* spelling, for fear you'd say "*Tod* is German for death: perhaps the name is symbolic." I myself use two *d*'s, partly in order to avoid that symbolism. But you see, I ended by not warning you at all, and that's because it just occurred to me that the double-*d Todd* is symbolic, too, and accurately so. *Tod* is death, and this book hasn't much to do with death; *Todd* is almost *Tod*—that is, almost death—and this book, if it gets written, has very much to do with almost-death. (3)

Familiar here is the characteristic pose of the Tristram Shandyesque narrator, the faux naïf whose bewildering digressions and insistently professed inability to tell a story turn out to be the story itself. The "almost death" in question here has to do, at least initially, with Todd's severe heart condition, which might cause him to keel over dead at any moment. Hence another familiar note is struck, this time the Scheherazadean leitmotiv of the story told, under precarious circumstances, in order to escape or cheat death (with the added twist that this heretofore formal compulsion emerges as the content, by and large, of the story).

Todd wants to avoid the possible death symbolism of his name, in a move typical of him that recurs at several points in the novel: after depicting an object or image that might well be read symbolically, he implores the reader not to read anything into them, a tactic he later generalizes into a rule of thumb: "So, reader, should you ever find yourself writing about the world, take care not to nibble at the many tempting symbols she sets squarely in your path, or you'll be baited into saying things you don't really mean, and offending the people you want most to entertain" (111). Here we see Todd shedding his earlier pose of incompetence, becoming more confident, and letting the virtuosity which is after all the real substance of this kind of feigned writerly inadequacy come dangerously close to the surface. As Couturier suggests in his essay on the novel, Todd's suspicion of symbol and cliché is an index to Barth's situation as a young writer in the mid-1950s, trying to remain within a modernist mode of narrative production and yet palpably feeling himself to be in the midst of a newly emergent aesthetic dispensation.[15] In this respect, his suspicions conform to the modernist dialectic of aesthetic progress, whereby previously employed images, tropes, and narrative devices are regarded as having become ossified and clichéd, and henceforth no longer usable (the result being a gradual reduction in what is "sayable," with a minimalist aesthetic being the logical telos toward which this dialectic moves). It is odd, though, to see this deployed so plaintively in the narrative itself, an indication of Barth's uncertainties and a prelude to the more usual sublimation of this impulse into the form itself (as in the later metafiction), where the older aesthetic materials are ruled out of bounds almost by definition.

A further example, in a rather different form, of the story's lessening of the semantic volume by way of avoiding older figurative and narrative materials occurs in relation to Todd's affair with Jane Mack and the relative nonissue of the paternity of the Macks' child Jeannine. The problems of adultery and paternity, which in earlier novels would probably have been explosive and tragedy-generating, are here fumbled with and rationalized into muddled inconsequentiality. This defusing of the family as a charged narrative nexus later finds its reverse but parallel image in the scrambled legal case Todd relates, where Colonel Morton ends up "suing his only-begotten son" (179).

Todd's attempts not to mean are, it seems to me, consistent with one of the more striking effects of the novel, given the date of its appearance: the detachment of the existential rhetoric from one of its most typical psychological concomitants, namely despair or angst. The novel thus departs markedly from those efforts, of only a few years before, of other young American writers to incorporate in some measure a "serious" existentialist thematic into their early works (Mailer's *The Naked and the Dead* and Bellow's *Dangling Man*, both from 1948, come to mind). Todd's nihilism is resolutely stoic and rational, even jaunty, his emotional detachment perfectly consistent, so much so that those rare points in the book when Todd actually does wish to evoke a sense of despair or horror are thereby undermined (these moments thus standing as symptomatic failures of the narrative), as when he seeks to convey to us the immediate cause of his decision to kill himself. He comes to realize, he tells us, that there will never be any way for him successfully to hide from himself the fact of his weak heart, that no amount of psychological prestidigitation (the adoption of this or that "mask") will ever allow him to regain that "mastery" of his will that he believes to have been vitiated by the proximity of death (and in a typical Barthian conjuncture, the protagonist's black mood is here precipitated by a bout of impotence):

> And suddenly my heart filled my entire body. It was not my heart that would burst, but my body, so full was it of my heart, and every beat was sick. Surely it would fail! I clapped my hand quickly to my chest, feeling for the beat; clutched at the window frame to keep from falling; stared at *nothing*, my mouth open, like a fish on the beach. And this not in pain, but in despair! . . . All I could do was clench my jaw, squint my eyes, and shake my head from side to side. But every motion pierced me with its own futility, every new feeling with its private hopelessness, until a battery of little agonies attacked from all sides, each drawing its strength from the great agony within me. (226)

As an attempt to conjure up a sense of despair, the scene is overly theatrical and quite unconvincing (particularly when, moments later, Todd's decision to kill himself returns him to cheerfulness). It never really suffices simply to tell us about such emotional states, which are probably better rendered through the recording of seemingly incidental or trivial activities, as for example in the great scene in *Crime and Punishment* where the nihilistic blankness attained by the doomed Svidrigailov is conveyed by his monotonous and repetitious swatting of flies.

In the end, however, it is (from the perspective of the overall interpretive economy we are here proposing) in the deeper interest of the narrative not to have a scene like this succeed, in that it can thereby remain faithful to its dominant texture of emotional passivity (its "failures" at one level translating into a different kind of achievement at another).[16] In general, Todd refrains from expressing any kind of emotional investment in even the people and events he is most heavily involved with, regarding them all with clinical detachment, and, like Bell, keeping reason and emotion strictly separate, as when he informs us, following his "change of mind," that "for the sake of convention I'd like to end the show with an emotional flourish, but though the progress of my reasoning from 1919 to 1937 was in many ways turbulent, it was of the essence of my conclusion that no emotion was necessarily involved in it" (251). We need not, of course, take this at face value, but the question remains why Barth himself would have interest in creating a narrative persona who claims to believe it. In any event, Todd's revision of existential rhetoric doubtless strikes one as a peculiarly American procedure, which, if it no longer, as here, seems very convincing as a lived personal philosophy, does nonetheless capture what has since become familiar as one of the dominant moods of the postmodern, what Todd variously describes as "unenthusiastic excitement," or the twin symbiotic gestures of piety and cynicism, or, most acutely, the "charm of the abyss." A current formulation of this mood is to be found in Lawrence Grossberg's dictum that it's not that nothing matters anymore, but that it doesn't matter that nothing matters.[17] This turns out to be the essential meaning of the final conclusion of Todd's *Inquiry* ("there's no final reason for living [or for suicide]"), which we do not learn until the end of the novel, and the only one of the group that has any resonance with the narrative as we experience it. Another word, finally, that brings to mind the mood in question here is that tiny expression that seems only to attain its fullest semantic specificity when uttered in the American context: *fun*.

Fun as I am invoking it here can be provisionally characterized as the continual effort to rearticulate what Benjamin described as *Erlebnis* as an affectively charged and "full" phenomenon, to cover over the essential lack that structures it. Benjamin contrasted Erlebnis with *Erfahrung*, both of which translate as "experience"; however, the latter refers to experience informed by collective social arrangements (and whose aesthetic corollary is storytelling), whereas the latter denotes its modern, privatized counterpart, one marked by a decline in the essential narratability of events.[18] The link between the individual subject and the world of larger human social reality is thus tendentially severed, and henceforth experience (which in Benjamin's view now constitutes a kind of nonexperience) retains only an "issueless private character" (158).[19]

The bored inhabitants of West's southern California were clearly afflicted with Erlebnis—with the crushing sense that nothing "happens" anymore, that there are no longer interesting or compelling events or activities. The upshot of this was the crowd scene at the end of *The Day of the Locust*, where, as I noted, we saw the sense of fun I am getting at here beginning to coalesce, though still festooned with violent and indeed pathological trappings. I remarked then that this dark and unrefined vision of fun would undergo further development and emerge in the midst of 1950s high Fordism in a rather different form, as something more pervasive and moodlike, at once more individualized and yet more of an obscure group imperative (as in that arch-contemporary rhetorical catchphrase popular a few years back, "are we having fun yet?"), and whose rearticulation in this form then, some fifteen years after *The Day of the Locust*, becomes one of the principal, if oblique, displays of *The Floating Opera*. This is now, following the absorption of the labor movement and the growth of the mass media (and Benjamin's thinking here includes a media component, with Erlebnis structured in part by the hurried and distracted consumption of information), a situation of intensified Erlebnis. This offers one possible contextualization for Barth's choice of a Tristram Shandy–type narrator, that is, one who dwells on the difficulty of constructing a narrative, and who is himself engaged in writing impossible narratives (Todd's various auto/biographical projects). In any event, fun strives to avoid any immediate association with anxiety or dread (unlike fear, which can be very "fun"), which is why Todd Andrews tells us that we should not, via the German, link his name to death, whereas Nathanael West, writing at a slightly different historical moment and with a correspondingly different sensibility, doubtless imagines just these sorts of symbolic affinities for his Tod Hackett.

Nor should we, meanwhile, take Todd's "almost death" to imply anything like "almost angst," as it leads rather in a different direction entirely, away from death and despair and toward the peculiar, irreal "time" of the mass media, particularly television. That is, the concept of Erlebnis will be taken up at length as a cognate of what Sartre theorized under the name of seriality, a paradoxical dynamic that posits people in groups that are fundamentally passive or inert, whose members operate in unison precisely by operating against one another, a dynamic that, for Sartre (and Benjamin, in a related way) displays a constitutive relation with modern media apparatuses.

With Erlebnis as we saw it delineated in West—as an affliction of the middle-class, and white, inhabitants of the Hollywood/New Deal fantasy space—comes a bleeding dry of "events," a mounting sense that nothing is happening anymore due to an inability to coordinate the content of daily life with any larger collective forces and destinies. *The Floating Opera* articulates a similar dynamic, in a more economical and even uncanny fashion, and one that avoids the use of stereotypical cultural material (the soulless midwesterners). I have in mind the peculiar temporal dislocations that arise from Barth's structuring of the "authorial position" of Todd. The story concerns one day in Todd's life, in June 1937, along with various episodes from earlier in his life. We know, however, that Todd is writing the narrative in 1954, and hence it is peculiar, and a matter of dim awareness throughout, that we do not learn of any other event or experience relating to him between that June day and the time of the story's composition.[20] This dim awareness does come into sharper focus at those not infrequent moments when Todd recalls us to the scene of writing, namely the hotel room where he has been living since 1930, by way of indicating how nothing has changed during the intervening years ("then, as now, the one window was dappled with little rings of dust," "the painting of the fishing boat that hung on the wall, and still does," and similar formulations). For the most part, then, we have our faces pressed up against the glass of 1937, only to have the reading mind wrenched, however momentarily, out of that temporal setting. In those brief instants we become cognizant of the 1937–54 period as a sheerly empty one, as we shift into the "present" of the book, readjusting our temporal sense as we cross the dead vacuum of years.

• • •

The emptiness of post-1937 time in the novel itself follows in the wake, and stands as a result, of the key nonevent of the novel, more important than the change of mind that is its putative climactic object: Todd's failed suicide attempt aboard the "floating opera" of the title. The latter is basically a large boat that, during the summer months, plies the waters of coastal North Carolina and Chesapeake Bay, and features a vaudeville and minstrel show. What is outrageous about Todd's suicide attempt is, of course, the fact that it takes place aboard the floating opera, during a performance, with a significant portion of the local Cambridge (Maryland) population on board, and involves a scheme to trigger an explosion in the boat's acetylene lighting system. If successful, his suicide will also be a mass murder, a consideration which does not seem to concern him at all. Strictly speaking, the element of murder breaches the narrow limits of Todd's "philosophy," which derived from an analysis of whether a given individual's existence was worth continuing, from that individual's point of view. In terms of the narrative, it has more in common with the episode in which Todd, without explanation, sends five thousand dollars to the wealthiest man in Cambridge. Todd imagines this as a pure gift, one that implies no reciprocal obligations on the receiver's part (and is thus another putatively "meaningless" act, on that desemanticized level of the story we examined earlier). Like the utopian *acte gratuit* of Gide, he wants this understood as a purely unmotivated act, one that cannot be traced to any definable characteristics of his "personality." Unfortunately for Todd, mass murder, however "gratuitous" in the execution, is one of those events that tend to be savagely recoded by posterity in terms of any number of constricting categories of psychological deviance or aberration (and indeed, his only moment of hesitation about committing suicide occurs when he imagines that the Macks will "misinterpret" the act).

Surely Barth, already uncertain of the possibilities for modernist narrative in mid-1950s America, must have sensed that the representation of the modernist acte gratuit, with its antinarrative impulse, was by this time itself a worn-out device, and no longer terribly effective in constructing a convincing narrative persona. I am speculating that its use here is indicative of a certain awareness on Barth's part that, when the X-ray machine is turned on, we can see how structurally unsound this discursive pastiche known as "Todd" really is. What this tells us, at least initially, is that we should avoid the common temptation to psychoanalyze Todd, to delve into his unconscious for the sources of his desire to destroy his fellow townsfolk, and so forth, as if he were a unified psychic entity.[21] This is confirmed by Patricia Tobin's important insight that there is a basic incommensurability between Todd as character and Todd the putative author of the text we read. Todd the character is burdened with obsessive habits (working, like his father, on his boat in good clothes, striving all the while to keep them perfectly clean; unchanging his two-biscuit breakfast; among others), pedantically interminable writerly exercises, and a callously debunking ironic sensibility (as when he demolishes Mister Haecker's pretense of a beautiful death, perhaps driving the old man into a suicide attempt). Todd the author is replete with the comic affability of Fielding and Sterne, the stylish use of double columns in the chapter "Calliope Music," and the elaborate comic parallels between the floating opera and his own story.[22] Why, indeed, would one characterize one's narrative as a kind of floating showboat ("you'll catch sight of it, lose it, spy it again; and it may require the best efforts of your attention and imagination to keep track of the plot as it sails in and out of view" [7]) when this would seem to be the perfect figure for that "imperfect communication" that plagues one? Todd's various masks (saint, cynic) are at once totalizing and unstable: each one putatively defines and exhausts the full range of his character, only to arrive at some crisis point and be shed in favor of some new, equally exclusive one. They thus strive toward an impossible closure, much in the manner of his *Inquiry* and related projects, and point toward a profound crisis of identity, wherein sources of a mature and stable identity cannot be found, which in turn implicates a deeper crisis of historicity itself.

At one level, this is signaled by what we might call a restriction of aesthetic materiality in evidence here. We have already noted the matter of agency, which in Dreiser was the occasion for manifold and palpable authorial and narrative investments; here it becomes something Todd ponders in his spare time (albeit fairly obsessively). The same holds true of irony, which does not—as in Conrad or Musil—live and breathe in the sentences themselves, but is reduced instead to the status of a character trait. A certain shrinkage of the aesthetic horizon is discernible, something confirmed by Barth's own doubts about his identity as a modernist writer and his misgivings—paralleling Bell's on the future of work in U.S. society—about the place and meaning of aesthetic labor in this period. Questions of career and vocation are certainly at issue here. The period prior to the writing of *The Floating Opera* was, Barth tells us in the preface to the novel, anxious and dispiriting, as he adopted and discarded various Joycean and Faulknerian styles, and eventually began considering whether to give up the whole writing enterprise altogether. In addition, as Heide Ziegler notes, Barth felt burdened by the conventions of the then popular existentialist novel, which tended to involve an impassioned and (as we observed earlier) anxiety-ridden search on the part of the protagonist for his "genuine essence," thus giving us one immediate cause for Barth's interest in creating a narrative entity such as Todd.[23] Barth was in effect struggling to escape the force of the central materialist tenet of existentialism, that existence precedes essence, that one's character arises from the choices made in the context of a situation one has been thrown into—an escape attempt that might well have helped render his narrative into an acute Geiger counter of those realms of hyperidealism we will examine shortly in terms of Sartrean seriality.

Hence the very difficulties of the aesthetic situation Barth found himself confronted with, and the ultimate choices he made in the face of these difficulties, allowed him to express his own considerable doubts about the value and indeed the very possibility of the modernist novelistic endeavor in the mid-1950s (in part by being virtuosic about these very doubts), including the possibility of not being able to fashion some sort of "identity" for himself through this labor. The "end of history" Barth conjures up in the pages of his novel is therefore at one level very specifically the end of modernism as a living cultural possibility, and "end" that affords his narrative a sharp resonance with other ends being articulated in this period. By the time Barth publishes his celebrated essay "The Literature of Exhaustion" in 1967, he is able to argue that a pervasive sense of artistic exhaustion, or a feeling that the dialectic of aesthetic progress has nowhere else to go, need not be an impediment to the serious writer, and in fact can be used as a springboard to artistic innovation. He is able to argue this, however, only after he himself has produced a series of acclaimed novels; this is not a position that the Barth of 1954 would have been confidently able to adopt. Todd's own indifference to his chosen career (he is a lawyer) conforms with his overall temperament but has a special resonance in this context: "I have no general opinions about the law, or about justice, and if I sometimes set little obstacles, books and slants, in the path of the courts, it is because I'm curious, merely, to see what will happen. . . . The law and I are uncommitted" (85). This is true at one level, although the lengthy sections of excruciating legalese we are treated to indicate a commitment of a rather different kind, a fixated investment in the rhetoric of the profession that suppresses its affective component beneath a sterile and exclusionary linguistic barricade, demonstrating in its own way the longing for, yet blocked access to, an older kind of career (in Barth's case, again, that of the modernist auteur).

Barth was far from being the only one in the 1950s worried about the fate of the modern novel. Numerous prominent critics and writers throughout this period—among them Lionel Trilling, Dwight MacDonald, Jack Kerouac, Gilbert Sorrentino, and Mary McCarthy—viewed the novel as an increasingly unviable form. For the writers, it was an especially difficult time: on one hand, writing in a realistic mode was proscribed by the politicized cultural terms then operative (since realism was the 1930s, leftism, Stalinism), whereas on the other hand, certain values characteristic of modernism were also felt to be oppressive and constricting (chief among them technical mastery and an intense investment in linguistic form).[24] Caught, then, in that interregnum described by Gramsci—between an old order not yet dead and a new one not yet born—serious novelistic production in the 1950s found itself peculiarly hampered and unable to locate itself at the cutting edge of cultural activity (a kind of fall from prominence from which it has perhaps never fully recovered). This is in contrast to, say, the realm of painting, which, relatively untouched by the political and aesthetic storms of the 1930s, and proceeding at its own rate of artistic uneven development, was able to elaborate in the postwar years the highly successful late modernist style of abstract expressionism.[25]

For the critic, meanwhile, the peril facing the novel was as often as not that worrisome and fiercely debated entity called "mass culture" (paired usually with "mass society"), which, during the 1950s, was frequently held responsible for strangling *all* real culture, not merely the novel. Deriving from both a conservative direction (T. S. Eliot, Ortega y Gasset), where the concern was with the unseemly spread of equality and the lack of respect for traditional authority, and a radical direction (Fromm, Adorno, and other Frankfurt School thinkers), where the principal interest was in explaining the appeal of fascism, the category of mass culture found favor primarily among those *cultural* intellectuals surrounding journals like *Partisan Review*, *Politics*, and *Dissent*, many of whom had followed a path from 1930s radicalism through to a postwar embrace of that constricted and embattled space of "cold war liberalism."[26] Much of the appeal of the category, of course, has to do with intellectuals of high cultural background confronting the enormous new expanses of commodified and mass-mediated cultural production generated after the war, and hence can be explained in terms of an elitist defense of educated taste. However, it should not be forgotten that the liberalism of many of these intellectuals was not simply window dressing, that some of the political positions they endorsed (like strong government support of health, education, and welfare, and a significant role for organized labor) are positions that today for example would put them well out on the left wing of the Democratic party, and that at the time the mass media and its cultural productions, with their uncritical jingoism and middle-class boosterism, were helping to stigmatize.

■ ■ ■

The issue of mass culture returns us at length to the fate of class in this era, as the "massification" of culture was itself widely held to be a further intensification of this process, a process by now often met with somewhat less approbation than had hitherto been accorded it in the tradition of American ideology. It is one thing to avoid (supposedly) a rigid class structure and the conflictual social dynamics that accompany it; it is another for society to be dissolved into an atomistic, undifferentiated mass incapable of supporting any interesting cultural or political activity. In his 1949 essay "Art and Fortune," Lionel Trilling argued that the "diminution of the reality of class, however socially desirable in many respects," has contributed to "the falling-off in the energy of ideas that once animated fiction."[27] The subtext of this argument, as Schaub notes, "seems to be that the obituary on the novel is a kind of allegory for the end or impossibility of socialism in the United States," with both the novel and socialism vanishing as social contradictions are absorbed by the new shapelessness of mass society.[28]

It remained for Trilling's protégé Richard Chase in his 1957 text *The American Novel and Its Tradition* to provide a full-blown exceptionalist theory of American fiction, that is, a theory that set American fiction in accord, rather than at odds, with both the dominant liberal interpretation of American history and the most visible and potent cultural forces of the day. What matter, Chase contended, if the novel depended on the energy of social contradiction—what American novelists in fact wrote were more properly characterized as romances, a genre that thrives in isolation from the pressure of society, and has constituted the great and enduring tradition of American novelistic literature. In taking this approach, one senses Chase, as a cultural critic, attempting to disengage himself from the pessimism typical of cultural liberals and to align himself with that other (probably more influential) wing of Cold War intellectual liberalism, more social scientific in cast (with figures like Louis Hartz, David Riesman, Seymour Martin Lipset, and Nathan Glazer), who saw in mass culture less a threat than a benign socialization mechanism in step with the "cultural pluralism" of American society.[29] One can discern an evident need for a move such as Chase's: with American literature being formally canonized during this period, and the fledgling discipline of American studies being elaborated, an elitist cultural pessimism—one which viewed the weak, and ever weakening, class character of the United States as a sterile ground for cultural production and a threat to any further aesthetic development—could hardly have been a terribly serviceable position for the tasks at hand. This is not to cast the notion of the romance as unabashedly popular—as it tendentially negates the real, the genre might well be articulated in terms of a formalist autonomy more sympathetic to highbrow tastes, as indeed Chase himself does at times. Yet, as Geraldine Murphy notes, "as a force field of dialectical oppositions, the romance resembles nothing so much as a microcosm of pluralist society, abuzz with irresolvable tensions and thereby inoculated against radical change."[30] It is thus in line with the more upbeat pluralist model of American society, and not at least initially hostile to a putative mass culture/society.[31]

Murphy also argues that the romance, described by Hawthorne as a kind of "neutral territory" between the real and the imaginary, resonated well with liberal notions of a pragmatic "vital center" between the extremes of communism and fascism. The phrase "vital center" had been coined by Arthur Schlesinger in his 1949 book of that name, a text worth looking at briefly, both for what it reveals about the highly contradictory aspirations of Cold War liberalism, and for the light it casts on *The Floating Opera*.[32] Indeed, it will be useful perhaps to assemble the peculiar "wish list" the book projects, a list that shows that the center, however vital, was, for those who would combine progressivism with anticommunism, an extremely narrow and precarious position. Schlesinger envisions a free society with a radically unfree human nature (the influence of Reinhold Niebuhr, with his stress on the inevitability of human fallibility and the sin of hubris, is everywhere in these pages, a part of that conservative "chastening" undergone by progressive thought in the period); a "new radicalism" with no meaningful involvement of workers, minorities, or the disenfranchised; vanguardism without a vanguard party (the remnants of FDR's brain trust, along with relative newcomers like Hubert Humphrey and Adlai Stevenson, who remake American society from on high); American-led global federalism without international conflict or peripheral resistance; capitalism without capitalists (because they do not perceive the general welfare, nor do they care much for culture or tradition), thanks to a strong Keynesian state; and, finally, the ultimate wish (characteristic, really, of all bourgeois thinking), economic competition and conflict without class conflict. Whatever sober political realism Schlesinger thinks he is propounding, the glaring impossibility of these goals marks him as utopian a dreamer as the rest of us.

This impossibility also marks the vital center as a kind of weird vanishing point, where the closer one comes to fixing it securely the closer it comes to disappearing, or mutating into something else altogether. Thus, despite the moral and political rectitude of the center, eternal vigilance is needed since, as Schlesinger memorably phrases it, "there is a Hitler, a Stalin, in every breast" (250). The moralistic intensity here effectively reduces politics to the vagaries of individual psychology, and creates fertile ground for sundry paranoid investments, since this "individual" appears on the face to be terribly unstable and unpredictable. What kind of person is it, indeed, who will defend the vital center one day and murder millions the next? It is, it seems to me, someone like Todd Andrews, a patchwork rhetorical construct who on further inspection dissolves into a set of initial discursive raw materials, and whose actions are incommensurate with anything we might piece together in terms of belief or psychological motivation. I am reminded, in this context, of those strenuous debates of the 1930s touched on in the last chapter, namely those that concerned whether or not the "new middle classes" of the period were going to follow the path of communism or fascism—in that case, too, a similar undecidability plagued the analysis.

What is emerging here, in these confusions about a middle-class group dynamic that can at the same time look radical or reactionary, or like separation and isolation, and about individuals and "beliefs" that can mutate perilously overnight, is what Sartre in the *Critique of Dialectical Reason* analyzed in terms of seriality.[33] A series is a human grouping that effectively has its principle of unity outside itself ("in the passive unity of the object"), such that, while each member of the series ignores all the others (absence or alterity functions here as a negative principle of unity), a homogeneous collective dynamic results. Sartre's initial example is the line of people waiting for a bus, an analysis that then leads him to the effects of radio broadcasts (and mass media generally), and, finally (and perhaps unsurprisingly), to the free market itself. Phenomena such as stock market panics vividly dramatize the workings of serial relations: one rushes to sell and get out, based on the fear that everyone else will do the same thing, which they in fact are doing and for the same reason, and hence, as Sartre notes, "everyone is the same as the Others in so far as he is Other than himself."[34] As Jameson explains, "in this sense seriality is a vast optical illusion, a kind of collective hallucination projected out of individual solitude onto an imaginary being thought of as 'public opinion' or simply 'they.' But public opinion does not exist, and it is rather the belief in it and the effects of such belief which 'unite' individuals in the series."[35] Seriality thus produces paradoxical anticollective collectivities, fundamentally passive groups that project an essentially statistical existence and that can then be polled as to what they believe, or what they will buy, and whose implicit response will always be "whatever you want us to."

It is evident that the middle classes as theorized by Gilbert Seldes in the 1930s, which was an attempt to delineate a group consciousness around a negative principle of unity—privatized consumerism—were already serialized entities, and much of the debate surrounding them was an attempt to give a kind of sociological density and reality to these odd, phantasmatic social "ungroupings" multiplying at the time, concurrent with growing white-collar strata and spreading notions of "the American way of life" (alternative and radical forms of consciousness were of course also burgeoning, which we saw clearly in the last chapter and which makes the 1930s so rich and contradictory).[36] Such an effort could not help but produce wildly varying interpretations, and generate unstable rhetorical configurations populated by incipient political monsters (the untrustworthy denizen of the vital center being an individualized "serial being"), creatures helping to populate that realm conventionally psychologized in terms of "paranoia." By the 1950s, this middle class meets, in the form of the new televisual apparatus, its technological embodiment, which intensifies the serial relations already active, and sends Seldes, in his pamphlet *The New Mass Media: Menace to a Free Society?* (1957), into alarmist fits about the potential mind-control powers of TV, itself a "serialized" reaction. Meanwhile, further developments since then in advertising and consumer marketing, in the absorption by the media of the political process, and in the intensity of fashion cycles, have only further solidified the basic serial texture of postmodern culture. Indeed, one is led to speculate about a possible "bonus" of collective affect associated with seriality, which despite the fact that seriality depends on an essential privatizing and disempowering dynamic, some sense or perception of group ties (even if to an abstract or statistical group) might not be generated at a certain level of serial density.

We can perhaps, finally, connect the foregoing with our earlier discussion of work and Bell's thoughts on changes in the labor process, for it is clear, as

Sartre argues, that the intensification of concerns with efficiency and of Taylorism can themselves be viewed as serializing processes, since these practices reconstitute the job outside the workers, pulling them away from reciprocal interactions and forcing their attention on external measures, thus creating the conditions for that passive unification in the object that is the basis of seriality. This gives a clearer sense of the intimate role Taylorism might play in that evaporation of class consciousness with which this chapter began, a clue as to the very process of psychic reorientation it entails. As a final speculation, then, it is interesting to consider whether Barth's own doubts about the viability of his chosen aesthetic activity (the "end of modernism") might have resonance here as well. This is not to suggest that the role of the modernist novelist has been "Taylorized." It is to consider, rather, whether Barth's narrative has been deflected toward a registration of serial culture precisely through its constitutive disconnection from an active historical progression—the "ending" that is not quite yet a beginning—analogous to the dismantling of collective potentiality represented by Taylorism. If modernism, as we argued in the last chapter, was enabled by a linkage to the multivalent guises and possibilities of revolution, then Taylorism and 1950s narrative alike register the waning, or outright repression, of that earlier situation and its (missed, but real) chances.

. . .

All of this still leaves us, finally, with Todd Andrews on board the floating opera, planning to annihilate himself and a good portion of Cambridge along with him. But this is not madness. As we have argued, Barth's text is not particularly interested in Todd's psychological makeup; rather, the peculiar exigencies of the aesthetic situation Barth found himself in led him to this discursive pattern called Todd, a pattern that reflects/participates in the growing serial realities of 1950s everyday life. The concluding sections of the book might nonetheless be viewed as analogous to the climax of *The Day of the Locust*, where a kind of disruption or "excess" also manifested itself in relation to the main character (one perhaps more specifically "psychic" in Tod Hackett's case), a disruption in both cases appearing in the midst of or in connection with a popular cultural event.

The nature of this popular cultural event in *The Floating Opera* is extremely interesting, and certain aspects of it allow us to clarify the connection between the novel and serial culture, particularly in its televisual form. The show on board the opera has vaudeville elements; however, the larger share of it is blackface minstrelsy, forms largely extinct in 1954, and even by 1937 no doubt endangered species. Thus with this initial choice, Barth is implicitly emphasizing historical passing, giving us forms of entertainment that were palpably on the way out (particularly as mounted in this curious shipboard fashion), entertainments about to be "blown up" after a fashion by the tide of history itself. But this is, as Todd asserted at the very outset of the story, not death, but almost death, and hence, as with his weak heart, we are poised on the brink of a catastrophe that never comes.

The audience, too, is threatened with elimination, a prospect Todd attempts to envision for us, but in a manner which, like his histrionic depiction of his despair, fails to engage us in the expected way:

> Calmly I regarded my companion Capt. Osborn, shouting hoarse encouragement to the *Robert E. Lee.* Calmly I thought of Harrison and Jane: of perfect breasts and thighs scorched and charred; of certain soft, sun-smelling hair crisped to ash. Calmly too I heard somewhere the squeal of an overexcited child, too young to be up so late: not impossibly Jeannine. I considered a small body, formed perhaps from my own and flawless Janes's, black, cracked, smoking. (243)

This language works to different effect than the visceral simplicity of West's violent passages (which themselves nonetheless had a kind of technological referent). The juxtaposition of "perfect" bodies with their utter destruction renders this a kind of logical exercise, and indeed tends to aestheticize any potential outrage here, a process aided by the verbs "consider" and "imagine," which in effect self-consciously turn these violent deaths into images for us, that is, derealize them and drain them of horror. Within the context of the general tone of comic detachment in the novel, such a passage rejoins that mood of "fun" we attempted to describe earlier—fun in the way that watching a tape of the space shuttle explosion can be fun: a specular rendering of violence or disaster that draws us into an indifferent fascination and whose avatar is the televised image.

Over and against this looming fate the rambunctiousness of the audience must be ranged. They do not sit back and idly watch the show; rather, they actively intervene in it, particularly when an uninspired Shakespearean recitation is thrust upon them.

> "Where's the minstrels?" someone shouted. "Bring on the minstrels!" More pennies sailed over the footlights.
> "The soliloquy from *Hamlet*," T. Wallace Whittaker whispered.
> "Go home!"
> "Take 'im away!
> "*To be or not to be: that is the question . . .*"
> "Ya-a-a-ah!"
> The audience was out of hand now. (236)

The hapless tragedian continues "undaunted" until, under a hail of pennies, he is dragged offstage by Captain Adam, the showboat's proprietor. Not only can they intervene, then; the audience can change the performance itself. This audience, like the very form of entertainment to which it corresponds, is on the way out as well, headed toward that serial recomposition in the media whose most salient trait, as Sartre argues, is the impotence the TV/radio audience members experience in the face of the "performances" they tune into: they cannot meaningfully respond to the television screen, which despite whatever remarks are cast in its direction will persist in beaming the images it chooses.[37] Nor is the frequent counsel about turning the set off an adequate rejoinder, since, as studies indicate, it is the rare household indeed where this actually occurs, eloquent testimony to that ineluctable moment of fascination Sartre alludes to, which has to do with the image as such but also significantly involves the awareness and study of one's entrapment as other in the serial unity of the TV audience. From the perspective of the networks and the media elites, meanwhile, the audience has "exploded" and vanished in a related fashion, becoming a relentlessly pursued statistical configuration of ratings and opinions generated out of serial fictionality.

This reading of the role of the showboat audience in the semantic economy of the novel also permits us at length to consider the setting of the novel, in a small Maryland city. Quite apart from this being Barth's actual hometown, within the novel this setting clearly affords a space of potential face-to-faceness, of daily reciprocal human interactions in the image of Main Street neighborliness. This has already been partly subverted through Todd's ironic debunking, and hence is itself headed for its own simulated rearticulation, the cackling and "cute" old men from the "Chorus of Oysters" chapter reappearing at last as wage-earning "greeters" at the local Wal-Mart (the store that helped eradicate the older town centers in the first place, the prescience of West's *A Cool Million* thus being demonstrated once again).

The issue of minstrelsy also requires some consideration in this context. There is an obvious pragmatic requirement here: Barth needs a show with an "explosion" to parallel/mock Todd's own planned one, something provided by the climax of the *Natchez vs. Lee* steamboat race, and which was evidently not an uncommon feature of such entertainments. Yet Todd himself takes brief time out to ponder the significance of the jokey banter of "Tambo and Bones," which is at the expense of the "educated" Mr. Interlocutor: "Tambo and Bones vindicated our ordinariness; made us secure in the face of mere book learning; their every triumph over Mr. Interlocutor was a pat on our backs. Indeed, a double pat: for were not Tambo and Bones but irresponsible Negroes?" (239). Ordinary, in other words, but not *too* ordinary. On the face of it, Todd's imagined participation in this ritual of plebeian communality might seem rather specious, since he is a Hopkins-educated lawyer. There is something of a middlebrow logic working here, with the high being cut down by the low—not, however, in the interests of that low but of an imagined middle, an ideological construct that can be projected onto a socially diverse group (Colonel Morton, for instance, the richest man in Cambridge, is in the audience).

To see what facilitates this, it is important to recall now the black residents of Cambridge, who, barred from the showboat's auditorium, must remain out on deck while the all-white audience inside enjoys what Dave Roediger calls "the first self-consciously *white* entertainers in the world."[38] The enormous popularity of minstrel shows among nineteenth-century working-class audiences was, as Roediger argues, instrumental in the eventual articulation of a self-consciously white working class, one that could imagine itself occupying a middling stratum of American society, beneath the owners but above slaves and indentured labor. White workers thus always had the ideological resources to view themselves above the truly lowest orders of society, which only eased the eventual adoption of a dominant middle-class ideology. Hence we have a nice allegory of the 1950s serial middle imaginatively revisiting one of its cultural conditions of possibility, bringing it forward in time to the very brink of its eclipse, when, with the explosion that climaxes the steamboat race, itself shadowed and structured by Todd's silent, serial explosion, the evening's performance as well as the historical existence of the form at once come to a close. This is all within the auditorium, however; outside, an African American population stands excluded, a population that will come to occupy the political center stage within a few years of *The Floating Opera*'s appearance (indeed, it will at that point assume the very mantle of opposition the white working class had by then largely abandoned). Middle-classlessness thus betrays here its connections to race, something I register at this late stage of our discussion not in any way to make up for what some readers have doubtless felt to be a palpable absence, but rather simply to mark the contours both of a middle-class form that ought never to be imagined as autonomous from other social practices and of a problematic for future research. Much the same pertains to my remarks on gender below.

In the end, then, the floating opera need not explode, preserving its status as the nonevent that changes everything and nothing. Todd's life will continue apace, much as before, although we as readers have only that empty time between 1937 and 1954 to match against this knowledge. "The concept of progress," wrote Benjamin, who, with his notion of Erlebnis, was already beginning to grasp some of the experiential dynamics of serial culture, "is to be grounded in the idea of catastrophe. That things 'just go on' *is* the catastrophe."[39] I suggest we interpret this in terms of a kind of "banalization of the event," a drawing of the new, the moment, down into the slack time of the everyday (progress and event being understood again as essentially temporal categories). If indeed television, as Doane suggests, "organizes itself around the event,"[40] with the catastrophe as the most privileged and fetishized form of event, then the paradoxical result is that such happenings are drained of their eventhood: derealized into an image and apprehended in alterity, as relating only to other people, they are drained of their temporal specificity, after a while seeming never to have happened at all. Serial culture is ordered around the sign of the permanent catastrophe, which, as epitomized by Todd's failed suicide, "never comes," issuing then in a dead time in which events no longer occur because time stands still. Already a mock explosion, the climax of the steamboat race signals the onset of Todd's epiphany: nothing has value, but it doesn't matter, nothing need change on account of this. In serial culture things will indeed go on, but a silence, a strange inertia, will be at their heart.

. . .

And so we come at last to a book, *The Old Man and the Sea*, that, unlike our other exhibits, seems actually to be about work, indeed in a rather vivid and sustained way. Yet I would like to muddy the waters at once by observing (and others have noted it) how closely the old man's labors resemble a sporting competition, and not merely because of the contest with the marlin, or his recurrent thoughts on DiMaggio. The entire construct of what, following Paul Smith, we might call the "cultural production" of Papa Hemingway— hunter, fisherman, world traveler, and so forth—mediates the isolate text, generating a level of secondary semantic signals or connotations and installing a kind of constitutive uncertainty about precisely what it is the old man is doing.[41] Indeed, work and sports maintain in Hemingway a striking and privileged relationship with one another, generated, as Jameson has argued, by the deepest formal and stylistic energies of the texts themselves:

> the experience of sentence production is the form taken in Hemingway's world by nonalienated work. Writing, now conceived as a *skill*, is then assimilated to the other skills of hunting and bullfighting, of fishing and warfare, which project a total image of man's active and all-absorbing technical participation in the outside world. . . . The Hemingway cult of machismo is just this attempt to come to terms with the great industrial [and, I would add, consumerist] transformation of America after World War I: it satisfies the Protestant work ethic at the same time that it glorifies leisure.[42]

Hemingway, then, becomes the response to Dreiser, in his articulation of an ideological program that reclaims the "feminized" world of consumption for male subjectivity.[43] An enormously successful program, no doubt, but are we still, at this late date, "around quitting time"?

Not, at first glance, with *The Old Man and the Sea* (1952), which in effect reverses the polarity of the standard Hemingway scenario: instead of sport giving off the signals of (unalienated) labor, we have work giving off signals of quite a few things, judging by the back-cover blurb, at least. There, this slim novel is at once characterized as a fable, a parable, a tragedy, and an epic—incompatible modes, one might have thought, but the novel does manage willy-nilly to hint at all of these. There are few other texts (outside socialist realism, in any case) that strive so diligently to dignify and elevate work, to invest it with a significance transcending its immediate practical context. The doggedness of the effort—which seems undertaken almost as a response to Bell's diagnosis of the disenchantment of work—leads Hemingway to some lamentable aesthetic choices, most notably the widely decried line about the man "feeling the nail go through his hands and into the wood," a moment when readers invariably tend to feel that they are having their noses rubbed in allegorical importance.[44] The question for us is whether or not the text can in fact succeed in its project of resignification, whether Hemingway can conjure forth an image of unalienated labor by focusing on work as such, rather than on some competitive and ritualized activity like the hunt or the bullfight.

I believe—unsurprisingly—that the answer here is "no," but the details of this failure should prove to be instructive. Hemingway attempts to posit the old man as a premodern subject, the inhabitant of an epic world of integral wholeness and (following the canonical Lukácsean conception) immanent meaning. Hence his talking to the fish, to his hands, to the stars—betokening a unified cosmos alive with purposeful forces, in which no hierarchy of existence obtains.[45] Coexisting in a syncretistic amalgam with the epic "consciousness" is a fitful, rather desultory Christianity (conforming to the old saw about the absence of atheists in foxholes, Santiago promises to say some Hail Marys at the Catholic shrine should he conquer the fish and arrive safely home), which, along with the aforementioned Christological motifs, lend a certain inflection to the epic materials: Odysseus was a lord of the manor, after all, whereas the figures of Christ, St. Peter, and DiMaggio's father (a fisherman himself) lead matters more toward the realm of the low-born.[46] The epic, world of maleness, traditionally, is now also a world of work.

Late in the story, after Santiago has fought off the first shark and awaits the arrival of others, his vague religious impulses emerge again as he begins musing on the subject of sin: "I have no understanding of it and I am not sure that I believe in it. Perhaps it was a sin to kill the fish. I suppose it was even though I did it to keep me alive and feed many people. But then everything is a sin" (105). Santiago senses, uneasily and uncertainly, that he has in some fashion committed offense against the marlin, though he realizes that putting it in religious terms is ultimately not terribly convincing, in that all efforts to harvest nature for the purpose of maintaining human culture then become tantamount to sin. I suspect that the reader, too, tends to dismiss Santiago's worries, and fails to see any grounds for attributing to his actions anything like sin. But I disagree: Santiago *has* "sinned" against the fish, though not in the way he is fitfully imagining. After he has killed the fish, he pauses a moment to marvel at its size: "He's over fifteen hundred pounds the way he is, he thought. Maybe much more. If he dresses out two-thirds of that at thirty cents a pound?" (97). A banal enough moment, from one perspective, yet the fall from a putative epic realm of wholeness could not be more complete. The world of exchange value, of quantitative equivalence, is the virtual antipode of the kind of immanent meaningfulness Santiago perceives in the world around him, a systematic and thorough negation of any pretense of natural or cosmic unity. The old man's language is itself an index of how forcibly he has leapt here from his previous context. The use of the American "cents," as opposed to the Cuban "centavos," in a text that is usually not reticent about employing the odd Spanish locution, lifts the old man from his place in an ordered universe and places him within the full hurricane rush of American modernity (and is a clue to the fact that *The Old Man and the Sea* is ultimately thinking about American realities rather than Cuban ones). We must leave aside the irrelevant question of whether, in the real world, we can find subjects who are at once premodern and yet deal in the world of monetary exchange. Within the semantic registers of the novel the level of unity and immanence and the level of value equivalence are strictly incompatible: the marlin cannot be at once noble, heroic, "my brother," and thirty cents a pound. This then is the real sin visited upon the fish, indeed the most crucial and lasting violence committed against it, rendering meaningless its specific place in the natural order.

Thus a certain "contamination" spreads about the end of the text, undermining the loftier allegorical levels. Or, better, it becomes a competing allegory, but now one of futility and the absurd: there is a marked Sisyphean quality to Santiago's labors, typical of Hemingway's ethic of stoic resignation and existential gritting of the teeth. "And what beat you," he asks himself, hauling home the fish's skeletal remains. " 'Nothing,' he said aloud. 'I went out too far' " (120). Nothing: the act was doomed from the outset, surrounded and consumed by nothing, the empty Camusian cosmos. The same holds true of the tourists at the end. They are very much Hemingway types, in their blithe ignorance, but also mark the revenge of alienated labor.

> "What's that?" she [the tourist] asked a waiter and pointed to the long backbone of the great fish that was now just garbage waiting to go out with the tide.
>
> "Tiburon," the waiter said. "Eshark." He was meaning to explain what had happened.
>
> "I didn't know sharks had such handsome, beautifully formed tails."
>
> "I didn't either," her male companion said. (126–27)

Is this not a stealing of the act, a bleeding away of the old man's work, his story, into anecdotal incomprehension (in rather Sartrean fashion, come to think of it)? From this perspective, the epic and salvational motifs crash against the rocks of alienation and existential gloom. The old man is defeated in multiple ways.

But the old man is not really all that down, at the end of the day. Immediately before invoking the specter of nothingness, a wave of calm overtakes him, a not unwelcome and perhaps even pleasurable sense of release: "Bed is my friend. Just bed, he thought. Bed will be a great thing. It is easy when you are beaten, he thought. I never knew how easy it was" (120). I suggest that, via the cunning of the utopian impulse, this moment of pure defeat is in reality the most hopeful (in the Blochian sense), the most positively charged in the entire story. Here, if only for an instant, we are afforded a glimpse of Morris's "epoch of rest."

To show this, it is necessary to reverse course and revisit the matter of sport and masculinity touched on at the outset. Christ, DiMaggio, Santiago: all men in pain, demonstrating in this world of men just what it means to be a man. This is formulated at one point with great clarity:

> "I'll kill [the fish] though," he said. In all his greatness and his glory."
>
> Although it is unjust, he thought. But I will show him what a man can do and what a man endures.
>
> "I told the boy I was a strange old man," he said. "Now is when I must prove it."
>
> The thousand times that he had proved it meant nothing. Now he

was proving it again. Each time was a new time and he never thought about the past when he was doing it. (66)

Like the injured DiMaggio stepping up to the plate once more, the old man must show again what he is made of. Here work and sport intertwine most intimately, the male ethos emerging as a pattern of serial endurance, without a past or a future. One can almost hear the dismissive voices of the spectators, should either DiMaggio or Santiago fail in their respective tasks: loser! what have you done for me lately? By deploying an ideal of sporting masculinity in the context of labor, Hemingway has managed to point to the ultimate sources of that ethos, and to the wellspring of its evident affective power. For what this pattern of male endurance, which must prove itself anew each time out, finally resembles is nothing so much as the conditions of wage work as such. By definition, only the labor performed that day counts for anything—what one did yesterday, or what one might do tomorrow, is of no consequence. The worker has no capital on which to rest, on which to establish himself, only a ceaseless punching of the clock. Interesting to speculate, then, if this was one of the reasons for the close interplay, during the first half of the twentieth century, between working-class culture and organized sports, particularly baseball, wherein an imaginary scene developed that transmuted a tyranny of time into the conditions of heroism— the working stiff as champion, or bum. Hemingway, by turning, late in his career, to work as such, suggests the ultimate ideological productivity of this particular masculine ethos, an ethos capable of transmuting abjection into heroism, form into content.

Hence, finally, the deeper functionality of the Homeric and Christian materials, which, aside from the surplus of meaning they seek to generate, signify continuity itself. That is, these allegorical levels—which revisit the enduring sources of Western culture—give rise to intimations of permanence, of cultural cohesion and tradition, the very opposite of the content of masculinity, which in effect has no reality beyond the actions of the here and now. Here is the intrinsic nihilism of capitalist organization, arising from a labor process that empties out the very substance of "culture" as such, and that the metaphysical categories of existentialism can little grasp.

So we are around quitting time after all, if only for a moment, when Santiago accepts his defeat and relaxes at last in his boat, a slave to the domination of lived time no longer; it is easy, indeed, to be defeated, at least on these terms. But it really is just a moment. As with Barth's reified philosophical doubts about agency, this moment in Hemingway is another index of the evident remove from Dreiser attained in the 1950s. Quitting time in *Sister Carrie* pervaded the very atmosphere of the novel, in an almost palpable way, serving as the vehicle and occasion for a range of writerly investments and perplexities. *The Old Man and the Sea*, despite the work-leisure nexus we can discern in semantic or symbolic terms, lacks this more material engagement with the problem so evident in the earlier novel, if only because in Hemingway we are in a certain sense actually working, something that, representationally speaking, was before to be avoided. Is this evidence, then, of the final eradication of work from the imagination—ironically enough, when we finally get to see it!—and the concomitant triumph of consumerism? Or rather of its utter hegemony? Of some wholly new middle-class dispensation? Time for a conclusion, where we can puzzle over some of these matters.

postscript

The Insistence of Class and

the Framing of Culture in the

American Scene

How, finally, to account for the "talismanic power" of the phrase "middle class?" As the most contradictory of the advanced industrial nations, and the one whose national specificity is so often expressed in a universalist idiom, the United States and the peculiarities of its national cultures are intensely and perhaps uniquely amenable to allegorical interpretation and investment. The lure of allegory has presented an almost irresistible temptation to generations of culturally inquisitive souls, both native born and foreign alike, all bent on capturing definitively the true meaning of the country's mythic origins and singular destiny. As a Montrealer weaned (like so many Canadians) on Bugs Bunny and *Gilligan's Island*, I became aware of many of the paradoxes of American life soon after my arrival in the United States for graduate study in the late 1980s. Chief among these, to my eyes, was the deep reluctance to discuss publicly or even acknowledge the social and political salience of class difference amid stunning disparities of wealth, the phrase "middle class" serving as a kind of overcoded substitute, a weird homeopathy that somehow invoked the word "class" while simultaneously emptying it of all conceptual content. It thus seemed to afford a nation that tries desperately to dream its way out of social class a method of acknowledging the matter and dispensing with it all at once.

I like to think, though, that I have managed something a little more concrete than the religiously inspired allegorical idealism of the "city on the hill" or "nature's nation" variety. I have sought instead to illuminate facets of what Slavoj Žižek likes to call the "national Thing" (to approach a psychoanalytic terminology I have thus far largely eschewed, for reasons of temperament fully as much as methodology), which hovers just beyond that particular concatenation of details (spaces, rituals, discourses, and so forth) that makes visible "the unique way a community *organizes its enjoyment.*"[1] In this regard, a certain discursive and structural consistency has become apparent, as the figure of the liminal in its various forms (work/leisure, motion/stasis, event/nonevent) has recurred throughout these pages, a pattern we might now try to disengage from its local interpretive contexts in order to formalize and inspect it a little more closely. In Žižek's Lacanian reckoning, the enjoyment of one's Thing is of course an ambivalent matter, since the Thing is never simply "present" unproblematically but is rather an effect of a process of serial othering (it exists and I believe in it only because others believe it exists), whereas "enjoyment" itself passes through the defile of the lack, and constitutes itself via a complex play of negativity and positivity.

The same holds true of the liminal modalities we have encountered, with their precarious and paradoxical efforts to remain suspended between states and spaces, fleetingly keeping open possible forms of both negation and affirmation of these states, an overall configuration I take to be central to the range of middle-class effects and affects, in both utopian and ideological forms. The dynamic or logic at issue here is not, it seems to me, that of the antinomy, with its implacable alternation between the opposing poles; nor does it seem to appear to conform to the dialectical model of the contradiction, which, although it shares much of the tension of the liminal, also implies or projects a temporal or historical arc, moving from origins to an imaginable future "solution" (as in the notorious moment of "synthesis" in Hegel, which is rather more complicated than its common caricatures might lead one to believe). The liminal, rather, remains suspended at a point where all options remain open, yet none can be definitively chosen or pursued, in a manner that might be described in terms of a stalled dialectic, a tempting yet ultimately frustrating state. Such a stalled dialectic is at the root of various noteworthy analyses of American culture, such as Lauren Berlant's notion of a utopian "present tense" encoded in American identity (inherited from the Puritans, in her scheme), that is, a sense of a utopian presence that is at once achieved and deferred, a configuration which works to dismantle and absorb forms of dissent.[2] The national-symbolic of "America" has for Berlant irremediably co-opted the utopian imagination as such, which leads her finally to a repudiation of all thoughts of utopia and the advocacy of locally based and denationalized identity politics. Berlant seeks a certain practice of designification: the avoidance of the symbolically charged "America" in favor of the more neutral and less ideologically totalizing "United States." In contrast, in my projected move from the mystified "middle class" to a focus on something like class as such, I would work to retain what might be called the "gambit of utopia," for I remain convinced that a socialist and universalist politics becomes untenable without it.

Observations such as Jean Baudrillard's typically extravagant (and, to some, irritating) claim that America is "utopia achieved" also figure into the present context.[3] Baudrillard's hyperbole is easy to mock, but there seems little doubt that he has hit on a certain key texture of desire and ideology in this country, whereby people are encouraged to take all national mythology as the simple, literal truth (indeed, the "theory effect" of *America* derives in part from Baudrillard's imagined effort to take every sign he encounters as literally as he thinks the "masses" do). As in Berlant, there is here an emphasis on temporal structuration, an emptying of the future as a meaningful category through a kind of pragmatic restlessness, by way of a drive to instantiate the imaginary in the immediate and a relentless will to concretization. This returns us to the thematic of time we invoked at the outset, to the notion that capitalism itself is a kind of infernal time machine, capturing and organizing lived time according to an alienating and exploitative logic. From this perspective the liminality of middle-classlessness emerges as a highly successful method of transmuting such a temporal trap into a generalized suspension, ambivalently poised just slightly above or beside the stream of time. Responses to the trauma of time under capitalism can thus take the form either of materially restructuring human time in a new way (which would be one way of characterizing the goal of socialism), or of trying to extricate oneself from capitalist time in some more ambivalent and imaginary fashion. Indeed, to recall for a moment Todd Andrews aboard the floating opera, we can discern a utopian aspect of Todd's failed suicide to which we have yet to call attention. Todd's invention of a kind of personal end of history for himself, while its ideological implications are ominous enough, does have its utopian side as well: Todd has managed to "quit time" in a fairly literal way, that is, by getting out of it altogether—an aspect of quitting time, given our previous focus on work and motion, that we have yet to appreciate sufficiently.

Perhaps the secret of the porch and the television lies here, with its serial audience and atemporal "event-images" resulting in a kind of forestalling of the future, together with a temporary resituating of the (nonetheless still present) flow of time such that it might be mediated by the individual subject rather than chiefly by the labor process. Indeed, this latter possibility has been suggested recently by Evan Watkins in his work on labor and consumer education. What television offers, to those subject to the controlled time patterns of industrial and service work alike, is "the possibility that you can tune 'in' or 'out' at will with no penalties attached. Thus, rather than some gratifying 'appropriation' of and 'identification' with what you see, the pleasure lies in your control over the duration of seeing, because this control is likely to be unavailable altogether at work, in lower-level service sector jobs especially."[4] A certain suggestion of agency is thus afforded by a medium whose other components—principally the derealization of events, not to mention the sheerly physical inertia of viewing—call agency and eventhood into question. We might return to the image of the channel-surfing TV viewer invoked in the introduction (in terms of a seductive pastoral-frontier synthesis) and recast it in these more precise terms: that is, the answer to the conundrum of the viewer's putative activity or passivity is neither one nor the other, but inescapably both, the conditions interpenetrating and simultaneously affirming and negating one another. It is this configuration that perhaps suggests TV viewing—even to Geoghegan atop the Hancock, where we began—as the most (stereo)typical middle-class site, the more privatized technological successor to the porch.

I have struggled at times to convince myself that part of the power of "middle class" lies in the very authenticity of its utopian component or drive, its insistent link to labor and class, a drive that, because it also remains constitutively tied to a pattern of stasis or inaction, cannot be articulated with any project that might further its actualization—a cutting off, again, of the perspective of the future for a certain fuzzy immediacy. One must imagine here a simultaneous conjoining of intense utopian and ideological effects and registers, which sometimes makes me think that the eccentric American socialist Leon Samson was right when he observed that "every concept of Socialism has its substitutive counter-concept in Americanism," and that, despite their stereotypically bitter opposition, they are curiously intertwined, the materialist and idealist sides of the same coin (to provide an overhasty image of the matter).[5] The great Trinidadian socialist C. L. R. James, echoing this line of thought, believed that he could perceive within the forms of American daily life and popular culture a kind of protorevolutionary impulse, an unquenchable desire for happiness that would in time express itself in radical political demands. Timothy Brennan, in his recent critical though not unsympathetic analysis of James's American period (basically the 1940s), formulates James's version of the national Thing as "an uncompromised hunger for what socialism alone could provide."[6] Brennan chastizes James for the latter's failure to appreciate the thin but diamond-hard wedge of reality that intrudes between any such radical impulses and actual political change, a wedge comprised of the massive and implacable effort that U.S. culture puts into tying all longings and their possible realizations strictly and exclusively to capitalist social forms. Hence the mythic status of the American Revolution as the "revolution to end all revolutions," all subsequent revolutions (save those that might with some ideological inventiveness be coded as repetitions of the fundamental American experience—the French, say, or the so-called "velvet revolutions" of Eastern Europe) being necessarily regarded as perverse and intrinsically totalitarian, precisely because they represent the irruption of the future into the present.

What James was most attracted to in American culture was its pragmatic, activity-oriented quality, which he saw expressed most fully in the workers' relation to the production process and which demonstrated that "the immense majority of American workers want to work and love handling the intricate scientific masses of machinery more than anything else in the world."[7] But here is the rub, since the many possible forms of such "handling" are in this period being increasingly dictated by forces and interests remote from the factory floor, the workers themselves coming to feel more and more like "cog[s] in a great machine, a piece of production as is a bolt of steel [or] a pot of paint." The fundamental issue, the great theme which in James's hands still electrifies, is once more that of control—the control, individual and collective, by people over both the conditions and the products of their labor. Work, human autonomy, and the shape of time come together in Marxism in a remarkable constellation, their dialectical interrelationship affirming, among other things, the radical openness of the future. "Labour is the living, form-giving fire," Marx wrote, in one of his more dramatic pronouncements on the subject, "it is the transitoriness of things, their temporality, as their formation by living time."[8] In this sense, the fact that humans must work to produce every aspect of their life worlds—and in so doing produce the always evolving social relations in which they are enmeshed—is at one with the fact that we live in history. Such considerations, which touch upon the outermost, perhaps ontological edges of Marxian thought, are invoked here to underscore a central, if sometimes submerged, theme of this book, namely that work as such is not to be grasped as simply a "good" in some moralistic sense (one that can easily become punitive and a mode of social discipline, as in the currently popular agenda of welfare reform and "workfare"). Work is, rather, the particular facet of necessity that attaches to the realm of "sensuous human activity," that multiform and ever expanding realm of praxis that is another of our distinguishing traits as a species; capitalism indeed enlarges some aspects of it (James's masses of technical machinery, for example), but also segments, speeds-up, routinizes, and in general pumps the life out of many of its other components. Work becomes "good" only under certain circumstances, whereas, from the other direction, the full expanse of human praxis can attain complete and "democratic" expression only if necessity in the form of work can itself be brought under democratic control. Thus I remain skeptical of analyses that call on the Left to abandon its traditional concern with labor.[9]

The question of work is thus at one with that of agency, an issue that has itself been persistent in these pages. From Dreiser's persistent bafflement over the action or inaction of his characters, to Cather's ambivalence over the process of producing; from Homer Simpson's tortured paralysis to Todd Andrews's probing of the sources of human actions: this set of concerns has in one fashion or another hovered around all of these novels. Work, as one of the paradigmatic forms or images of creative agency in bourgeois society, but debased under capitalist rationalization, lies within the political unconscious of these texts as something to be at once disavowed and embraced, affirmed and negated, and tortuously negotiated throughout. For the problematic of agency must be a matter of both individual and collective agency: our ceaseless attempts to "master history," to wrest a measure of security and control in the face of its inexorable flows and exigencies—whether as individuals or as members of groups with whom we identify—are everywhere mediated by the configuration of the mode of production as a whole, with its overarching and subversive dynamics of dispersal and fragmentation. Only a collective response to this system will finally be adequate, one that might guarantee a degree of power to everyone and hence allow "agency" in its fullest sense to come into being as if for the first time.

Agency is such a problem for middle-classlessness because what is desired, but also inscrutably feared and resisted, is a perpetual present wherein actions—and their literary concomitant of plot and narrative—can lead only into an equally ambivalent future. A contemporary summa of these concerns, and a spiritual descendant of the texts we have looked at, is surely Don DeLillo's *White Noise*, which obsessively hovers over the problem of agency and in so doing produces a key literary presentation of the middle-class imaginary for our time. "May the days be aimless. Let the seasons drift. Do not advance the action according to a plan."[10] So muses Jack Gladney, the novel's protagonist, a middle-aged academic worried about his own mortality: no plot, he reasons, then no death. But plotlessness is in its own way just as unnerving. Gladney inhabits a world of random and inexplicable occurrences, in which a stray cloud of toxic gas is no less sublimely life-threatening (but also life-affirming) than the sudden rearrangement of the shelves at the local supermarket. This is history as experienced by the purely privatized middle class, as the sum of unintended consequences produced by a mass of equally inscrutable intentions. DeLillo's achievement (in this not unlike Baudrillard) is to utterly accept this situation at face value, in a kind of mutation of Swiftian satire in which the deadpan adoption of the discourse peculiar to this realm is maintained while at the same time the secure location of a moral or critical consciousness (like Swift's) is forsaken. DeLillo's sentences embrace these characters and situations, evincing much humor and affection, while the overall effect is increasingly uncanny and disturbing.

So Jack conceives of his own "plot" to reinsert himself into the flow of events, to assert a measure of control over his own destiny. His plan is to kill his wife's secret Svengali and possible lover, the maker of a narcotizing wonder drug whose putative effect is precisely to relieve oneself of the burden of the future, through the eradication of one's fear of death. This effort, though, is clumsy and painstakingly literal, with Jack reformulating his plan over and over again in his head, like a child fumbling to form its first words with alphabetic blocks: "This was my plan. Enter unannounced, gain his confidence, wait for an unguarded moment, take out the Zumwalt, shoot him three times in the viscera for maximum slowness of agony, put the gun in his hand to suggest a lonely man's suicide, write semi-coherent things on the mirror, leave Stover's car in Treadwell's garage" (306). This stark desire to accede to narrative suggests Jack groping along the inner walls of his privatized world, searching for escape. This scene takes place near a foundry—abandoned, naturally—in the old Germantown section of Iron City (Jack himself lives in Blacksmith), places suggestive of since vanished ethnic and working-class communities, pointing to a truth that the novel does not and cannot countenance as such: that "escape" of the sort that Jack seeks is not a matter of individual will, but must involve a larger collective dynamic (the older collective glue of religion is itself subverted in the story, with the postmodern nuns at the end who simulate belief for the benefit of the multitudes).

So Jack's attempt at narrative redemption ends inconclusively and unsatisfyingly—with a bang *and* a whimper, as it were. Agency dissipates back into the round of daily life at the conclusion, and *White Noise* is subsequently overtaken by events, either prescient or sadly outdated, depending on one's perspective. Paranoid conspiracy narratives now saturate the pop-cultural landscape, wherein mysterious and disturbing events of uncertain origin and purpose threaten the American way of life. A faceless corporate-bureaucratic entity—the Agency, the Bureau, the Force—typically occupies an ambiguous narrative position, at once causally linked to the events yet involved in their solution and exposure at the same time. Contemporary cultural studies, meanwhile, often abandoning what it takes to be the clunky "productionist" model of Marxism (without necessarily grasping in full what this model signifies and entails), attempt to relocate agency in the realm of consumption and consumerism itself. Consumers now "produce" varied and potentially subversive lifestyles for themselves, refashioning the commodity world in their own image. But even Carrie Meeber understood that the most seductive component of shopping was the pleasurable suspension before a range of enticing goods, the act of buying some particular thing and taking it home always emerging as something of a baleful denouement of this process, the ability of any commodity to remain an active vessel of libidinal investment being an extremely uncertain question. More to the point, consumption can never finally take one too far from production, as Watkins notes in one of the more striking formulations of *Throwaways*. He discusses what he calls the education of taste, which centrally involves the expansion of the necessary, or that domain of goods one simply "must" have in order to be viewed as a full-fledged participant in consumer society: "More and more people more and more of the time must work more and more in order simply to keep up with this proliferation of the necessary. Educating taste is then less a matter of inducing consumption than of inducing work."[11] Cultural studies, for its part, frequently recognizes some of these problems, generally restricting the scope and subversiveness of the putative agency of consumption to a series of (properly interminable) coping strategies, thus rendering an acknowledged weakness with respect to the mode of production as a whole as a new sort of strength (the work of Michel de Certeau being central here).

I take these developments as signs and symptoms of a middle-class imaginary being stressed and stretched by fin de siècle pressures new and sundry. Chief among these is what we might (perhaps too rapidly) invoke in terms of the new and much discussed economic globalism. The main consequence of this from our present perspective is the erosion undergone in the competitive stature of the U.S. economy, resulting in a fundamentally altered relationship between capital and American labor. Throughout much of this century, the United States had managed, sometimes piecemeal, sometimes in quantum leaps, to improve its position in the world economy, attaining a state of insular near autonomy in the decades following World War II (as indicated for example by the sharply diminished volume of foreign trade during these years). This helped make capital a little more pliable in its struggles with the working class, a little more open to thoughts of the general welfare. The reduction of work time and the increased access to material goods afforded in part by this situation helped materially to support the various affects of middle-classlessness we have looked at. But all of this is now eroding, and the current ideological climate emphasizes, instead of security, scenarios of disruption, dislocation, and rapid and unpredictable change. Such disturbing forces call forth a need for appropriately postmodern "flexible subjectivities," a need promoted, as Roger Rouse acutely observes, as "the bourgeoisie has increasingly tried to inculcate in most workers the kind of subjectivity that it previously sought to foster solely among people in the reserve army."[12]

Under this new dispensation the middle-class imaginary begins producing panic images and scenarios, which betray deeper desires. So we get the recent Hollywood/media infatuation with generation-X and slackers: young, hip, underemployed college graduates (not, that is, unemployed adult workers), drifting through time without a clear purpose, a group the media felt duty-bound to moralize about but who clearly offered a utopian image of release from overwork and time constraints. Even their "hipness"—typically connoted through a dense and punning web of allusions to old TV shows and pop songs—seems a weirdly redeemed version of the working conditions of those youngish media professionals largely responsible for the sudden attention lavished on slackers in the first place: anonymous, endlessly repeated bits of pop culture refashioned into signs of individuality and style, a transition from heteronomy to autonomy devoutly to be wished by harried yuppies whose corporate workplaces squelch individual creativity (the otherwise lackluster film *Reality Bites* is instructive on all of this). The ever expanding universe of television talk shows, meanwhile, offers to media pundits concerned about the fate of civilization an image of threatened privacy, of personal lives bled dry by a voracious sensationalism. But things are exactly the reverse. If talk shows are symptomatic of anything it is of hyperprivatization, as bits of "personal" narrative (but in reality they are becoming as familiar and generic as snippets of *The Brady Bunch*) are flung out into the mediascape in an effort to conjure into being, by way of serialized fascination/revulsion, a long-vanished public sphere, or at least some mediatory space that might suggest that individual lives have a meaningful relationship to larger historical events and processes.

It is this latter we signally lack today, a situation Benjamin had begun to grasp with his notion of Erlebnis, or (non)experience, a disjunction between the time of the subject and the time of history, brought about through an absence of sufficient narrative mediation. Hence class as a category, considered in its full spectrum of cultural ramifications, as an enveloping frame for human practice and belief, stands as one way of facilitating these kinds of connections, at the level of knowledge, at least—the domain of the aesthetic, of narrative and representation, would be another, very different way (though the affinities between these two "mapping" strategies help explain at least some of the interest Marxism has historically shown in aesthetic matters). Class retains, however, an ineradicable economic dimension, which signifies first and foremost a mode of alienation, as both the products of labor and time itself are stolen away from the individual. If this unavoidable materialist aspect troubles some people, then so be it: one cannot fault the method for a fault in the matter, as Adorno once put it. Still, criticisms of the sort offered by Wai-Chee Dimock, in her elaborate contribution to the collection *Rethinking Class*, remain common today.[13] Of the many sins with which she charges Marxism, the worst is that its concept of class inevitably impoverishes lived experience when applied to actual people, that "difference" and diversity are somehow occluded or repressed. There is a certain element of truth here: even the most miserable and impoverished existence will in its specificity "go beyond" the analytic instruments called upon to explain the origin and consequence of that misery in the first place. Such specificity ought not, however, to be used simply to ratify the social situation in question.

But Dimock attempts to trump class analysis by offering workers who more or less seemed to enjoy what they were doing. Surely, for Marxism, this is inadmissible, or at best an instance of blinkered false consciousness? Her examples are mid-nineteenth-century New England millworkers, young petty bourgeois women venturing forth from the home as wage earners for the first time in an effort to support their declining families. Rather than experiencing a world principally of exploitation, these women discover, in contrast to their relatively constricted domestic and familial circumstances, a factory floor peopled by exotic strangers and teeming with the excitements and intricacies of life such as they had never before known them. Do not these stories, then, show "class" to be the blunt instrument it is and must remain? Perhaps, but only if one insists on the most reductive and mechanical reading of the theory. The bourgeoisie, as Marx famously noted, has had a historically progressive role, putting an end to all "feudal, patriarchal, idyllic" social relations (well, perhaps not *all*), throwing hitherto provincial and cloistered populations out into a dizzyingly new and "democratized" world. So there is nothing especially surprising about the fresh realms of experience encountered by these women. More seriously, what Dimock's analysis lacks (and this is true of many such critiques) is a temporal perspective, some registration of lived *durée*. Imagine, that is, fast-forwarding twenty years or so: Are any of the now no longer young women still working the looms, and are they still feeling the same exhilaration? Or have they since retreated back into a more middle-class environment? A generation later, are their children working similar factory jobs, and if so what are their experiences? Proletarianization, in other words, does not happen all at once, and the full range of its effects requires time to manifest itself in the bodies and spirits of those subjected to it. Snapshots such as Dimock provides can be historically misleading, and fail to do the theoretical work asked of them. In the end, her strenuous march through Marx, Melville, Durkheim, Althusser, Rebecca Harding Davis, and much else manages only to reinvent the feeblest individualism: please respect the precious uniqueness of individual experience.

I have attempted to provide in these chapters at least one way of registering and thinking about what might be called the "cultural presence" of social class in its specifically capitalist sense, one way of mediating between the realms of consciousness and linguistic production on one hand and the mechanisms of the labor and class processes on the other. There are doubtless other ways to do this, and much work needs to be done in this vein of left cultural and intellectual practice. Indeed, the relative poverty of descriptive and analytical resources attending the class-culture conjuncture is a large part of the oft-noted underdevelopment of class theory in Marxism. Progress on this front will require holding together in the mind what are at first glance two seemingly opposed views, both of which tend to induce a certain scandalous reaction today among left scholars and intellectuals (not to mention everyone else). The first is that class is much more than an economic category, that the range of its effects extends to the deepest layers of culture, language, and subjectivity. The second is that class is at the very same time wholly, indeed ruthlessly, economic, which, as we noted at the outset, makes it conceptually distinct from those other categories—race, gender, ethnicity—with which it is frequently grouped. As an impersonal economic mechanism, class possesses an at least semiautonomous moment with respect to ideology and conscious human intention, requiring no particular cultural motivation. That this situation sometimes makes class less immediately palpable within the boundaries of daily life and work cannot be doubted. The sole "privilege" (often derided these days) it affords politically is that it offers large groups of otherwise very different sorts of people something in common to talk about and act upon.

notes

ONE *Class, Middle Class, and the Modalities of Labor*

1 Thomas Geoghegan, *Which Side Are You On? Trying to Be for Labor When It's Flat on Its Back* (New York: Farrar, Straus, and Giroux, 1991), 123, emphasis in original.

2 Ibid. The reference here is to Francis Fukuyama's notion of an "end of history," that is, the final and irrevocable victory of liberal capitalism.

3 See Evan Watkins, *Throwaways: Work Culture and Consumer Education* (Stanford: Stanford University Press, 1993).

4 Eli Zaretsky, "American Exceptionalism and Working-Class History," *Rethinking Marxism* 3, 1 (1990): 138.

5 Benjamin DeMott, *The Imperial Middle: Why Americans Can't Think Straight about Class* (New York: William and Morrow, 1990).

6 Loren Baritz, *The Good Life: The Meaning of Success for the American Middle Class* (New York: Knopf, 1989).

7 Karl Marx, "On the Jewish Question," in *Early Writings*, ed. Tom Bottomore (New York: McGraw-Hill, 1963), 13.

8 Fredric Jameson, "Marx's Purloined Letter," *New Left Review* 209 (1995): 86–120.

9 In tracking the disjunctions among the levels of class structure, class formation, and class consciousness, I follow Nick Salvatore's formulation: "A society can witness class formation, experience at times severe class conflict, and yet rarely find even moments in its history when a consistent and coherent consciousness of those 'objective' conditions informed the public actions and expressed ideology of working people." "Response to Sean Wilentz," *International Labor and Working Class History* 26 (1984): 26.

10 See Reeve Vanneman and Lynn Weber Cannon, *The American Perception of Class* (Philadelphia: Temple University Press, 1987), in which the authors contend that "the failure of working-class protest is not equivalent to the failure of working-class consciousness" (15). There is certainly a good measure of truth in this, and their own emphasis on the sheer power of American capital, its remarkable dominance of the state apparatus, is a necessary corrective to those analyses that invoke ideology alone, or the surfeit of commodities (American workers bought off, e.g.). But they tend finally to discount the very notion of ideological domination, seeing this as a species of "blaming the victim." Ideology, however, is not like a drug, to which the weak-willed succumb; rather, it is a material force in its own right, one which, moreover, comes in many forms (forms from which intellectuals—and not just workers—are scarcely exempt). I also feel that Vanneman and Cannon's methodology (a form of sociological survey) restricts the matter of class too narrowly to the (certainly crucial) occupational level. People might grasp some jobs as inherently more working-class, others as more middle-class (and in terms of such factors as control and autonomy, not just income alone), but class as I understand it runs a circuit among economic, social, and cultural levels: a man who places himself in the working class occupationally might well see himself as middle-class in a variety of other ways (and experience middle-classlessness as I describe it here).

11 F. Scott Fitzgerald, *The Great Gatsby* (New York: Scribner's, 1953), 57.

12 On this, see the remarks in the opening methodological essay of Franco Moretti's *Signs Taken for Wonders*, rev. ed., trans. Susan Fischer et al. (London: Verso, 1988), where Moretti invokes the "simplifying" power of literature, which allows us to grasp sociohistorical patterns in a purer form.

13 For a discussion of capitalist dynamics in these terms, see Harry Cleaver, *Reading Capital Politically* (Austin: University of Texas Press, 1980). For reflections on alienated labor as the "ultimate category" of this mode of production and of Marxian analysis, see Fredric Jameson, "Marxism and Historicism," in *The Ideologies of Theory*, vol. 2, *Syntax of History* (Minneapolis: University of Minnesota Press, 1988), 148–77.

14 E. P. Thompson, "Time, Work-Discipline, and Industrial Capitalism," *Past and Present* 38 (1967): 56–97.

15 Karl Marx, *Capital*, vol. 1, trans. Ben Fowkes (New York: Vintage, 1977), 375. For an excellent, technical, but lucid exposition of the centrality of time for Marx's basic method, see Moishe Postone, *Time, Labor, and Social Domination: A Reinterpretation of Marx's Critical Theory* (Cambridge: Cambridge University Press, 1993).

16 Juliet Schor, *The Overworked American: The Unexpected Decline of Leisure in America* (New York: Basic Books, 1991). Many academics are beginning to feel this dynamic acutely, as increasing teaching loads and class sizes erode what had been one of the most attractive features of the profession, namely an autonomy of work practices that afforded first and foremost a certain amount of free time for individual scholarly pursuits. It is worth noting, also, that the upward pressure on working time can manifest itself in various ways. A recent news report out of Oregon, for example, described one county's efforts to attract a manufacturing plant by locally suspending (with the good wishes of the state legislature) state labor laws regarding overtime pay; in effect, work that would normally have counted as time-and-a-half or double-time was reconverted into the regular pay scale, leaving workers faced with the prospect of working more hours in order to maintain their standard of living.

17 For a defense of Marx's prediction concerning the tendential polarization of classes under capitalism, see Immanuel Wallerstein, "Marx and History: Fruitful and Unfruitful Emphases," in *Race, Nation, Class: Ambiguous Identities*, by Etienne Balibar and Immanuel Wallerstein (London: Verso, 1991), 125–34.

18 Andre Gorz, *Paths to Paradise: On the Liberation from Work,* trans. Malcolm Imrie (London: Pluto Press, 1985), 103.

19 "Art is an anticipation of how work should be employed under a highly productive regime." Georges Sorel, *Réfléctions sur la violence* (Paris, 1950), 53, quoted in Fredric Jameson, *Marxism and Form: Twentieth-Century Dialectical Theories of Literature* (Princeton: Princeton University Press, 1971), 145.

20 See Watkins, *Throwaways*, for an attempt to address this problematic. Marx's own description of the complex interlinkage among these moments of the economic circuit can be found in his preface to *Grundrisse*.

21 David Montgomery, *The Fall of the House of Labor* (Cambridge: Cambridge University Press, 1987), 279.

22 Raymond Williams, *Television: Technology and Cultural Form* (New York: Schocken, 1974).

23 Michael Denning, " 'The Special American Conditions': Marxism and American Studies," *American Quarterly* 38, 3 (1986): 356–80.

24 Racial and gender interpellation involves a similar fixing. However, some forms of identity politics struggle with the burden of having to retain the identities in question, even if this is understood as entailing some form of transformation.

25 The observations of John Dos Passos are apposite here: "People are formed by their trades and occupations much more than by their opinions. The fact that a man is a shoesalesman or a butcher is in every respect more important than that he's a republican or a theosophist." Quoted in Michael Denning, *The Cultural Front: The Laboring of American Culture in the Twentieth Century* (London: Verso, 1996), 178.

One might well wonder if such patterns of determination still obtain today, given the much discussed fluidity of the labor market—the increasing use of "temp" labor, the notion that people can expect to change jobs five or more times over the course of their working lives, and so forth. I believe such patterns are overstated, however: one will tend to stay in sales, for example, even if the place of work changes. More to the point, what tends to generate the sense these days of an increasing disarticulation between work and identity is the strong focus of the media and entertainment industries on youth culture (where labor is by and large bracketed, a meaningless activity between periods of "fun") and, if work is in fact the subject, the middle and upper corporate levels (where "self-fashioning" is typically foregrounded more strongly). The focus on youth, moreover, affords the representation of people (frequently well-off and college-educated) who have yet to settle down into anything like a steady job, let alone a "career."

26 Karl Marx, *The German Ideology*, in *The Marx-Engels Reader*, ed. Robert Tucker (New York: Norton, 1978), 160.

27 In the Marxian canon, Adorno comes most readily to mind with respect to the critique of identity. In Adorno, this critique is conducted at an essentially philosophical level (chiefly in terms of how exchange value casts a pall on our conceptual systems), but the critique has social and political guises as well, in the effort to show how our social relations screen off and repress the manifold heterogeneity of the real. In Marx, this suppressed realm of difference is best grasped through use value. For the existentialist expression of this theme, contemporaneous with Marx's early writings, I recall Kierkegaard's great line: "We literally do not want to be what we are!"

28 Lee Edelman, "The Future Is Kid Stuff: Queer Theory, Disidentification, and the Death Drive," *Narrative* 6, 1 (1998): 18–30.

29 Etienne Balibar, "From Class Struggle to Classless Struggle?" in *Race, Nation, Class*, by Balibar and Wallerstein, 153–84.

30 Peter Hitchcock, *Oscillate Wildly: Space, Body, and Spirit of Millennial Materialism* (Minneapolis: University of Minnesota Press, 1999), 150, emphasis in original. See also Jameson's discussion of these matters, on which I draw here, in *Marxism and Form*, 297.

TWO *The Burden of Toil:* Sister Carrie *as Urban Pastoral*

1 Theodore Dreiser, *Sister Carrie* (New York: Signet, 1961), 7. All further references are cited in the text.

2 Philip Fisher, *Hard Facts: Setting and Form in the American Novel* (New York: Oxford University Press, 1987), 129.

3 See Mike Davis, *Prisoners of the American Dream* (London: Verso, 1986), ch. 1, and Richard Slotkin, *The Fatal Environment: The Myth of the Frontier in the Age of Industrialization, 1800–1890* (New York: Atheneum, 1985), 33–47.

4 William Cronon, *Nature's Metropolis: Chicago and the Great West* (New York: Norton, 1991).

5 Hamlin Garland, *Rose of Dutcher's Cooley*, quoted in ibid., 13.

6 I allude, of course, to the title of Leo Marx's classic study of the pastoral form in

America, *The Machine in the Garden: Technology and the Pastoral Ideal in America* (New York: Oxford University Press, 1964). By "garden in the machine," I have in mind later attempts to imagine a naturalized space of pastoral disengagement within the context of a fuller industrial and technological order (an effort undertaken, as we shall see, by certain features of the Chicago fair of 1893).

7 Indeed, Dreiser later invoked a related idiom in his account of his recovery from depression, *An Amateur Laborer* (ed. Richard Dowell [Philadelphia: University of Pennsylvania Press, 1983]), only in a putatively nonfictional mode, as if such language indicated a marked feature of his own personality:

> I had never fancied that being what I was, an excitable and high-flown sentimentalist, I could be happy in the long-contented sense of the word; but as for bliss, that ecstasy that seizes one at the sight of a beautiful landscape, that flows in with the possibility (fancied) of peace, that rises like bubbles to the brain when the night falls in beauty . . . when love and life and pleasure crowd as nascent possibilities upon the brain—I have had that all my days. (102)

This text, from 1903, offers remarkable intertextual connections with *Sister Carrie*, not least because Dreiser presents himself as living, three years after the novel first appeared, that downward spiral of depression and poverty embodied in the fictional Hurstwood. Many of the same motifs and turns of phrase—of feeling oneself an outsider, locked out of "Life," the gradual extinction of the will—return in the later text, prompting questions about a possible incomplete shift of authorial registers, the novelistic discourse somehow shaping the later (never completed) manuscript.

8 See Theodor Adorno, *Minima Moralia*, trans. E. F. N. Jephcott (London: Verso, 1978), 157. My sense of the utopian accents in these passages in general owes much to Adorno, whose own language was occasionally marked by related yearnings: "No differently will the world one day appear, almost unchanged, in its constant feast-day light, when it stands no longer under the law of labour, and when for the home-comers duty has the lightness of holiday play" (*Minima Moralia*, 112).

9 Peter Bürger, *Theory of the Avant-Garde*, trans. Michael Shaw (Minneapolis: University of Minnesota Press, 1984). The fate of this avant-garde strategy of cultural revolution was, Bürger notes, tied to the wider fate of the failed western European socio-political revolutions of the 1910s and 1920s. For more on the dialectic of utopia and ideology in Kant's aesthetic, see Terry Eagleton, *The Ideology of the Aesthetic* (Oxford: Blackwell, 1990).

10 Cronon, *Nature's Metropolis*, 347. On suburbanization more generally, see Robert Fishman, *Bourgeois Utopias: The Rise and Fall of Suburbia* (New York: Basic Books, 1987).

11 Cronon, *Nature's Metropolis*, 349.

12 L. Marx, *Machine in the Garden*, 129–30. For Marx's later reflections on this theme, see his "Pastoralism in America," in *Ideology and Classic American Literature*, ed. Sacvan Bercovitch and Myra Jehlen (Cambridge: Cambridge University Press, 1986), 36–69.

13 William Empson, *Some Versions of Pastoral* (New York: New Directions, 1974), 11.

14 Ibid., 18.

15 I am drawing here on William Appleman Williams, *The Contours of American History* (New York: Norton, 1961). In Williams's narrative, the former, more conservative (that is, authentically tory) values underwrote a concern with the public good or "common weal," which might have fostered in time (as for example in Canada) a political culture more receptive to social democratic initiatives.

16 Richard Lehan, "*Sister Carrie*: The City, the Self, and the Modes of Narrative Discourse," in *New Essays on Sister Carrie*, ed. Donald Pizer (Cambridge: Cambridge University Press, 1991), 79.

17 Theodore Dreiser, *Newspaper Days* (New York, 1965), quoted in Guy Szuberla, "Dreiser at the World's Fair: The City without Limits," *Modern Fiction Studies* 17 (1977): 369–79.

18 For recent treatments of the fair, see Alan Trachtenberg, *The Incorporation of America: Culture and Society in the Gilded Age* (New York: Hill and Wang, 1982), ch. 7, and Robert W. Rydell, *All the World's a Fair* (Chicago: University of Chicago Press, 1984), ch. 2. Rydell focuses on the sprawling Midway (the other chief component of the exposition), whose many exhibits were marked by a notable efflorescence of crude racial and imperial ideologies.

19 Dreiser, in the St. Louis *Republic*, 23 July 1893, quoted in Szuberla, "Dreiser at the World's Fair," 373.

20 Such work would include Michael Davitt Bell, *The Problem of American Realism* (Chicago: University of Chicago Press, 1993), and Alan Trachtenberg, "Who Narrates? Dreiser's Presence in *Sister Carrie*," in *New Essays*, ed. Pizer, 87–122.

21 Cronon, *Nature's Metropolis*, 349.

22 Fisher, *Hard Facts*, 154.

23 Michael Rogin, "Nature as Politics and Nature as Romance in America," in *Ronald Reagan, the Movie, and Other Episodes in Political Demonology* (Berkeley: University of California Press, 1987), 169–89.

24 Sigfried Giedion, *Space, Time, and Architecture* (Cambridge: Harvard University Press, 1954).

25 As Althusser remarks, "the distinction between the public and the private is a distinction internal to bourgeois law. . . . The domain of the State escapes it because the latter is 'above the law': the State, which is the State *of* the ruling class . . . is the precondition for any distinction between public and private." *Lenin and Philosophy and Other Essays*, trans. Ben Brewster (New York: Monthly Review, 1971), 144.

26 Compare here the remark of Leon Samson, a socialist and student of American exceptionalism who devised an elaborate account of Americanism as a kind of substitute socialism: "The emancipation of labour—is in America the emancipation of the American from labour." *The American Mind: A Study in Socio-Analysis* (New York: Jonathan Cape and Harrison Smith, 1932), 54.

27 In this context, I am reminded of the observation Adorno and Horkheimer made in the *Dialectic of Enlightenment* (120–67) with respect to the increasingly industrial

character of leisure and mass cultural pursuits in the twentieth century. Leisure was coming to look more like work, something that, far from harming the attractiveness of this sphere, would seem (from our present perspective) rather to heighten its capacity for stimulating utopian impulses.

28 Martha Banta, *Taylored Lives: Narrative Productions in the Age of Taylor, Veblen, and Ford* (Chicago: University of Chicago Press, 1993), 188.

29 I am grateful to Susan Hegeman for this point.

30 Amy Kaplan, *The Social Construction of American Realism* (Chicago: University of Chicago Press, 1988), 155.

31 Ibid., 149.

32 Fisher, *Hard Facts*, 157.

33 Kaplan, *Social Construction*, 156.

34 Trachtenberg, "Who Narrates?" 104.

35 Christopher Wilson, "The Rhetoric of Consumption: Mass-Market Magazines and the Demise of the Gentle Reader, 1880–1920," in *The Culture of Consumption*, ed. Richard W. Fox and Jackson Lears (New York: Pantheon, 1983), 39–64.

36 Margaret Morse, "An Ontology of Everyday Distraction: The Freeway, the Mall, and Television," in *Logics of Television*, ed. Patricia Mellencamp (Bloomington: Indiana University Press, 1990), 193–221.

37 A good account of Dreiser's work with *Ev'ry Month* can be found in Ellen Moers, *The Two Dreisers* (New York: Viking, 1969), 32–43. See also Kaplan, *Social Construction*, 117–25.

38 See Georg Simmel, "The Metropolis and Mental Life," in *The Sociology of Georg Simmel*, ed. Kurt Wolff (Glencoe, Ill.: Free Press, 1950), 405–20.

39 I am drawing here on Franco Moretti's discussion of that seminal daydreamer and *flâneur*, Leopold Bloom. See "The Long Goodbye: *Ulysses* and the End of Liberal Capitalism," in *Signs Taken for Wonders*, rev. ed., trans. Susan Fischer et al. (London: Verso, 1988), 182–208.

40 Gerard Genette, *Figures of Literary Discourse* (New York: Columbia University Press, 1982), 138–39.

41 Fredric Jameson, *The Political Unconscious: Narrative as a Socially Symbolic Act* (Ithaca: Cornell University Press, 1981), 104.

42 M. D. Bell, *Problem of American Realism*, 159.

43 Mark Seltzer, *Bodies and Machines* (New York: Routledge, 1992), 17–20 and *passim*. The same phrase might well be applied to *An American Tragedy*, where the murder scene and the trial dramatize at length the identical concern.

44 In an extension of this line of thought, John O'Neill argues that "we need to think of the *work of consumption* in order to begin to understand what is required of us in the collection, display, and disposal of commodities that service the collective representation of a scientific and technical society." *Five Bodies: The Human Shape of Modern Society* (Ithaca: Cornell University Press, 1985), 102 (emphasis in original). From our present perspective, and in line with Horkheimer and Adorno on the industrializa-

tion of leisure, it emerges that consumption is capable of bearing intense libidinal and utopian investment fully as much from its likeness to work as from its difference.

45 See Walter Benn Michaels, *The Gold Standard and the Logic of Naturalism* (Berkeley: University of California Press, 1987), 29–58. Michaels would seem to argue that *Sister Carrie* offers nothing in the way of a critique of capitalist logic—indeed, that it fairly celebrates this.

46 For this compelling historical argument, see James Livingston, *Pragmatism and the Political Economy of Cultural Revolution, 1850–1940* (Chapel Hill: University of North Carolina Press, 1994). Livingston's subsequent argument about the decreasing salience of class in America strikes me as more dubious, however, venturing in its own way onto an exceptionalist terrain.

47 Lori Merish, " 'The Hand of Refined Taste' in the Frontier Landscape: Caroline Kirkland's *A New Home, Who'll Follow?* and the Feminization of American Consumerism," *American Quarterly* 45, 4 (1993): 485–523. This is not to deny the striking religious and gender inflections, discussed by Merish, of this *mission civilisatrice* in the American context.

   I recall here the scene in Anouilh's *Beckett*, where Beckett suggests the adoption of the fork—a new utensil in twelfth-century Europe—to a skeptical King Henry II ("All the royals on the Continent are using it," Beckett says in effect). Henry, not about to part with his barbarian ways so readily, first brandishes the fork as a weapon at a dinner table of rowdy noblemen, before displaying his newfound civility by spearing a piece of meat.

48 Neil Harris, *Cultural Excursions: Marketing Appetites and Cultural Tastes in Modern America* (Chicago: University of Chicago Press, 1990), 177.

49 See Fredric Jameson, "Conversations on the New World Order," in *After the Fall: The Failure of Communism and the Future of Socialism*, ed. Robin Blackburn (London: Verso, 1991), 255–68.

50 See Donald Pizer, *The Novels of Theodore Dreiser* (Minneapolis: University of Minnesota Press, 1976), 77–78.

51 Moers, *Two Dreisers*, 102.

52 At the end of chapter 24, Hurstwood is also locked out—this time out of his house, by his estranged wife, thus preventing him from taking the actions he had planned, individual agency evaporating once more.

53 See Georg Lukács, *History and Class Consciousness: Studies in Marxist Dialectics*, trans. Rodney Livingstone (Cambridge: MIT Press, 1971).

54 The classic account of Taylorism remains that of Harry Braverman, *Labor and Monopoly Capital: The Degradation of Work in the Twentieth Century* (New York: Monthly Review, 1974). I have also benefited from the discussions of Taylorism found in Alfred Sohn-Rethel, *Intellectual and Manual Labour: A Critique of Epistemology*, trans. Martin Sohn-Rethel (Atlantic Highlands, N.J.: Humanities Press, 1978); Michael Burawoy, *The Politics of Production* (London: Verso, 1985); and David Montgomery, *The Fall of the House of Labor* (Cambridge: Cambridge University Press, 1987).

55 Stanley Aronowitz, "Marx, Braverman, and the Logic of Capital," in *The Politics of Identity: Class, Culture, and Social Movements* (New York: Routledge, 1992), 76–124.

56 Ibid., 90.

57 Etienne Balibar, preface to *Race, Nation, Class: Ambiguous Identities*, by Etienne Balibar and Immanuel Wallerstein (London: Verso, 1991), 4.

58 Antonio Gramsci, "Americanism and Fordism," in *Selections from the Prison Notebooks*, ed. and trans. Quentin Hoare and G. Nowell Smith (New York: International Publishers, 1971), 277–320. Gramsci's optimism in this matter should be balanced against the views of others, such as Sohn-Rethel and Sartre, who argue variously that the conditions of work employ the worker, not the other way around, and that these conditions essentially inform the content of any daydream they might occasion. In general, it is probably best to remain aware of both the enabling and disabling, or utopian and ideological, aspects generated by the historical innovations precipitated through capitalist modernization.

59 Similar problems inform Walter Benn Michaels's interesting essay "An American Tragedy, or The Promise of American Life," *Representations* 25 (1989): 71–98, where Michaels mistakenly suggests that the application of the external time/motion standard to discrete labor processes represents a "bypassing of individual judgment," when it is far more crucially a dismantling of collective organization. This business of the "standard," and the subsequent standardized mass culture generated by it, fascinates both Michaels and Seltzer, largely because it inspires the insistent new historicist thematics of personhood/personation (that is, the seeming paradox of people developing a sense of self by embracing standardized culture), a theme susceptible to mystification unless the energies, at once abstract and collective, of such processes of modernization are duly registered.

60 The political and cultural diversity of the pre–World War I period (roughly 1880 through 1917) was intense. Works I have found to convey an especially rich sense of this diversity include Herbert Gutman, *Work, Culture, and Society in Industrializing America* (New York: Random House, 1976); Lawrence Goodwyn, *Democratic Promise: The Populist Moment in America* (New York: Oxford University Press, 1976); Olivier Zunz, *The Changing Face of Inequality* (Chicago: University of Chicago Press, 1982); Roy Rosenzweig, *Eight Hours for What We Will: Workers and Leisure in an Industrial City, 1870–1920* (Cambridge: Cambridge University Press, 1983).

61 See Gilles Deleuze and Félix Guattari, *Anti-Oedipus: Capitalism and Schizophrenia*, trans. Robert Hurley et al. (Minneapolis: University of Minnesota Press, 1984). The authors use these terms to designate a process whereby capital functionally dismantles and rearticulates older forms and patterns, thus generating a certain freedom (a "decoded flow") that it at once attempts to integrate (with varying degrees of success) into its own logic.

62 Morse, "Ontology," 204.

63 On class tourism, see June Howard, *Form and History in American Literary Naturalism* (Chapel Hill: University of North Carolina Press, 1985), 99–101, 152–56; Alan

Trachtenberg, "Experiments in Another Country: Stephen Crane's City Sketches," in *American Realism: New Essays*, ed. Eric Sundquist (Baltimore: Johns Hopkins University Press, 1982), 138–54; and Kaplan, *Social Construction*, 44–46.

64 On the structure of tourism, see Dean MacCannell, *The Tourist* (New York: Schocken, 1976). It seems to me, in recalling Carrie's wanderings in downtown Chicago and New York, that MacCannell's analysis of tourism might well be deployed more fully in reading the novel.

65 "If the fundamental premise of any Marxian social psychology lies in the well-nigh ontological attraction and force of gravity of the achieved collective as such, then the envy and nostalgia of elites for the realer people of the underclasses is at once given." Fredric Jameson, *Postmodernism, or, The Cultural Logic of Late Capitalism* (Durham: Duke University Press, 1991), 342.

66 Stephen Crane, "An Experiment in Misery," in *Stephen Crane: Stories and Tales*, ed. R. W. Stallman (New York: Vintage, 1961), 38.

67 I am drawing on Kaplan's fine discussion of these materials.

THREE *Willa Cather and the Ambivalence of Hierarchy*

1 Willa Cather, *The Professor's House* (New York: Vintage, 1973), 172. Further references are cited in the text.

2 See Steven J. Ross, *Working-Class Hollywood: Silent Film and the Shaping of Class in America* (Princeton: Princeton University Press, 1998); Roy Rosenzweig, *Eight Hours for What We Will: Workers and Leisure in an Industrial City, 1870–1920* (Cambridge: Cambridge University Press, 1983).

3 For some of Cather's comments on movies and her audience, see the *New York Times* and *Bookman* interviews in L. Brent Bohlke, ed., *Willa Cather in Person: Interviews, Speeches, and Letters* (Lincoln: University of Nebraska Press, 1986). Jo Ann Middleton discusses these issues in *Willa Cather's Modernism* (Rutherford, N.J.; Fairleigh Dickinson University Press, 1990).

4 Deborah Carlin, *Cather, Canon, and the Politics of Reading* (Amherst: University of Massachusetts Press, 1992), 170.

5 Frederick Jackson Turner, quoted in Henry Nash Smith, *Virgin Land: The American West as Symbol and Myth* (Cambridge: Harvard University Press, 1960), 297.

6 Willa Cather, *A Lost Lady* (New York: Vintage: 1972), 9–10. Further references are cited in the text.

7 Willa Cather, *My Ántonia* (Boston: Houghton Mifflin, n.d.), 76.

8 For this position, see Merrill Maguire Skaggs, *After the World Broke in Two: The Later Novels of Willa Cather* (Charlottesville: University Press of Virginia, 1990), 24–62.

9 Nina Schwartz, "History and the Invention of Innocence in *A Lost Lady*," *Arizona Quarterly* 46, 2 (1990): 33–53.

10 Sharon O'Brien, "Becoming Noncanonical: The Case against Willa Cather," *American Quarterly* 40, 1 (1988): 110–26.

11 This overview also provides us with a possible angle on a very different, if nonetheless related, topic, namely the influence of *A Lost Lady* on Fitzgerald's writing of *The Great Gatsby* (an influence Fitzgerald noted, but did not spell out in detail). *A Lost Lady* awakened Fitzgerald to a certain problematic of social representation, particularly the use of affective dynamics to chart shifting class textures. I have written on this at greater length in my "*The Great Gatsby* and the Social Poetics of Ressentiment: Fitzgerald Reads Cather" (forthcoming in *Modern Fiction Studies*).

12 Marilyn R. Chandler, *Dwelling in the Text: Houses in American Fiction* (Berkeley: University of California Press, 1991), 202–3.

13 Fritz Oehlschlaeger, "*Indisponibilité* and the Anxiety of Authorship in *The Professor's House*," *American Literature* 62, 1 (1990): 84.

14 I do not accede to the common argument (made by both Chandler and Skaggs, for example) that equates the professor with the figure of the artist. When St. Peter lectures his students (67–69) on the identity of art and religion as communal binding agents, it seems to me that his own isolation and religious skepticism place him at a certain remove from these spheres.

15 Walter Benn Michaels has drawn attention to a general concern in American fiction of the 1920s with "keeping the family intact by saving sisters from marriage to—or, at least intercourse with—strangers." Michaels goes on to link this concern with debates over the nature of American citizenship and the construction of cultural identity. See "The Vanishing American," *American Literary History* 2, 2 (1990): 220–41.

16 Among these studies is an immersion in the *Aeneid*, the epic of the founding of imperial Rome. Tom's newly attained disinterested humanism, not unlike the professor's with respect to his series on the Spanish "adventurers" (leaders of a murderous colonial juggernaut), is thus shadowed by a history of plunder and exploitation: hence another ironic parable in the novel is the transformation by spellbound intellectuals of political and economic machinations into benign cultural "designs."

17 See Erik Olin Wright, *Classes* (London: Verso, 1985).

18 On this history, and on professionalization among cultural intellectuals more generally, see Bruce Robbins, *Secular Vocations: Intellectuals, Professionalism, Culture* (London: Verso, 1993).

19 Alexander Inglis's *Principles of Secondary Education*, one of the key texts in the development of middle-class educational discourse, appeared in 1918. For a nuanced Gramscian reading of this work, which deals more generally with educational ideology as well, see Evan Watkins, *Work Time: English Departments and the Circulation of Cultural Value* (Stanford: Stanford University Press, 1989).

20 I stress this because I am cognizant of the 1920s period fascination with the southwestern natives as artisanal producers of various sorts (i.e., as anything but proletarian). I suggest merely that, once drawn within the frame of the story, the natives, whatever their real-life characteristics, become imagined characters themselves and hence as multivalent as Tom Outland himself.

21 Thomas Strychacz has identified other, similar moments and patterns (Tom's "rever-

ence" for the Blue Mesa is at a certain level indistinguishable from the Marselluses acquisitiveness; the professor's modest beach house is symbolically allied to the opulent estate of Outland). See "The Ambiguities of Escape in Willa Cather's *The Professor's House*," *Studies in American Fiction* 15 (1987): 49–61.

22 Eve Kosofsky Sedgwick, "Across Gender, across Sexuality: Willa Cather and Others," *South Atlantic Quarterly* 88, 1 (1989): 68.

23 Michaels, "Vanishing American," 234.

24 Key texts in the debate include those of Sharon O'Brien, " 'The Thing Not Named': Willa Cather as a Lesbian Writer," *Signs* 9 (1984): 571–93, and *Willa Cather: The Emerging Voice* (New York: Oxford University Press, 1987); and Sandra Gilbert and Susan Gubar, *No Man's Land*, vol. 2, *Sexchanges* (New Haven: Yale University Press, 1989).

25 Putting things this way—suspended, as it were, between process and product—suggests an interesting parallel with the argument of Walter Benn Michaels, cited above. For Michaels, the invention of cultural pluralism in the 1920s (as exemplified in novels like *The Professor's House* and Zane Grey's *The Vanishing American*) involves setting in place a logic that suspends the issue of cultural identity between nature and history: between an inherited identity and one acquired through learning. Both poles remain active. Although I would hesitate to specify the precise nature of this parallel, it is worth observing that both open up a certain problematic of reification, that is, the whole business of getting from process to product, from the flux of production to the finished item, a concern Jameson has argued marks much of the writing from the modernist period. Michaels has more recently produced the full-length version of his argument in *Our America: Nativism, Modernism, and Pluralism* (Durham: Duke University Press, 1995).

26 Another 1925 novel that might be seen as refusing the notion of a contradictory class location is Dreiser's *An American Tragedy*, where Clyde Griffiths, at once working-class and bourgeois, fails to occupy successfully a niche in the Lycurgus social structure.

27 Christopher Benfey, " 'The Other Side of the Rug': Cather's Narrative Underpinnings," *American Literary History* 6, 3 (1994): 140–54.

28 Frank Lentricchia, "The Resentments of Robert Frost," *American Literature* 62, 2 (1990): 175–200.

29 In general, she achieved this by forbidding her work to be anthologized and by preventing her publishers—Houghton Mifflin and later Knopf—from issuing cheap editions, keeping the texts too expensive for widespread educational distribution.

30 See Joan Shelley Rubin, *The Making of Middlebrow Culture* (Chapel Hill: University of North Carolina Press, 1992); Janice Radway, *A Feeling for Books: The Book-of-the-Month Club, Literary Taste, and Middle-Class Desire* (Chapel Hill: University of North Carolina Press, 1997).

31 Van Wyck Brooks, " 'Highbrow' and 'Lowbrow,' " in *Critics of Culture: Literature and Society in the Early Twentieth Century*, ed. Alan Trachtenberg (New York: Wiley and Sons, 1976), 45.

32 A nice irony, then, that Tom is schooled precisely by such jesuitical types.

33 For a discussion of the foundation, see Carlin, *Cather, Canon*, 3–6.

34 See Skaggs, *After the World Broke in Two*, and Susan Rosowski, *The Voyage Perilous: Willa Cather's Romanticism* (Lincoln: University of Nebraska Press, 1986).

35 David Stineback, "No Stone Unturned: Popular Versus Professional Evaluations of Willa Cather," *Prospects* 25 (1982): 167–76.

36 John Guillory, *Cultural Capital: The Problem of Literary Canon Formation* (Chicago: University of Chicago Press, 1993).

37 Radway, *A Feeling for Books*.

FOUR *New Frontiers in Hollywood: Mobility and Desire in* The Day of the Locust

1 This is the epigraph West originally had intended to head *The Day of the Locust*. He deleted it in galley proof.

2 Nathanael West, *Miss Lonelyhearts and The Day of the Locust* (New York: New Directions, 1962), 59. Further references are cited in the text.

3 See Otto Friedrich, *City of Nets: A Chronicle of Hollywood in the 1940s* (New York: Random House, 1986).

4 See Lewis Corey, *The Crisis of the Middle Class* (New York: Covici, Friede, 1935), especially chs. 6, 7, 10. "Lewis Corey" was the pseudonym of the Italian American Luigi Fraina. Fraina first came to prominence after World War I, emerging as one of the most important theorists of Leninism in America. His fifteen minutes of Hollywood fame came in 1980, when Paul Sorvino portrayed him in Warren Beatty's *Reds*.

5 R. A. Lawson, *The Failure of Independent Liberalism, 1930–1941* (New York: Putnam, 1971).

6 Paul Buhle, *Marxism in the United States* (London: Verso, 1991), ch. 5.

7 Alfred Bingham, *Insurgent America: Revolt of the Middle Classes* (New York: Harper Brothers, 1935), 62, emphasis in original. Further references are cited in the text.

8 On Technocracy, see William E. Akin, *Technocracy and the American Dream: The Technocrat Movement, 1900–1941* (Berkeley: University of California Press, 1977), and Howard P. Segal, *Technological Utopianism in American Culture* (Chicago: University of Chicago Press, 1985).

9 The key documents of the recent debate on this issue are collected in Pat Walker, ed., *Between Labor and Capital* (Boston: South End Press, 1979).

10 See Lawrence W. Levine, "American Culture and the Great Depression," *Yale Review* 62, 4 (1985): 196–223; Warren Susman, "The Culture of the Thirties," *Culture as History: The Transformation of American Society in the Twentieth Century* (New York: Pantheon, 1984), 150–183.

11 The continued lack of reflection by the Left on the dimension of cultural revolution is evident in some recent attempts to propound a model of "market socialism" (John Roemer and Robin Blackburn come to mind). The putative denizens of their hypothetical planned market economies bear a strong resemblance to the inhabitants of present-day bourgeois society.

12   Perry Anderson, "Modernity and Revolution," in *Marxism and the Interpretation of Culture*, ed. Carry Nelson and Larry Grossberg (Urbana: University of Illinois Press, 1988), 325.

13   Ibid., 329, emphasis in original.

14   Jameson in particular has highlighted this feature of modernism. See, for example, the "Existence of Italy" chapter of *Signatures of the Visible* (New York: Routledge, 1990).

15   For examples of this recent work on the New Deal, see Steve Fraser and Gary Gerstle, eds., *The Rise and Fall of the New Deal Order, 1930–1980* (Princeton: Princeton University Press, 1989), and Richard M. Valelly, *Radicalism in the States: The Minnesota Farmer-Labor Party and the American Political Economy* (Chicago: University of Chicago Press, 1989).

16   On the continued political ambivalence of state intervention, see Robert Meister, *Political Identity: Thinking Through Marx* (Oxford: Blackwell, 1990), especially ch. 6; John Clarke, "Hard Times: The American New Right and Welfare," in *New Times and Old Enemies: Essays on Cultural Studies and America* (London: Harper Collins, 1991), 113–52.

17   Charles Alexander, *Here the Country Lies: Nationalism and the Arts in Twentieth-Century America* (Bloomington: Indiana University Press, 1980), 191. See also Arthur Ekirch, *Ideologies and Utopias: The Impact of the New Deal on American Thought* (Chicago: Quadrangle Press, 1969). For a very rich and suggestive examination of the intersections between nationalism and progressive working-class politics in this period, see Gary Gerstle, *Working-Class Americanism: The Politics of Labor in a Textile City, 1914–1960* (Cambridge: Cambridge University Press, 1989).

18   On this, see Susman's "Culture and Communications" chapter in *Culture as History*, 252–70.

19   Alfred Kazin, introduction to *The Day of the Locust*, by Nathanael West (New York: Signet, 1983), xvii.

20   Hollywood and the film industry were the stock-in-trade of a certain strain of Menckenesque cultural criticism as well. For an example that had early on impressed West, and had established the basic representational coordinates he would employ, see Louis Adamic's autobiographical *Laughing in the Jungle* (New York: Harper and Brothers, 1932), especially ch. 17, "The Enormous Village."

21   James F. Light, *Nathanael West: An Interpretive Study* (Evanston: Northwestern University Press, 1961), 175.

22   Thomas M. Strychacz, *Modernism, Mass Culture, and Professionalism* (Cambridge: Cambridge University Press, 1993), 187, 191.

23   A more even-handed treatment of the problem of mass culture has become much more common in the most recent criticism on West, as critics react to the stark, Cold War liberal elitism that informs much of the earlier work on *The Day of the Locust*. In addition to Strychacz, Rita Barnard's *The Great Depression and the Culture of Abundance: Kenneth Fearing, Nathanael West, and Mass Culture in the 1930s* (Cambridge:

Cambridge University Press, 1995) is another recent text that more subtly explores West's ambivalent relationship to mass culture, and that has shaped my own thinking on the topic.

24 For Auden's comments on West, see Jay Martin, *Nathanael West: The Art of His Life* (New York: Farrar, Straus, and Giroux, 1970), 161–62.

25 Mathew Roberts, "Bonfire of the Avant-Garde: Cultural Rage and Readerly Complicity in *The Day of the Locust,*" *Modern Fiction Studies* 42, 1 (1996): 61–90. I regret that this study, as well as Jonathan Veitch's fine *American Superrealism: Nathanael West and the Politics of Representation in the 1930s* (Madison: University of Wisconsin Press, 1997), came to my attention too late for me to make proper use of their many insights.

26 This point is not lost on Matt Groening, the creator of the animated TV series *The Simpsons.* Groening's cartoon takes an almost perverse pleasure in juxtaposing the advertising industry's inflated claims to happiness with the flimsy junk and disappointing experiences received by Homer and the family: *all of your desires will be mocked, everything is a lie.* Of course, none of this gives anyone pause anymore.

27 See Fredric Jameson, "Beyond the Cave: Demystifying the Ideology of Modernism," in *The Ideologies of Theory,* vol. 2, *Syntax of History* (Minneapolis: University of Minnesota Press, 1988), 115–32.

28 For two very different examinations of some of the cultural mythography of southern California, see Kevin Starr, *Material Dreams: Southern California through the 1920s* (New York: Oxford University Press, 1990), and Mike Davis, *City of Quartz: Excavating the Future in Los Angeles* (London: Verso, 1990).

29 Gilbert Seldes, *The Years of the Locust* (Boston: Little, Brown, 1933), 16.

30 Henry Wallace, *New Frontiers* (New York, 1934), quoted in Michael Rogin, *Ronald Reagan, the Movie, and Other Episodes in Political Demonology* (Berkeley: University of California Press, 1987), 179.

31 See the discussion of this and other exhibits in Miles Orvell, *The Real Thing: Imitation and Authenticity in American Culture, 1880–1940* (Chapel Hill: University of North Carolina Press, 1989), 180–85.

32 See Dick Hebdige, *Hiding in the Light* (London: Routledge, 1988), 59.

33 Jameson, *Signatures,* 183.

34 Ibid., 184.

35 Max Horkheimer and Theodor W. Adorno, *Dialectic of Enlightenment,* trans. John Cumming (New York: Continuum, 1972), 130.

36 The evolution of David Lynch's *Twin Peaks* TV series is instructive here. Lauded initially for its formal inventiveness, the series slouched fairly rapidly toward a bloody finale remarkable for its misogyny and cynicism. This conclusion might well be grasped as an outgrowth of Lynch's own reactionary politics, but it also represents a formal reaction to the petrifaction of the show's stylistic ingenuity, a kind of exhausted rage directed at the very reifying apparatus of cultural production that afforded its initial success.

37 For a discussion of this aspect of their argument, see Fredric Jameson, *Late Marxism: Adorno, or, The Persistence of the Dialectic* (London: Verso: 1990), 145–50.

38 See Peter Bürger, *Theory of the Avant-Garde*, trans. Michael Shaw (Minneapolis: University of Minnesota Press, 1984). For the surrealist attack on narrative, see in particular Breton's First Manifesto of Surrealism, in *Manifestoes of Surrealism* (Ann Arbor: University of Michigan Press, 1969). See also Veitch, *American Superrealism*, and Roberts, "Bonfire," for further discussion of West's avant-gardist sensibilities.

39 Raymond Williams has paid particular attention to the ironies of this "ruse of History." See *The Politics of Modernism* (London: Verso, 1989).

40 Gilbert Seldes, *Your Money and Your Life: A Manual for the "Middle Classes"* (New York: Whittlesey House, 1938), 116–17, emphasis in original.

41 This, of course, refers to the "slave morality" of Christianity that triumphs over the ethos of the aristocracy. See essay 1 of *On the Genealogy of Morals* in Nietzsche, *On the Genealogy of Morals and Ecce Homo*, ed. and trans. Walter Kauffman (New York: Vintage, 1969). For a suggestive deconstruction of the Nietzschean paradox, see Geoffrey Harpham's chapter on Nietzsche in *The Ascetic Imperative in Criticism and Culture* (Chicago: University of Chicago Press, 1987).

42 Theodor Adorno, *Aesthetic Theory*, trans. C. Lenhardt (London: Routledge, 1984), 31–32.

43 We should note the similar dynamics at play in *Miss Lonelyhearts* (a work West once imagined would be "in the form of a comic strip"), where another constitutive element of modernism identified by Adorno is foregrounded, namely the "guilt of art," the stain of privilege and "uselessness" that affixes to the institution of art as such, but that the individual artifact must negotiate in its own way (becoming thereby another component of modernist self-consciousness). The "lost" and cynical newspapermen of the novella wander a blasted urban landscape, sarcastically invoking the traditions of Western art and literature, now hopelessly juxtaposed against the misery of the setting itself.

44 Strychacz, *Modernism*, 182–83.

45 For a thorough working through of the machinec metaphor in the novel, see Robert Edenbaum, "From American Dream to Pavlovian Nightmare," in *Nathanael West: The Cheaters and the Cheated*, ed. David Madden (Deland, Fla.: Everett Edwards, 1973), 201–16.

46 For an eloquent discussion of the seductiveness of machinec metaphors, see Richard Dienst, *Still Life in Real Time: Theory after Television* (Durham: Duke University Press, 1994), 38–40.

47 West strove for such effects throughout his writing: compare here the dream sequence in *Miss Lonelyhearts* in which the sacrifice of the lamb is botched.

48 Nathanael West, "Violence in America," in *The Writings of Nathanael West*, ed. Alistair Wisker (New York: St. Martin's, 1990), 78.

49 Linda Williams, *Hard Core: Power, Pleasure, and the "Frenzy of the Visible"* (Berkeley: University of California Press, 1989), ch. 3.

50 Jameson, *Signatures*, 211.

51 L. Williams, *Hard Core*, ch. 2.

52 See Richard Slotkin, *Regeneration through Violence: The Mythology of the American Frontier, 1600–1860* (Middletown, Conn.: Wesleyan University Press, 1973).

53 Seldes, *Years of the Locust*, 177.

54 Strychacz, *Modernism*, 190.

55 This image of an irresistible molar force affording a certain molecular free play has long struck me as at least in part West's dark parody of Huck Finn adrift on the Mississippi, often considered an archetypal image of American freedom. But Twain's vision is itself ambiguous: the river, after all, leads where it wants to, and this is sometimes into unpleasant and even dangerous situations. What looks like freedom can, with only the slightest twist of the lens, come to look like its virtual opposite.

56 Michael Denning, *Mechanic Accents: Dime Novels and Working-Class Culture in America* (London: Verso: 1987), 79.

57 In this capacity, Tod invites comparison with Philip Marlowe, hero of Raymond Chandler's *The Big Sleep* (1939), a novel that features a social geography with interesting similarities to *The Day of the Locust*'s.

58 Philip Fisher, *Hard Facts: Setting and Form in the American Novel* (New York: Oxford University Press, 1987), 7.

59 Quoted in Veitch, *American Superrealism*, xiii.

60 For discussions of the image of the dream dump, see Levon Mueller, "Malamud and West: The Tyranny of the Dream Dump," in *Cheaters and Cheated*, ed. Madden, 221–34; Barnard, *Great Depression*, 320–25.

61 Alfred Kazin, *On Native Grounds: An Interpretation of Modern American Prose Literature* (New York: Harcourt Brace Jovanovich, 1982 [1942]), 504.

62 Ibid., 498.

63 See Mike Davis, *Prisoners of the American Dream* (London: Verso, 1986), 81–82.

64 Lawrence Grossberg, *We Gotta Get Out of This Place: Popular Conservatism and Postmodern Culture* (New York: Routledge, 1992), 239.

65 I thus cannot assent to the interpretation of the crowd scene offered recently by Philip Brian Harper, who reads this as a politically positive "systemic rupture" enacted by the "socially marginalized" crowd. See *Framing the Margins: The Social Logic of Postmodern Culture* (New York: Oxford University Press, 1994), 52–54. The lack of historical reflection in this book, and its reduction of the modernism/postmodernism problem to issues of "fragmented subjectivity," tend in any case to render its interpretive framework somewhat less than compelling.

66 Michael Denning, *The Cultural Front: The Laboring of American Culture in the Twentieth Century* (London: Verso, 1996).

67 Perhaps a final remark on "The Burning of Los Angeles" is in order here as well. On one hand, it occupies the place of the novum, of the modernist utopian moment of aesthetic innovation. On the other hand, its thematics seem rather obvious, even heavy-handed: that is, like Tod's decoding of Homer's garbled speech, it too makes

"the usual kind of sense" of the fractured text it reflects on, being marked as a kind of degraded realism or even kitsch. It thus fails on one level, yet succeeds on another in connoting the utopian and ideological weave of the text.

FIVE *Into the 1950s: Fiction in the Age of Consensus*

1 George Romney, quoted in Nelson Lichtenstein, "From Corporatism to Collective Bargaining: Organized Labor and the Eclipse of Social Democracy in the Postwar Era," in *The Rise and Fall of the New Deal Order, 1930–1980*, ed. Steve Fraser and Gary Gerstle (Princeton: Princeton University Press, 1989), 126.

2 Quoted in ibid., 142. For another invocation of the Treaty of Detroit, in the context of a compressed but sharply observed discussion of the nature of Fordism, see Richard Godden, *Fictions of Capital: The American Novel from James to Mailer* (Cambridge: Cambridge University Press, 1990), ch. 6.

3 Another factor we might point to would be the post–World War II mass growth of suburbanization, which Stanley Aronowitz points to as *the* principal shatterer of older class lines in terms of family, friendship, and consumption patterns. See *The Politics of Identity: Class, Culture, and Social Movements* (New York: Routledge, 1992), 35. The epigraph from Levitt adds the (probably unintended) twist that once the worker arrives in the suburbs, he is faced with ever more work to do: the burden of toil, if not lifted, is at least transferred to a domestic, and hopefully less alienated, realm (the situation for women presumably remaining somewhat different).

4 Alain Lipietz, *Mirages and Miracles: The Crises of Global Fordism*, trans. David Macey (London: Verso, 1987), 37–38. The basic work on Fordism remains Michel Aglietta, *A Theory of Capitalist Regulatiom: The U.S. Experience*, trans. David Fernbach (London: Verso, 1979).

5 It is difficult, in retrospect, not to regard the Treaty of Detroit and others of its ilk as finally amounting to something of a Faustian bargain for American workers. For a time, they enjoyed an unprecedented standard of living, and, as the specter of competition as such was temporarily held at bay, and as IBM and other large corporations began making "no layoff" pledges to their white-collar staffs, a substantial measure of what Bingham had identified as the overarching middle-class desire was attained: security. But with security comes a certain letting down of one's guard, and working people today find themselves unprepared for global capital's inevitable Mephisthophelean return.

6 James O'Connor, *Accumulation Crisis* (Oxford: Blackwell, 1984), 75. See also Andrew Ross *No Respect: Intellectuals and Popular Culture* (New York: Routledge, 1989), 43, on the Cold War politico-cultural project of "quarantining" and "lobotomizing" notions of class from the "national mind."

7 Jean-François Lyotard, *The Postmodern Condition: A Report on Knowledge*, trans. Brian Massumi (Minneapolis: University of Minnesota Press, 1984), 80.

8 Daniel Bell, *The End of Ideology: On the Exhaustion of Political Ideas in the Fifties* (Glencoe, Ill.: Free Press, 1960), ch. 13. Further references are cited in the text.

9 The key earlier reference is Robert Lynd and Helen Merrell Lynd, *Middletown: A Study in Contemporary American Culture* (New York: Harcourt, 1929). For a discussion of the centrality of work satisfaction to 1920s professional/managerial ideology, see Tom Lutz, "'Sweat or Die': The Hedonization of the Work Ethic in the 1920s," *American Literary History* 8, 2 (1996): 259–83.

10 Juliet Schor, *The Overworked American: The Unexpected Decline of Leisure in America* (New York: Basic Books, 1991).

11 John Barth, *The Floating Opera and The End of the Road* (New York: Anchor Doubleday, 1989), 218. All further references are cited in the text. A comment like this marks vividly the historical distance we have traveled from a writer like Dreiser, for whom the status of actions was in effect materially problematic and the locus of frank narrative and representational uncertainty. In the 1950s, we meet this problem in the form of a reified "philosophical concern." We shall develop this below.

12 Maurice Couturier has usefully cataloged the numerous metafictional devices in the text, which work to undermine the more "serious" philosophical and autobiographical levels of the narrative, and which point the way toward the more developed metafictional extravagances of Barth's later novels. See "From Displacement to Compactness: John Barth's *The Floating Opera*," *Critique: Studies in Contemporary Fiction*, 33, 1 (1991): 3–21.

13 See Fredric Jameson, *The Political Unconscious: Narrative as a Socially Symbolic Act* (Ithaca: Cornell University Press, 1981), 259.

14 Reported in Franco Moretti, *Modern Epic: The World System from Goethe to García Márquez*, trans. Quintin Hoare (London: Verso, 1996), 72.

15 Barth has, perhaps anachronistically, always clung to a modernist conception of the artist, with the novelist as a godlike figure who elaborates vast, encyclopedic fictional worlds into which the reader must wholly submerge him or herself. See his comments in *The Friday Book: Essays and Other Nonfiction* (New York: Putnam's, 1984), 29ff.

16 Indeed, when Barth in his next novel, *The End of the Road* (1958), strives for somewhat greater emotional realism and an increased charge of anxiety, the results are equivocal, with certain scenes having an undeniable power (of a kind absent from *The Floating Opera*), but the narrative as a whole is finally less interesting.

17 See Lawrence Grossberg, "Another Boring Day in Paradise," *Minnesota Review* 12, 2 (1984): 112–31. Andy Warhol's slogan "bored but hyper" would be yet another, related effort to pithily characterize (or, in Warhol's case, also create) this mood.

18 Walter Benjamin, *Illuminations*, ed. Hannah Arendt, trans. Harry Zohn (New York: Schocken, 1969). See in particular the essays on Leskov and Baudelaire.

19 The interpretive dilemma this situation places the subject in is then theorized by Benjamin through the concept of allegory.

20 We do learn one fact about Todd during these years, itself a kind of nonevent that only too obviously ratifies the effect in question: that he has not had sex since 1937.

21 This is, for example, the approach of Charles Harris, who, in his *Passionate Virtuosity* (Urbana: University of Illinois Press, 1983), attempts to construct an elaborate typol-

ogy of Barth's characters based on Jungian archetypes and allied myth-critical notions (e.g., Joseph Campbell).

22 Patricia Tobin, *John Barth and the Anxiety of Continuance* (Philadelphia: University of Pennsylvania Press, 1992), 28–30.

23 Heide Ziegler, *John Barth* (London: Methuen, 1987), 25.

24 Thomas Hill Schaub provides a good overview of the terms of cultural discourse among critics and writers of the period, and of the aesthetic difficulties entailed by them, in his *American Fiction in the Cold War* (Madison: University of Wisconsin Press, 1991), 25–67.

25 For an account of how the polarized Cold War cultural context provided a fertile site of reception for this style, see Serge Guilbaut, *How New York Stole the Idea of Modern Art*, trans. A. Goldhammer (Chicago: University of Chicago Press, 1983).

26 On this history, see Patrick Brantlinger, *Bread and Circuses: Theories of Mass Culture as Social Decay* (Ithaca: Cornell University Press, 1986).

27 Lionel Trilling, *The Liberal Imagination* (New York: Scribner's, 1976 [1950]), 262.

28 Schaub, *American Fiction*, 47.

29 For the distinction between liberal dissenters and liberal pluralists I am drawing on here, see Ross, *No Respect*, 43ff. For a useful summary and critique of the pluralist position, see Michael Rogin, *The Intellectuals and McCarthy: The Radical Specter* (Cambridge: MIT Press, 1967), 9–31.

30 Geraldine Murphy, "Romancing the Center: Cold War Politics and Classic American Literature," *Poetics Today* 9, 4 (1988): 737–47.

31 For some interesting, if preliminary, remarks on the role that discourses of cultural pluralism, beginning in the 1940s, had in ideologically defusing patterns of class identification and class consciousness, see the conclusion of Gary Gerstle's superb monograph on the textile workers of Woonsocket, Rhode Island: *Working-Class Americanism: The Politics of Labor in a Textile City, 1914–1960* (Cambridge: Cambridge University Press, 1989). As Gerstle notes, the genius of cultural pluralism, then articulated in particular around the question of race, lay in the effort to recast sentiments such as "capitalists exploit workers" as manifestations of racism.

32 Arthur Schlesinger, *The Vital Center: The Politics of Freedom* (New York: Da Capo, 1988 [1949]). References are cited in the text.

33 Jean-Paul Sartre, *Critique of Dialectical Reason*, vol. 1, trans. Alan Sheridan-Smith (London: Verso, 1991), 256–93. For an essay that attempts to link seriality, television, and postmodernism, see Arthur Kroker, "Television and the Triumph of Culture: Three Theses," *Canadian Journal of Political and Social Theory* 9, 3 (1985): 37–47.

34 Sartre, *Critique*, 260.

35 Fredric Jameson, *Marxism and Form: Twentieth-Century Dialectical Theories of Literature* (Princeton: Princeton University Press, 1971), 248.

36 Warren Susman has noted that the phrase "the American way of life" was not in common usage before the advent of the Depression. See his *Culture as History: The*

Transformation of American Society in the Twentieth Century (New York: Pantheon, 1984), 150–83.

37 Jean Baudrillard makes a similar argument in his critique of Hans Magnus Enzensberger. See *For a Critique of the Political Economy of the Sign*, trans. Charles Levin (St. Louis: Telos Press, 1981), 172.

38 Dave Roediger, *The Wages of Whiteness: Race and the Making of the American Working Class* (London: Verso, 1991), 117. See also Eric Lott, *Love and Theft: Blackface Minstrelsy and the American Working Class* (New York: Oxford University Press, 1993).

39 Walter Benjamin, "Central Park," quoted in Mary Ann Doane, "Information, Crisis, Catastrophe," in *Logics of Television,* ed. Patricia Mellencamp (Bloomington: Indiana University Press, 1990), 229.

40 Ibid., 222.

41 Paul Smith, *Clint Eastwood as Cultural Production* (Minneapolis: University of Minnesota Press, 1994).

42 Jameson, *Marxism and Form*, 412.

43 Recall, too, the numerous advertisements Hemingway appeared in, especially in the 1940s and 1950s. Such a project of reclamation must always be a fraught one: consumption and images of traditional male power/potency can never quite mix, at least in the Marxian view, since, as we have noted, consumption represents a substitute praxis, after production and hence effective human control of the social have been forsaken. For a stimulating discussion of gender issues in Hemingway, see Nancy Comley and Robert Scholes, *Hemingway's Genders* (New Haven: Yale University Press, 1994).

44 Ernest Hemingway, *The Old Man and the Sea* (New York: Scribner/Collier, 1986), 107. Further references are given in the text.

45 For an account of Homeric elements in the novel, see Kathleen Morgan and Luis Losada, "Santiago in *The Old Man and the Sea:* A Homeric Hero," *Hemingway Review* 12, 1 (1992): 35–51.

46 My thanks to Frank Lentricchia for first alerting me to several of these aspects of the novel.

POSTSCRIPT *The Insistence of Class and the Framing of Culture in the American Scene*

1 Slavoj Žižek, *Tarrying with the Negative: Kant, Hegel, and the Critique of Ideology* (Durham: Duke University Press, 1993), 201, emphasis in original.

2 Lauren Berlant, *The Anatomy of National Fantasy: Hawthorne, Utopia, and Everyday Life* (Chicago: University of Chicago Press, 1991), especially ch. five.

3 Jean Baudrillard, *America*, trans. Chris Turner (London: Verso, 1988), 75–106.

4 Evan Watkins, *Throwaways: Work Culture and Consumer Education* (Stanford: Stanford University Press, 1993), 145.

5 Leon Samson, "Americanism as Surrogate Socialism," in *Failure of a Dream? Essays in*

the History of American Socialism, ed. John Laslett and Seymour Martin Lipset (New York: Anchor, 1974), 426.

6 C. L. R. James, *American Civilization*, ed. Anna Grimshaw and Keith Hart (Oxford: Blackwell, 1993), especially ch. six; Timothy Brennan, *At Home in the World: Cosmopolitanism Now* (Cambridge: Harvard University Press, 1997), 233.

7 James, *American Civilization*, 167.

8 Karl Marx, *Grundrisse*, trans. Martin Nicolaus (New York: Vintage, 1973), 166.

9 See, for instance, Maria Milagros López, "Post-Work Selves and Entitlement 'Attitudes' in Peripheral Postindustrial Puerto Rico," *Social Text* 38 (1994): 111–35. López argues that the Left's historic emphasis on labor prevents it from valorizing the cultural achievements of those groups, such as those she studies in Puerto Rico, who, forced outside the domain of wage labor, turn to a reliance on the state and over time develop antibourgeois sentiments grounded in the structuring of their lived time according to their own needs and desires. She concentrates in particular on the gender relations at issue, and there is much of value in her discussion; certainly when thinking about the industrialized core countries it seems as if an older masculinism, one that persists in measuring self-worth in terms of "bringing home the bacon," has hampered efforts to create communal practices of joy such as these often female-centered groups have (though perhaps the protagonists of *The Full Monty* are on their way to such a breakthrough?). Still, for purposes of formulating more general political strategies, one must balance these cultural innovations against the specificities of their origin (the peculiar position of Puerto Rico) and their forthright dependence on the bourgeois state. It seems likely that such *souci de soi* and arts of living will be of great importance to cultural revolutions of the future; they should, however, be grasped as objects of political desire and struggle fully as much as practices fully realizable in the present and transferable to other contexts.

10 Don DeLillo, *White Noise* (New York: Penguin, 1986), 98. Further references are cited in the text.

11 Watkins, *Throwaways*, 161.

12 Roger Rouse, "Thinking Through Transnationalism: Notes on the Cultural Politics of Class Relations in the Contemporary United States," *Public Culture* 7 (1995): 391.

13 Wai-Chee Dimock, "Class, Gender, and a History of Metonymy," in *Rethinking Class*, ed. Michael Gilmore and Wai-Chee Dimock (New York: Columbia University Press, 1994).

bibliography

Adamic, Louis. *Laughing in the Jungle*. New York: Harper and Brothers, 1932.

Adorno, Theodor. *Aesthetic Theory*. Trans. C. Lenhardt. London: Routledge, 1984.

——. *Minima Moralia*. Trans. E. F. N. Jephcott. London: Verso, 1978.

Aglietta, Michel. *A Theory of Capitalist Regulation: The U.S. Experience*. Trans. David Fernbach. London: Verso, 1979.

Akin, William E. *Technocracy and the American Dream: The Technocrat Movement, 1900–1941*. Berkeley: University of California Press, 1977.

Alexander, Charles. *Here the Country Lies: Nationalism and the Arts in Twentieth-Century America*. Bloomington: Indiana University Press, 1980.

Althusser, Louis. *Lenin and Philosophy and Other Essays*. Trans. Ben Brewster. New York: Monthly Review, 1971.

Anderson, Perry. "Modernity and Revolution." In *Marxism and the Interpretation of Culture*, ed. Carry Nelson and Larry Grossberg. Urbana: University of Illinois Press, 1988.

Aronowitz, Stanley. *The Politics of Identity: Class, Culture, and Social Movements*. New York: Routledge, 1992.

Aronowitz, Stanley, and William DiFazio. *The Jobless Future: Sci-Tech and the Dogma of Work*. Minneapolis: University of Minnesota Press, 1994.

Auerbach, Erich. *Mimesis: The Representation of Reality in Western Literature*. Trans. Willard Trask. Princeton: Princeton University Press, 1953.

Balibar, Etienne, and Immanuel Wallerstein. *Race, Nation, Class: Ambiguous Identities*. London: Verso, 1991.

Banta, Martha. *Taylored Lives: Narrative Productions in the Age of Taylor, Veblen, and Ford*. Chicago: University of Chicago Press, 1993.

Baritz, Loren. *The Good Life: The Meaning of Success for the American Middle Class*. New York: Knopf, 1989.

Barnard, Rita. *The Great Depression and the Culture of Abundance: Kenneth Fearing, Nathanael West, and Mass Culture in the 1930s*. Cambridge: Cambridge University Press, 1995.

Barth, John. *The Floating Opera and The End of the Road*. New York: Anchor Doubleday, 1989.

——. *The Friday Book: Essays and Other Nonfiction*. New York: Putnam's, 1984.

Baudrillard, Jean. *America*. Trans. Chris Turner. London: Verso, 1988.

——. *For a Critique of the Political Economy of the Sign*. Trans. Charles Levin. St. Louis: Telos Press, 1981.

Bell, Daniel. *The End of Ideology: On the Exhaustion of Political Ideas in the Fifties*. Glencoe, Ill.: Free Press, 1960.

Bell, Michael Davitt. *The Problem of American Realism*. Chicago: University of Chicago Press, 1993.

Benfey, Christopher. " 'The Other Side of the Rug': Cather's Narrative Underpinnings." *American Literary History* 6, 3 (1994): 140–54.

Benjamin, Walter. *Illuminations*. Ed. Hannah Arendt. Trans. Harry Zohn. New York: Schocken, 1969.

Bercovitch, Sacvan. *The American Jeremiad*. Madison: University of Wisconsin Press, 1978.

——. *The Office of the Scarlet Letter*. Baltimore: Johns Hopkins University Press, 1991.

Bercovitch, Sacvan, and Myra Jehlen, eds. *Ideology and Classic American Literature*. Cambridge: Cambridge University Press, 1986.

Berlant, Lauren. *The Anatomy of National Fantasy: Hawthorne, Utopia, and Everyday Life*. Chicago: University of Chicago Press, 1991.

Bingham, Alfred. *Insurgent America: Revolt of the Middle Classes*. New York: Harper Brothers, 1935.

Biskind, Peter. *Seeing Is Believing: How Hollywood Taught Us to Stop Worrying and Love the Fifties*. New York: Pantheon, 1983.

Bloch, Ernst. *The Utopian Function of Art and Literature: Selected Essays*. Trans. Jack Zipes and Frank Mecklenburg. Cambridge: MIT Press, 1988.

Blumin, Stuart M. *The Emergence of the Middle-Class: Social Experience in the American City, 1760–1900*. Cambridge: Cambridge University Press, 1989.

Bohlke, L. Brent, ed. *Willa Cather in Person: Interviews, Speeches, and Letters*. Lincoln: University of Nebraska Press, 1986.

Bowlby, Rachel. *Just Looking: Consumer Culture in Dreiser, Gissing, and Zola*. New York: Methuen, 1985.

Brantlinger, Patrick. *Bread and Circuses: Theories of Mass Culture as Social Decay*. Ithaca: Cornell University Press, 1986.

Braverman, Harry. *Labor and Monopoly Capital: The Degradation of Work in the Twentieth Century*. New York: Monthly Review, 1974.

Brennan, Timothy. *At Home in the World: Cosmopolitanism Now*. Cambridge: Harvard University Press, 1997.

Breton, Andre. *Manifestoes of Surrealism*. Ann Arbor: University of Michigan Press, 1969.

Brooks, Van Wyck. " 'Highbrow' and 'Lowbrow.' " In *Critics of Culture: Literature and Society in the Early Twentieth Century*, ed. Alan Trachtenberg. New York: Wiley and Sons, 1976.

Buhle, Paul. *Marxism in the United States*. London: Verso, 1991.

Burawoy, Michael. *The Politics of Production*. London: Verso, 1985.

Bürger, Peter. *Theory of the Avant-Garde*. Trans. Michael Shaw. Minneapolis: University of Minnesota Press, 1984.

Carlin, Deborah. *Cather, Canon, and the Politics of Reading*. Amherst: University of Massachusetts Press, 1992.

Carmichael, Virginia. *Framing History: The Rosenberg Story and the Cold War*. Minneapolis: University of Minnesota Press, 1993.

Cather, Willa. *A Lost Lady*. New York: Vintage, 1972.

——. *My Ántonia*. Boston: Houghton Mifflin, n.d.

——. *The Professor's House*. New York: Vintage, 1973.

Certeau, Michel de. *The Practice of Everyday Life*. Trans. Stephen Rendall. Berkeley: University of California Press, 1984.

Chandler, Marilyn R. *Dwelling in the Text: Houses in American Fiction*. Berkeley: University of California Press, 1991.

Chase, Richard. *The American Novel and Its Tradition*. New York: Anchor Doubleday, 1957.

Clarke, John. *New Times and Old Enemies: Essays on Cultural Studies and America*. London: Harper Collins, 1991.

Cleaver, Harry. *Reading Capital Politically*. Austin: University of Texas Press, 1980.

Comley, Nancy, and Robert Scholes. *Hemingway's Gender's*. New Haven: Yale University Press, 1994.

Corey, Lewis. *Crisis of the Middle Class*. New York: Covici, Friede, 1935.

Corkin, Stanley. "*Sister Carrie* and Industrial Life: Objects and the New American Self." *Modern Fiction Studies* 33, 4 (1987): 605–18.

Couturier, Maurice. "From Displacement to Compactness: John Barth's *The Floating Opera*." *Critique: Studies in Contemporary Fiction* 33, 1 (1991): 3–21.

Crane, Stephen. *Stories and Tales*. Ed. R. W. Stallman. New York: Vintage, 1961.

Cronon, William. *Nature's Metropolis: Chicago and the Great West*. New York: Norton, 1991.

Cross, Gary. *Time and Money: The Making of Consumer Culture*. New York: Routledge, 1993.

Davis, Mike. *City of Quartz: Excavating the Future in Los Angeles*. London: Verso, 1990.

———. *Prisoners of the American Dream*. London: Verso, 1986.

Deleuze, Gilles, and Félix Guattari. *Anti-Oedipus: Capitalism and Schizophrenia*. Trans. Robert Hurley et al. Minneapolis: University of Minnesota Press, 1984.

DeLillo, Don. *White Noise*. New York: Penguin, 1986.

DeMott, Benjamin. *The Imperial Middle: Why Americans Can't Think Straight about Class*. New York: William and Morrow, 1990.

Denning, Michael. *The Cultural Front: The Laboring of American Culture in the Twentieth Century*. London: Verso, 1996.

———. *Mechanic Accents: Dime Novels and Working-Class Culture in America*. London: Verso, 1987.

———. " 'The Special American Conditions': Marxism and American Studies." *American Quarterly* 38, 3 (1986): 356–80.

Dienst, Richard. *Still Life in Real Time: Theory after Television*. Durham: Duke University Press, 1994.

Dimock, Wai-Chee. "Class, Gender, and a History of Metonymy." In *Rethinking Class: Literary Production and Social Formations*, ed. Michael Gilmore and Wai-Chee Dimock. New York: Columbia University Press, 1994.

Doane, Mary Ann. "Information, Crisis, Catastrophe." In *Logics of Television*, ed. Patricia Mellencamp. Bloomington: Indiana University Press, 1990.

Dreiser, Theodore. *An Amateur Laborer*. Ed. Richard Dowell. Philadelphia: University of Pennsylvania Press, 1983.

———. *An American Tragedy*. Cleveland: World Publishers, 1946.

———. *Sister Carrie*. New York: Signet, 1961.

Eagleton, Terry. *The Ideology of the Aesthetic*. Oxford: Blackwell, 1990.

Edelman, Lee. "The Future Is Kid Stuff: Queer Theory, Disidentification, and the Death Drive." *Narrative* 6, 1 (1998): 18–30.

Edenbaum, Robert. "From American Dream to Pavlovian Nightmare." In *Nathanael West: The Cheaters and the Cheated*, ed. David Madden. Deland, Fla.: Everett Edwards, 1973.

Ehrenreich, Barbara. *Fear of Falling: The Inner Life of the Middle Class*. New York: Pantheon, 1989.

Eisenstein, Sergei. "*An American Tragedy*." *Close Up* 10, 2 (1933): 109–32.

Ekirch, Arthur. *Ideologies and Utopias: The Impact of the New Deal on American Thought*. Chicago: Quadrangle Press, 1969.

Ellis, William A. *The Theory of American Romance*. Ann Arbor: UMI Research Press, 1989.

Empson, William. *Some Versions of Pastoral*. New York: New Directions, 1974.

Fisher, Philip. *Hard Facts: Setting and Form in the American Novel*. New York: Oxford University Press, 1987.

Fishman, Robert. *Bourgeois Utopias: The Rise and Fall of Suburbia.* New York: Basic Books, 1987.

Fitzgerald, F. Scott. *The Great Gatsby.* New York: Scribner's, 1953.

Fox, Richard W., and Jackson Lears, eds. *The Culture of Consumption.* New York: Pantheon, 1983.

Fraser, Steve, and Gary Gerstle, eds. *The Rise and Fall of the New Deal Order, 1930–1980.* Princeton: Princeton University Press, 1989.

Friedrich, Otto. *City of Nets: A Chronicle of Hollywood in the 1940s.* New York: Random House, 1986.

Genette, Gerard. *Figures of Literary Discourse.* New York: Columbia University Press, 1982.

Geoghegan, Thomas. *Which Side Are You On? Trying to Be for Labor When It's Flat on Its Back.* New York: Farrar, Straus, and Giroux, 1991.

Gerstle, Gary. *Working-Class Americanism: The Politics of Labor in a Textile City, 1914–1960.* Cambridge: Cambridge University Press, 1989.

Giedion, Sigfried. *Space, Time, and Architecture.* Cambridge: Harvard University Press, 1954.

Gilbert, Sandra, and Susan Gubar. *No Man's Land.* Vol. 2, *Sexchanges.* New Haven: Yale University Press, 1989.

Gilmore, Michael, and Wai-Chee Dimock, eds. *Rethinking Class: Literary Production and Social Formations.* New York: Columbia University Press, 1994.

Godden, Richard. *Fictions of Capital: The American Novel from James to Mailer.* Cambridge: Cambridge University Press, 1990.

Goodwyn, Lawrence. *Democratic Promise: The Populist Moment in America.* New York: Oxford University Press, 1976.

Gorz, Andre. *Paths to Paradise: On the Liberation from Work.* Trans. Malcolm Imrie. London: Pluto Press, 1985.

Gramsci, Antonio. *Selections from the Prison Notebooks.* Ed. and trans. Quentin Hoare and G. Nowell Smith. New York: International Publishers, 1971.

Grossberg, Lawrence. "Another Boring Day in Paradise." *Minnesota Review* 12, 2 (1984): 112–31.

——. *We Gotta Get Out of This Place: Popular Conservatism and Postmodern Culture.* New York: Routledge, 1992.

Guilbaut, Serge. *How New York Stole the Idea of Modern Art.* Trans. A. Goldhammer. Chicago: University of Chicago Press, 1983.

Guillory, John. *Cultural Capital: The Problem of Literary Canon Formation.* Chicago: University of Chicago Press, 1993.

Gutman, Herbert. *Work, Culture, and Society in Industrializing America.* New York: Random House, 1976.

Harper, Philip Brian. *Framing the Margins: The Social Logic of Postmodern Culture.* New York: Oxford University Press, 1994.

Harpham, Geoffrey Galt. *The Ascetic Imperative in Criticism and Culture.* Chicago: University of Chicago Press, 1987.

Harris, Charles. *Passionate Virtuosity*. Urbana: University of Illinois Press, 1983.

Harris, Neil. *Cultural Excursions: Marketing Appetites and Cultural Tastes in Modern America*. Chicago: University of Chicago Press, 1990.

Harvey, David. *The Condition of Postmodernity: An Enquiry into the Origins of Cultural Change*. Oxford: Blackwell, 1989.

Hebdige, Dick. *Hiding in the Light*. London: Routledge, 1988.

Hemingway, Ernest. *The Old Man and the Sea*. New York: Scribner/Collier, 1986.

Hitchcock, Peter. *Oscillate Wildly: Space, Body, and Spirit of Millennial Materialism*. Minneapolis: University of Minnesota Press, 1999.

Horkheimer, Max, and Theodor W. Adorno. *Dialectic of Enlightenment*. Trans. John Cumming. New York: Continuum, 1972.

Howard, June. *Form and History in American Literary Naturalism*. Chapel Hill: University of North Carolina Press, 1985.

James, C. L. R. *American Civilization*. Ed. Anna Grimshaw and Keith Hart. Oxford: Blackwell, 1993.

Jameson, Fredric. "Beyond the Cave: Demystifying the Ideology of Modernism." *The Ideologies of Theory*, vol. 2, *Syntax of History*. Minneapolis: University of Minnesota Press, 1988.

——. "Conversations on the New World Order." In *After the Fall: The Failure of Communism and the Future of Socialism*, ed. Robin Blackburn. London: Verso, 1991.

——. *Late Marxism: Adorno, or, The Persistence of the Dialectic*. London: Verso, 1990.

——. *Marxism and Form: Twentieth-Century Dialectical Theories of Literature*. Princeton: Princeton University Press, 1971.

——. "Marxism and Historicism." In *The Ideologies of Theory*, vol. 2, *Syntax of History*. Minneapolis: University of Minnesota Press, 1988.

——. "Marx's Purloined Letter." *New Left Review* 209 (1995): 86–120.

——. *The Political Unconscious: Narrative as a Socially Symbolic Act*. Ithaca: Cornell University Press, 1981.

——. *Postmodernism, or, The Cultural Logic of Late Capitalism*. Durham: Duke University Press, 1991.

——. *Signatures of the Visible*. New York: Routledge, 1990.

Jehlen, Myra. "The Novel and the Middle Class in America." In *Ideology and Classic American Literature*, ed. Sacvan Bercovitch and Myra Jehlen. Cambridge: Cambridge University Press, 1986.

Kaplan, Amy. *The Social Construction of American Realism*. Chicago: University of Chicago Press, 1988.

Kazin, Alfred. Introduction to *The Day of the Locust*, by Nathanael West. New York: Signet, 1983.

——. *On Native Grounds: An Interpretation of Modern American Prose Literature*. New York: Harcourt Brace Jovanovich, 1982 [1942].

Kroker, Arthur. "Television and the Triumph of Culture: Three Theses." *Canadian Journal of Political and Social Theory* 9, 3 (1985): 37–47.

Lawson, R. A. *The Failure of Independent Liberalism, 1930–1941*. New York: Putnam, 1971.

Le Goff, Jacques. *Time, Work, and Culture in the Middle Ages*. Trans. Arthur Goldhammer. Chicago: University of Chicago Press, 1980.

Lehan, Richard. "*Sister Carrie*: The City, the Self, and the Modes of Narrative Discourse." In *New Essays on Sister Carrie*, ed. Donald Pizer. Cambridge: Cambridge University Press, 1991.

Lentricchia, Frank. "The Resentments of Robert Frost." *American Literature* 62, 2 (1990): 175–200.

Levine, Lawrence W. "American Culture and the Great Depression." *Yale Review* 62, 4 (1985): 196–223.

Lichtenstein, Nelson. "From Corporatism to Collective Bargaining: Organized Labor and the Eclipse of Social Democracy in the Postwar Era." In *The Rise and Fall of the New Deal Order, 1930–1980*, ed. Steve Fraser and Gary Gerstle. Princeton: Princeton University Press, 1989.

Light, James F. *Nathanael West: An Interpretive Study*. Evanston: Northwestern University Press, 1961.

Lipietz, Alain. *Mirages and Miracles: The Crises of Global Fordism*. Trans. David Macey. London: Verso, 1987.

Livingston, James. *Pragmatism and the Political Economy of Cultural Revolution, 1850–1940*. Chapel Hill: University of North Carolina Press, 1994.

López, Maria Milagros. "Post-Work Selves and Entitlement 'Attitudes' in Peripheral Post-industrial Puerto Rico." *Social Text* 38 (1994): 111–35.

Lott, Eric. *Love and Theft: Blackface Minstrelsy and the American Working Class*. New York: Oxford University Press, 1993.

Lukács, Georg. *History and Class Consciousness: Studies in Marxist Dialectics*. Trans. Rodney Livingstone. Cambridge: MIT Press, 1971.

Lutz, Tom. "'Sweat or Die': The Hedonization of the Work Ethic in the 1920s." *American Literary History* 8, 2 (1996): 259–83.

Lynd, Robert, and Helen Merrell Lynd. *Middletown: A Study in Contemporary American Culture*. New York: Harcourt, 1929.

Lyotard, Jean-François. *The Postmodern Condition: A Report on Knowledge*. Trans. Brian Massumi. Minneapolis: University of Minnesota Press, 1984.

MacCannell, Dean. *The Tourist*. New York: Schocken, 1976.

Madden, David, ed. *Nathanael West: The Cheaters and the Cheated*. Deland, Fla.: Everett Edwards, 1973.

Martin, Jay. *Nathanael West: The Art of His Life*. New York: Farrar, Straus, and Giroux, 1970.

Marx, Karl. *Capital*. Vol. 1. Trans. Ben Fowkes. New York: Vintage, 1977.

——. *The German Ideology*. In *The Marx-Engels Reader*, ed. Robert Tucker. New York: Norton, 1978.

——. *Grundrisse*. Trans. Martin Nicolaus. New York: Vintage, 1973.

——. "On the Jewish Question." In *Early Writings*, ed. Tom Bottomore. New York: McGraw-Hill, 1963.

Marx, Leo. *The Machine in the Garden: Technology and the Pastoral Ideal in America.* New York: Oxford University Press, 1964.

——. "Pastoralism in America." In *Ideology and Classic American Literature,* ed. Sacvan Bercovitch and Myra Jehlen. Cambridge: Cambridge University Press, 1986.

Meister, Robert. *Political Identity: Thinking Through Marx.* Oxford: Blackwell, 1990.

Mellencamp, Patricia, ed. *Logics of Television.* Bloomington: Indiana University Press, 1990.

Merish, Lori. " 'The Hand of Refined Taste' in the Frontier Landscape: Caroline Kirkland's *A New Home, Who'll Follow?* and the Feminization of American Consumerism." *American Quarterly* 45, 4 (1993): 485–523.

Michaels, Walter Benn. "An American Tragedy, or The Promise of American Life." *Representations* 25 (1989): 71–98.

——. *The Gold Standard and the Logic of Naturalism.* Berkeley: University of California Press, 1987.

——. *Our America: Nativism, Modernism, and Pluralism.* Durham: Duke University Press, 1995.

——. "The Vanishing American." *American Literary History* 2 (1990): 220–41.

Middleton, Jo Ann. *Willa Cather's Modernism.* Rutherford, N.J.: Fairleigh Dickinson University Press, 1990.

Mitchell, Arnold. *The Nine American Lifestyles.* New York: Anchor Doubleday, 1983.

Moers, Ellen. *The Two Dreisers.* New York: Viking, 1969.

Montgomery, David. *The Fall of the House of Labor.* Cambridge: Cambridge University Press, 1987.

Moretti, Franco. *Modern Epic: The World System from Goethe to García Márquez.* Trans. Quintin Hoare. London: Verso, 1996.

——. *Signs Taken for Wonders.* Rev. ed. Trans. Susan Fischer et al. London: Verso, 1988.

——. *The Way of the World: The* Bildungsroman *in European Culture.* Trans. A. Sbragia. London: Verso, 1987.

Morgan, Kathleen, and Luis Losada. "Santiago in *The Old Man and the Sea:* A Homeric Hero." *Hemingway Review* 12, 1 (1992): 35–51.

Morse, Margaret. "An Ontology of Everyday Distraction: The Freeway, the Mall, and Television." In *Logics of Television,* ed. Patricia Mellencamp. Bloomington: Indiana University Press, 1990.

Mueller, Levon. "Malamud and West: The Tyranny of the Dream Dump." In *Nathanael West: The Cheaters and the Cheated,* ed. David Madden. Deland, Fla.: Everett Edwards, 1973.

Murphy, Geraldine. "Romancing the Center: Cold War Politics and Classic American Literature." *Poetics Today* 9, 4 (1988): 737–47.

Nietzsche, Friedrich. *On the Genealogy of Morals and Ecce Homo.* Ed. and trans. Walter Kauffman. New York: Vintage, 1969.

O'Brien, Sharon. "Becoming Noncanonical: The Case against Willa Cather." *American Quarterly* 40 (1988): 110–26.

——. "'The Thing Not Named': Willa Cather as a Lesbian Writer." *Signs* 9 (1984): 571–93.

——. *Willa Cather: The Emerging Voice*. New York: Oxford University Press, 1987.

O'Connor, James. *Accumulation Crisis*. Oxford: Blackwell, 1984.

Oehlschlaeger, Fritz. "*Indisponibilité* and the Anxiety of Authorship in *The Professor's House*." *American Literature* 62, 1 (1990): 74–86.

O'Neill, John. *Five Bodies: The Human Shape of Modern Society*. Ithaca: Cornell University Press, 1985.

Orvell, Miles. *The Real Thing: Imitation and Authenticity in American Culture, 1880–1940*. Chapel Hill: University of North Carolina Press, 1989.

Pizer, Donald. *The Novels of Theodore Dreiser*. Minneapolis: University of Minnesota Press, 1976.

Pizer, Donald, ed. *New Essays on Sister Carrie*. Cambridge: Cambridge University Press, 1991.

Porter, Carolyn. *Seeing and Being: The Plight of the Participant Observer in Emerson, James, Adams, and Faulkner*. Middletown, Conn.: Wesleyan University Press, 1981.

Postone, Moishe. *Time, Labor, and Social Domination: A Reinterpretation of Marx's Critical Theory*. Cambridge: Cambridge University Press, 1993.

Quirk, Tom. "Fitzgerald and Cather: *The Great Gatsby*." *American Literature* 54 (1982): 576–91.

Radway, Janice. *A Feeling for Books: The Book-of-the-Month Club, Literary Taste, and Middle-Class Desire*. Chapel Hill: University of North Carolina Press, 1997.

Reising, Russell. *The Unusable Past: Theory and the Study of American Literature*. New York: Methuen, 1986.

Robbins, Bruce. *Secular Vocations: Intellectuals, Professionalism, Culture*. London: Verso, 1993.

Roberts, Mathew. "Bonfire of the Avant-Garde: Cultural Rage and Readerly Complicity in *The Day of the Locust*." *Modern Fiction Studies* 42, 1 (1996): 61–90.

Roediger, Dave. *The Wages of Whiteness: Race and the Making of the American Working Class*. London: Verso, 1991.

Rogin, Michael. *The Intellectuals and McCarthy: The Radical Specter*. Cambridge: MIT Press, 1967.

——. *Ronald Reagan, the Movie, and Other Episodes in Political Demonology*. Berkeley: University of California Press, 1987.

Rosenzweig, Roy. *Eight Hours for What We Will: Workers and Leisure in an Industrial City, 1870–1920*. Cambridge: Cambridge University Press, 1983.

Rosowski, Susan. *The Voyage Perilous: Willa Cather's Romanticism*. Lincoln: University of Nebraska Press, 1986.

Ross, Andrew. *No Respect: Intellectuals and Popular Culture*. New York: Routledge, 1989.

Ross, Steven J. *Working-Class Hollywood: Silent Film and the Shaping of Class in America*. Princeton: Princeton University Press, 1998.

Rouse, Roger. "Thinking Through Transnationalism: Notes on the Cultural Politics of Class Relations in the Contemporary United States." *Public Culture* 7 (1995): 353–402.

Rubin, Joan Shelley. *The Making of Middlebrow Culture*. Chapel Hill: University of North Carolina Press, 1992.

Rydell, Robert W. *All the World's a Fair*. Chicago: University of Chicago Press, 1984.

Salvatore, Nick. "Response to Sean Wilentz." *International Labor and Working Class History* 26 (1984): 25–30.

Samson, Leon. "Americanism as Surrogate Socialism." In *Failure of a Dream? Essays in the History of American Socialism*, ed. John Laslett and Seymour Martin Lipset. New York: Anchor, 1974.

——. *The American Mind: A Study in Socio-Analysis*. New York: Jonathan Cape and Harrison Smith, 1932.

Sartre, Jean-Paul. *Critique of Dialectical Reason*. Vol. 1. Trans. Alan Sheridan-Smith. London: Verso, 1991.

——. "Individualism and Conformism in the United States." In *Literary and Philosophical Essays*, trans. Annette Michelson. New York: Criterion, 1955.

Schaub, Thomas Hill. *American Fiction in the Cold War*. Madison: University of Wisconsin Press, 1991.

Schlesinger, Arthur. *The Vital Center: The Politics of Freedom*. New York: Da Capo, 1988 [1949].

Schor, Juliet. *The Overworked American: The Unexpected Decline of Leisure in America*. New York: Basic Books, 1991.

Schwartz, Nina. "History and the Invention of Innocence in *A Lost Lady*." *Arizona Quarterly* 46, 2 (1990): 33–53.

Sedgwick, Eve Kosofsky. "Across Gender, across Sexuality: Willa Cather and Others." *South Atlantic Quarterly* 88, 1 (1989): 53–72.

Segal, Howard P. *Technological Utopianism in American Culture*. Chicago: University of Chicago Press, 1985.

Seldes, Gilbert. *The Years of the Locust*. Boston: Little, Brown, 1933.

——. *Your Money and Your Life: A Manual for the "Middle Classes."* New York: Whittlesey House, 1938.

Seltzer, Mark. *Bodies and Machines*. New York: Routledge, 1992.

Simmel, Georg. *The Sociology of Georg Simmel*. Ed. Kurt Wolff. Glencoe, Ill.: Free Press, 1950.

Skaggs, Merrill Maguire. *After the World Broke in Two: The Later Novels of Willa Cather*. Charlottesville: University Press of Virginia, 1990.

Slotkin, Richard. *The Fatal Environment: The Myth of the Frontier in the Age of Industrialization, 1800–1890*. New York: Atheneum, 1985.

——. *Regeneration through Violence: The Mythology of the American Frontier, 1600–1860*. Middletown, Conn.: Wesleyan University Press, 1973.

Smith, Henry Nash. *Virgin Land: The American West as Symbol and Myth*. Cambridge: Harvard University Press, 1960.

Smith, Paul. *Clint Eastwood as Cultural Production*. Minneapolis: University of Minnesota Press, 1994.

Sohn-Rethel, Alfred. *Intellectual and Manual Labour: A Critique of Epistemology*. Trans. Martin Sohn-Rethel. Atlantic Highlands, N.J.: Humanities Press, 1978.

Sollors, Werner. *Beyond Ethnicity: Consent and Descent in American Culture*. New York: Oxford University Press, 1986.

Starr, Kevin. *Material Dreams: Southern California through the 1920s*. New York: Oxford University Press, 1990.

Stineback, David. "No Stone Unturned: Popular Versus Professional Evaluations of Willa Cather." *Prospects* 25 (1982): 167–76.

Strychacz, Thomas. "The Ambiguities of Escape in Willa Cather's *The Professor's House*." *Studies in American Fiction* 15 (1987): 49–61.

———. *Modernism, Mass Culture, and Professionalism*. Cambridge: Cambridge University Press, 1993.

Sundquist, Eric, ed. *American Realism: New Essays*. Baltimore: Johns Hopkins University Press, 1982.

Susman, Warren. *Culture as History: The Transformation of American Society in the Twentieth Century*. New York: Pantheon, 1984.

Szuberla, Guy. "Dreiser at the World's Fair: The City without Limits." *Modern Fiction Studies* 17 (1977): 369–79.

Thompson, E. P. "Time, Work-Discipline, and Industrial Capitalism." *Past and Present* 38 (1967): 56–97.

Tobin, Patricia. *John Barth and the Anxiety of Continuance*. Philadelphia: University of Pennsylvania Press, 1992.

Trachtenberg, Alan. "Experiments in Another Country: Stephen Crane's City Sketches." In *American Realism: New Essays*, ed. Eric Sundquist. Baltimore: Johns Hopkins University Press, 1982.

———. *The Incorporation of America: Culture and Society in the Gilded Age*. New York: Hill and Wang, 1982.

———. "Who Narrates? Dreiser's Presence in *Sister Carrie*." In *New Essays on Sister Carrie*, ed. Donald Pizer. Cambridge: Cambridge University Press, 1991.

Trilling, Lionel. *The Liberal Imagination*. New York: Scribner's, 1976 [1950].

Valelly, Richard M. *Radicalism in the States: The Minnesota Farmer-Labor Party and the American Political Economy*. Chicago: University of Chicago Press, 1989.

Vanneman, Reeve, and Lynn Weber Cannon. *The American Perception of Class*. Philadelphia: Temple University Press, 1987.

Veblen, Thorstein. *The Theory of the Leisure Class*. Harmondsworth: Penguin, 1979.

Veitch, Jonathan. *American Superrealism: Nathanael West and the Politics of Representation in the 1930s*. Madison: University of Wisconsin Press, 1997.

Walker, Pat, ed. *Between Labor and Capital*. Boston: South End Press, 1979.

Wallace, Henry. *New Frontiers*. New York: Putnam's, 1934.

Watkins, Evan. *Throwaways: Work Culture and Consumer Education*. Stanford: Stanford University Press, 1993.

——. *Work Time: English Departments and the Circulation of Cultural Value.* Stanford: Stanford University Press, 1989.

West, Nathanael. *The Collected Works of Nathanael West.* Harmondsworth: Penguin, 1976.

——. *Miss Lonelyhearts and The Day of the Locust.* New York: New Directions, 1962.

Williams, Linda. *Hard Core: Power, Pleasure, and the "Frenzy of the Visible."* Berkeley: University of California Press, 1989.

Williams, Raymond. *The Politics of Modernism.* London: Verso, 1989.

——. *Television: Technology and Cultural Form.* New York: Schocken, 1974.

Williams, William Appleman. *The Contours of American History.* New York: Norton, 1961.

Wilson, Christopher. "The Rhetoric of Consumption: Mass-Market Magazines and the Demise of the Gentle Reader, 1880–1920." In *The Culture of Consumption*, ed. Richard W. Fox and Jackson Lears. New York: Pantheon, 1983.

Wisker, Alistair, ed. *The Writings of Nathanael West.* New York: St. Martin's, 1990.

Wright, Erik Olin. *Classes.* London: Verso, 1985.

Zaretsky, Eli. "American Exceptionalism and Working-Class History." *Rethinking Marxism* 3, 1 (1990): 135–56.

Ziegler, Heide. *John Barth.* London: Methuen, 1987.

Žižek, Slavoj. *Tarrying with the Negative: Kant, Hegel, and the Critique of Ideology.* Durham: Duke University Press, 1993.

Zunz, Olivier. *The Changing Face of Inequality.* Chicago: University of Chicago Press, 1982.

index

Robert Seguin is Visiting Assistant Professor of English at
SUNY College at Brockport.

Library of Congress Cataloging-in-Publication Data
Seguin, Robert.
Around quitting time : work and middle-class fantasy in
American fiction / by Robert Seguin.
p. cm. — (New Americanists)
Includes bibliographical references and index.
ISBN 0-8223-2675-2 (cloth : alk. paper)
ISBN 0-8223-2670-1 (pbk. : alk. paper)
1. American fiction—20th century—History and criticism.
2. Middle class in literature. 3. Literature and society—
United States—History—20th century. 4. Social change
in literature. 5. Work in literature. 6. Labor in literature.
7. Fantasy in literature. 8. Class consciousness in literature.
9. Working class in literature. 10. United States—Social
conditions—20th century. I. Title. II. Series.
PS374.W64 S44 2001
813'.509355—dc21   00-046257